DE PROPRIETATIBUS LITTERARUM

edenda curat

C. H. VAN SCHOONEVELD

Indiana University

Series Maior, 1

THE MEANING

OF

POETIC METAPHOR

An Analysis in the Light of Wittgenstein's Claim

that Meaning is Use

by

MARCUS B. HESTER

Wake Forest College
Winston Salem, N.C.

1967

MOUTON & CO.

THE HAGUE · PARIS

Printed in The Netherlands by Mouton & Co., Printers, The Hague.

To Joan

ACKNOWLEDGMENTS

A book in philosophy grows out of an environment of ideas, and thus one should always have misapprehensions about signing his name as author. My misapprehensions are unusually great since this work is essentially my dissertation, submitted in partial fulfillment of the requirements for the degree of Doctor of Philosophy at Vanderbilt University. The most significant changes made since then are in the first chapter, changes which, hopefully, reflect a more adequate understanding of Wittgenstein. My debt to thinkers I have read will be evident in the text. Here I wish to acknowledge my debt to those who taught me by showing me what philosophy is. Dr. Donald Sherburne very patiently directed my work and helped to strengthen it both with his insights in aesthetics and his many stylistic suggestions. Dr. John Compton helped directly with the sections on phenomenology and indirectly in being himself a model of rigor and excellence. Dr. Clement Dore stimulated my first interests in analytic philosophy and helped with the chapter on Wittgenstein. I am indebted to many others who were not directly involved in the writing of this work. Especially I must mention Dr. Philip Hallie and Dr. Samuel Stumpf.

My contemporaries constantly challenged my ideas and made an inestimable impact on them. We tested each other's thoughts at every coffee break and at every lunch hour. I am especially grateful to Dr. Robert Shaw and Dr. Ed Harris. Finally, the source of all my general inspiration, my constant companion in this writing, my most familiar model of the beautiful, the graceful, and the sensitive, and the typist who spent months on this manuscript is my wife. This book must be dedicated to her.

Winston-Salem, North Carolina
November, 1965

MARCUS B. HESTER

TABLE OF CONTENTS

INTRODUCTION

The question of the meaning of poetic metaphor suggests two possible procedures. One can analyze how or why the language in the metaphor means. This approach leads to a theory of meaning[1] of poetic metaphor. Or one can survey the definitions of metaphor in the history of literature and philosophy and generalize from these theories to an adequate definition of metaphor. I shall not follow this latter procedure because, first, a very excellent dissertation on metaphor using the comprehensive survey method has been done by Douglas Charles Berggren at Yale University.[2] Second, several of the major theories of metaphor in the history of philosophy and literature will be mentioned and

[1] I have chosen the phrase "theory of meaning of poetic metaphor" instead of the phrase "semantic of poetic metaphor" for this reason. Wittgenstein in arguing that the method of philosophy is grammatical implies that a semantical theory need not consider the traditional problems of epistemology. I shall not argue whether in fact semantics can be done without epistemology because such an argument would have to prove a conception of philosophy. Such an argument would have to establish that philosophy cannot be purely grammatical. This work in no way intends to prove what philosophy is or should be. I have thus chosen to call my analysis a "theory of meaning" instead of a "semantic" in order to avoid this particular debate. In choosing this phrase I have left myself the possibility of considering semantical *and* epistemological points which metaphor raises. This broader conception is demanded by metaphor because metaphor involves imagery and imagery calls for an analysis of the mode in which this imagery is realized, namely reading. I call my analysis of reading "epistemological" because this study of reading is a treatment of the way metaphorical meaning is known. An adequate response to the question of how one knows or determines a metaphor's meaning would be the answer that one reads the metaphor. My analysis of metaphor then does not claim to be a grammatical analysis. I shall analyze the *act* of reading and the *act* of seeing as. Since I shall analyze the acts of reading and seeing as, I shall omit quotation marks when using either "reading" or "seeing as" in my own sense. When I do put quotes around "seeing as" I shall be using the phrase in Wittgenstein's sense. Wittgenstein clearly intended to be analyzing only the *concept* of "seeing as".

[2] Douglas Charles Berggren, "An Analysis of Metaphorical Meaning and Truth". Unpublished Ph.D. dissertation, Dept. of Philosophy, Yale University (1959).

commented on as I develop my thesis. Third, disagreements as to definitions of metaphor can best be settled by considering the theory of meaning of poetic metaphor. That the historical disagreements lie in the area of a theory of meaning can be seen from a brief examination of several of these definitions.

A. DEFINITIONS OF METAPHOR

Aristotle says:

Metaphor consists in giving the thing a name that belongs to something else; the transference being either from genus to species, or from species to genus, or from species to species, or on grounds of analogy. . . . That from analogy is possible whenever there are four terms so related that the second (B) is to the first (A), as the fourth (D) to the third (C); for one may then metaphorically put D in lieu of B, and B in lieu of D.[3]

Aristotle here clearly states the analogy view of metaphor. Such a view, emphasizing proportionality in metaphor, is most adequate to the more cognitive types of metaphor. The analogy view can adequately deal with the rigorous explicit metaphors of the metaphysical poets, for example, Donne or Marvell, but is inadequate with regard to the implicit suggestiveness of the romantic or symbolist poet, for example, Wordsworth or Eliot. Also the analogy view of metaphor is fairly adequate with regard to models of science, a type of metaphor.

On the other hand, Aristotle says: "Metaphor, moreover, gives style clearness, charm, and distinction as nothing else can: and it is not a thing whose use can be taught by one man to another." [4] This view of metaphor argues that it is essentially a decoration or ornament to enliven style. This understanding of metaphor differs quite radically from the view of metaphor as analogy. The ornamental view of metaphor emphasizes its noncognitive function. This strand of Aristotle's thought has been taken up by present-day emotive theorists. One wonders if these dual strands in Aristotle's thought may not indicate inconsistency rather than catholicity of mind.

Turning to contemporary thought we see a great interest in metaphor

[3] W. D. Ross (ed.), *The Works of Aristotle* (Oxford, The Clarendon Press, 1959), XI, 1457b 7-18.
[4] *Ibid.*, 1405a 8-9.

which has further complicated the matter by a flood of definitions. Charles Morris states:

A sign is *metaphorical* if in a particular instance of its occurrence it is used to denote an object which it does not literally denote in virtue of its signification, but which has some of the properties which its genuine denotata have.[5]

Ogden and Richards argue:

Metaphor, in the most general sense, is the use of one reference to a group of things between which a given relation holds, for the purpose of facilitating the discrimination of an analogous relation in another group.[6]

This general definition of metaphor seems to place Ogden and Richards in the analogy tradition stemming from Aristotle. However, when metaphor is qualified as *poetic* metaphor, it functions not symbolically or referentially, as does cognitive language, but emotively.[7] Thus, poetic metaphor is merely an ornament as far as referential significance is concerned.

That this view is a latter-day ornamental view is clearly indicated by Richards' further analysis in *Principles of Literary Criticism*. There he states: "Metaphor is a semi-surreptitious method by which a greater variety of elements can be wrought into the fabric of the experience." [8] In another early work Richards argues that poetic statements are not real statements but pseudo-statements. In his pseudo-statement view, he seems to mean to assert that metaphor causes emotion and does not refer like scientific statements.[9] He apparently does not notice that to say metaphor causes emotions is quite a different assertion from saying that metaphor in poetry is non-referential. Descriptive psychology investigates emotional causes while theories of meaning deal with the referential status of poetic language.

However, in fairness to Richards it must be pointed out that his excellent critical practices and his theoretical analysis of metaphor in *The*

---

[5] Charles Morris, *Sign, Language and Behavior* (New York, Prentice-Hall, Inc., 1946), p. 136.
[6] C. K. Ogden and I. A. Richards, *The Meaning of Meaning*, 10th ed. (London, Routledge & Kegan Paul Ltd., 1960), p. 213.
[7] *Ibid.*, pp. 148-49.
[8] I. A. Richards, *Principles of Literary Criticism* (New York, A Harvest Book, First published in 1925), p. 240.
[9] Morris Weitz (ed.), *Problems in Aesthetics: An Introductory Book of Readings* (New York, The Macmillan Co., 1959), pp. 456-57. (Originally published in Richards, *Science and Poetry*, London, Kegan Paul, Trench, Trubner & Co., 1935.)

Philosophy of Rhetoric show an important change from his earlier view that poetic statements are pseudo-statements and, thus, that metaphor is a semi-surreptitious element of style. In this later work he understands metaphor to be an interaction of tenor and vehicle. "Tenor" is further defined as the original idea or the principal subject, while "vehicle" is the borrowed idea or what the subject resembles.[10] His later analysis of the many subtle relations between tenor and vehicle, relations which vary from cognitive similarity to emotional disparity, is a significant improvement on his earlier view of metaphor. His later interactive view of metaphor ceases to stress that metaphor is merely emotive language.

Max Black consciously reacts against the emotive view of poetry held by the early Richards[11] and argues instead that metaphorical statements are interactive. By this he means that the metaphorical elements, while remaining distinct, draw out and emphasize certain implications of each other while suppressing other irrelevant qualities.[12] This view is similar to Morris' statement of the nature of metaphor. It is also similar to Richards' own later view.

Another view which emphasizes with Black the interactive nature of metaphor is the tensive view of metaphor. Philip Wheelwright introduces his version of this position by contrasting the poverty of literal language or "steno" language with the rich, tensive fullness of poetry.[13] He explicitly develops this view in relation to metaphor. Metaphor exhibits two complementary but tensive tendencies – epiphor and diaphor. Epiphor means that metaphors are contagious. They tend to implicate wider and wider contexts in their semantic plenitude of implication.[14] Diaphor, on the other hand, is a type of inward focus, an internal juxtaposition of qualities which gives the poem the concrete status of a presented object. The best metaphors display a fusion of diaphor and epiphor, the tension of which gives the metaphor its power.[15]

Martin Foss is another tension theorist. He says: "Metaphor is a

---

[10]   I. A. Richards, *The Philosophy of Rhetoric* (New York, Oxford University Press, 1936), p. 96.
[11]   Max Black, "Some Questions about Emotive Meaning", *The Philosophical Review*, LVII (March, 1948), pp. 111-26.
[12]   Max Black, *Models and Metaphors: Studies in Language and Philosophy* (Ithaca, N.Y., Cornell University Press, 1962), pp. 44-45.
[13]   Philip Wheelwright, *Metaphor and Reality* (Bloomington, Ind., Indiana University Press, 1962), pp. 35-65.
[14]   *Ibid.*, pp. 72-77.
[15]   *Ibid.*, pp. 78-90.

process of tension and energy, manifested in the process of language, not in the single word." [16] The essence of metaphor is a personification, a stylization of nature. Art makes material come alive by infusing the world with the ego.[17] Stylization raises the question of the subjectivity of art because style introduces nonobjective factors. Foss meets this question directly by arguing that stylized materials in art and poetry are not distortions but represent drives towards the highest unity of life, the personality.[18] In contrast to the dynamism of metaphor, the symbol is stable. Only the known can be represented symbolically. Science, using symbols for the purpose of fixing and closing the system of knowledge, reduces truth.[19] Only metaphor can represent reality because the conatus of substance leaves every fragmentary symbol.[20] Foss's whole argument is based on the point that metaphor is more suitable to expressing truth than the symbol because reality is dynamic.

A final, very helpful tension theory is that held by Douglas Berggren to whom I have already referred the reader in connection with his historical survey of theories of metaphor. Berggren argues that metaphor involves both dual (or more) references which are separated by a recognized type boundary and a textural principle of transference which transgresses but does not obliterate the boundary.[21] The "textural principle of transference" seems to mean an emotional charge or force which causes the intuition of a relation between the parts of the metaphor. Berggren draws this view from the expression theorists.[22] Berggren also recognizes, with Wheelwright, the double tendency of metaphor to implicate wider contexts and to focus inwardly. His particular terms for this duality are "centrifugal" and "centripetal". The former term designates the plurisignative nature of metaphor; the latter designates the conjunctive use of several metaphors to focus on the same phenomena.[23]

Within this framework Berggren analyzes several types of metaphor. First, the isolated pictorial, as the words designate, involves a relation of isolated images. Berggren credits the ornamental view with observing

---

[16] Martin Foss, *Symbol and Metaphor in Human Experience* (Princeton, Princeton University Press, 1949), p. 61.
[17] *Ibid.*, pp. 111-13.
[18] *Ibid.*, p. 147.
[19] *Ibid.*, p. 103.
[20] *Ibid.*, p. 42.
[21] Berggren, p. 383.
[22] *Ibid.*, pp. 263-94.
[23] *Ibid.*, pp. 399-403.

this type.[24] Second, there is the structural metaphor involving the relation of structures. Gestalt perception is involved in this type, credited to Aristotle's doctrine of analogy.[25] Finally, there is the textural metaphor based on an emotional intuition of similarity or disparity. Croce and Collingwood are credited for emphasizing this type.[26] The three appeal respectively to empirical intuition, intellectual intuition and lyrical intuition.[27] This classification of types is significant especially in view of the wide difference in types of metaphor, for instance, the difference in the metaphors of the metaphysical poet and the modern symbolist poet. The cognitively rigorous metaphors of the metaphysical poet, for example, those of Donne, are what Berggren calls structural metaphors. The vague suggestiveness of the metaphors of the symbolist poet, for example, those of Eliot, are what Berggren calls textural metaphors. At present I shall emphasize Berggren's basic definition of metaphor which points out that it is equally necessary for type boundaries to be transgressed while the individual parts of the metaphor remain distinct. The parts of the metaphor must be related but not absorbed into each other. This quite important point is made again by Berggren in a recent article. There he points out that metaphor can lose its life, its tension of parts, by being transformed either into myth or literal language.[28] Berggren's pointing out that metaphor may lose its tension either in myth or literal language is a significant insight which will appear again very shortly when I consider poetic metaphor's nearest "cousins".

Now we must attend to the nature of the disagreement among these theories. The theorists are agreed that metaphor involves two parts. (I shall hereafter borrow Richards' terms, "tenor" and "vehicle", to refer to these parts. I shall also follow his understanding of these terms. Thus, "tenor" will mean the original idea or main subject, while "vehicle" will mean the borrowed idea compared to this subject.) The disagreement arises as to the nature of the relation between these parts and, thus, how the whole metaphor is related to our body of knowledge. The theorists vary from the extreme analogical view, emphasizing the cognitive significance of metaphor, to the extreme ornamental view, emphasizing that metaphor is an interesting curlicue or embellishment which en-

[24] *Ibid.*, p. 215.
[25] *Ibid.*, p. 130.
[26] *Ibid.*, p. 266.
[27] *Ibid.*, pp. 115-16.
[28] Douglas Berggren, "The Use and Abuse of Metaphor, I", *The Review of Metaphysics*, XVI (Dec., 1962), pp. 243-44.

livens style. Ogden and the early Richards, in emphasizing that poetic metaphor is a semi-surreptitious element of emotional significance only, line up on the ornamental end. Max Black and the later Richards, emphasizing that metaphorical tenor and vehicle interact heightening certain qualities in each other while suppressing others, are beginning to see that metaphor is not just a prose ornament but has certain characteristics unique to itself. Thus, they take a step toward the analogical emphasis because they are moving away from the view that the metaphor simply causes or has emotional content. The tension theorists, especially Foss and Wheelwright, in emphasizing that metaphor is somehow more suited to express "reality" than literal language take still another step toward the analogical end. They not only deny that the significance of metaphor is that of an emotional cause, but argue positively that metaphor is more suited to express "reality" than even literal language. The views vary from those which say poetic metaphor makes no assertive or truth claim to those which say that metaphor is more fitted to the expression of truth than even literal language. These arguments are clearly over what could variously be called the "cognitive" status of metaphor or the "referential" status of metaphor. Such disputes are also clearly in the area of a theory of meaning. My third reason then for not using the historical survey procedure is that *these* historical disputes can be best settled by reaching a theory of meaning of poetic metaphor. Of course, I do not intend to disparage the significance of an historical approach to other problems.

B.   POSITIVE STATEMENT OF PROCEDURAL METHOD

The basic procedural methodology of this book will involve presenting examples of metaphors and generalizing from these examples to a theory of meaning of poetic metaphor. The specific questions metaphor must answer in order to provide a satisfactory theory of meaning will be drawn mainly from Wittgenstein's later philosophy. Specifically, my procedural methodology will involve a dialogue between Wittgenstein's theory of meaning,[29] criticisms and elaborations of it, and poetic metaphor. Poetic metaphors do not have voices so I shall call on authorities

---

[29]   Wittgenstein did not believe he held any *philosophical* theories. When I refer to his "theory of meaning" I do not mean he did have a philosophical theory of meaning. I am using "theory", as it is often used, as loosely synonymous with "view" or "views". In this loose sense he does have a "theory of meaning".

on poetic language – literary critics. From this dialogue between authorities on meaning (Wittgenstein and others) and authorities on poetic
metaphor (literary critics) a theory of meaning of poetic metaphor is
expected.

My calling this technique a "dialogue" between theorists and examples intends to emphasize an analogy between the present method
and scientific procedure. The examples chosen represent a body of
unassimilated material. The material has not been hand-picked but is
claimed to be representative. Examples of romantic metaphor, classical
metaphor, and shades between will be presented. These examples then
are the body of data which the theory here being developed must
describe. This theory must be adequate to this body of data and must
show a flexibility which implies that it would not be embarrassed by
an unexpected example. The method of this book then is scientific in
the sense that it claims adequacy to the examples.

However, two significant problems arise from the statement that I
intend to reach a theory of meaning of poetic metaphor by means of a
dialogue between general theories of meaning and examples of poetic
metaphor. (I have used the word "theories" in the plural because I shall
include several theories briefly, but only Wittgenstein's in detail.) First,
it is not clear what I mean by a "theory of meaning" and, thus, what I
intend to do. Second, in view of the historical dispute already noted over
a definition of metaphor, it is not clear that *examples* of metaphor can
be selected without objection. How can I select examples without a
definition? I shall deal with these problems in the order stated.

1. *Theory of Meaning*

What I mean by "theory of meaning" can be clarified ostensively. Of
course, I mean my own theory as it is developed in Chapter III. I also
mean Wittgenstein's theory as it is developed in his later writings. However, I can do more than point to my own and Wittgenstein's theory.
By "theory of meaning" I understand those theories which deal with
the relation of signs, both verbal and nonverbal, to contexts. These
contexts may be other signs, as in the case of analytic statements, or
particular experiences or physical situations, as in the case of synthetic
statements. The context of a verbal utterance includes the rest of our
language, our behavior, and the physical world. I have already indicated
(above, p. 13, footnote 1) that the theory of meaning of poetic meta-

phor will involve epistemological considerations because a significant
part of the context of such language is imagery. Thus, I shall have to
analyze the mode in which such imagery is realized, namely reading.[30]
I have also indicated that perhaps Wittgenstein would deny that his
analysis of meaning as use involved such epistemological considerations.
He might claim that his grammatical method did not involve epistemology. Thus, why should his theory be included under the same
phrase as mine since I explicitly state that my analysis will involve some
epistemological considerations?

My reply is, first, that Wittgenstein's later philosophy clearly does
appeal to grounds other than grammatical ones. In "The Blue Book",
in attacking the view that "expecting" involves some prior mental
rehearsal, Wittgenstein states:

A gun is fired in my presence and I say: "This crash wasn't as loud as I had
expected." Someone asks me: "How is this possible? Was there a crash,
louder than that of a gun, in your imagination?" I must confess that there
was nothing of the sort.[31]

I quite agree with Wittgenstein that "there was nothing of the sort".
However, the reason I agree with Wittgenstein here is that in fact introspection tells me that "expecting" does not involve such a prior
rehearsal. Wittgenstein's appeal here to introspection or self-knowledge
is not at all peculiar to this example. Stanley Cavell goes so far as to
argue that Wittgenstein's real method is an appeal to self-knowledge.[32]

Second, just because I shall argue that a theory of meaning of poetic
metaphor involves epistemological considerations does not commit me
to the view that a theory of meaning of *literal* statements involves such
considerations. I can consistently hold that Wittgenstein's analysis of
literal statements is not in the main epistemological and that such an
analysis is quite adequate with regard to literal language, while still
holding that an analysis of metaphor involves such considerations.

Third, Wittgenstein's analysis of meaning in his later philosophy is
clearly a theory of meaning in the minimal sense implied by my defini-

---

[30] The term "reading" by no means excludes hearing the poem. In fact it is
probably true that a silently read poem is "heard" in the "mind's ear".
[31] Ludwig Wittgenstein, *Preliminary Studies for the "Philosophical Investigations"*, generally known as: *The Blue and Brown Books* (Oxford, Basil Blackwell,
1960), p. 40. (Hereafter *The Blue and Brown Books* will be referred to as *"Blue
Book"*.)
[32] Stanley Cavell, "The Availability of Wittgenstein's Later Philosophy", *The
Philosophical Review*, LXXI (Jan., 1962), p. 89.

tion of such a theory. In *The Blue and Brown Books* and in the *Philosophical Investigations*, Wittgenstein is clearly dealing with the question: How are signs related to their contexts? In "The Blue Book" Wittgenstein presents the example of squaring cardinal numbers to show what is involved in "understanding" with regard to analytic procedures. If someone asks me to square this series: 1, 2, 3, 4, and I write 1, 4, 9, 16, then I have demonstrated that I understand the meaning of "squaring" because I have proceeded in accordance with the general rule of squaring.[33] In the *Philosophical Investigations* a similar example is further elaborated. Even if I can cite the formula for "squaring" I am not said to know how to go on with the series unless I actually apply the formula and continue the series.[34] In short: "The grammar of the word 'knows' is evidently closely related to that of 'can', 'is able to'. But also closely related to that of 'understands'. ('Mastery' of a technique, [*sic*].)" [35] Understanding the meaning of certain words such as "squaring" can be demonstrated by producing other signs in accordance with a rule.

Wittgenstein gives words whose meanings involve observational contexts a similar treatment. To test someone's understanding of the word "red" we might order him to fetch us a red flower. The person ordered may carry a chart of colors, may imagine red, or may simply pick the flower. None of the three alternate ways is *the* process of understanding "red". Rather understanding is shown by actually fetching a flower whose color is commonly called "red".[36] The same point is expanded in the *Philosophical Investigations* with regard to the primitive language-game in section 2. Both species of meaning, one demonstrating understanding of signs by production of other signs in accordance with a rule and one demonstrating understanding of signs by indicating an observational context conventionally designated by that sign, fall under Wittgenstein's classical statement of the meaning of signs: "But if we had to name anything which is the life of the sign, we should have to say that it was its *use*." [37] Wittgenstein's analysis of meaning as use is clearly a theory of meaning in that it shows how signs are related to their contexts; namely, they are related by use.

[33] *Blue Book*, p. 13.
[34] Ludwig Wittgenstein, *Philosophical Investigations*, trans. G. E. M. Anscombe (New York, The Macmillan Co., 1960), sec. 179. (Hereafter the *Philosophical Investigations* will be referred to as "*Investigations*".)
[35] *Ibid.*, # 150.
[36] *Blue Book*, p. 3.
[37] *Ibid.*, p. 4.

This general theory of meaning will be expanded only in so far as it is relevant to an analysis of the meaning of poetic metaphor. An example will help to adumbrate the relevance of Wittgenstein's analysis to the meaning of poetic metaphor. Suppose Columbus in speaking to Queen Isabella said: "The world is like this orange." The Queen might query him further by asking: "What do you mean, Columbus? Is the world orange in color?" Columbus would answer: "No. I meant the world is like the orange in that both have a spherical shape." Columbus has responded by pointing out in what *relevant* sense the world is like an orange. In place of his original metaphorical statement, Columbus provides a literal restatement. This restatement cites a predicate, "spherical", which can be literally asserted of both the world and the orange. We could call Columbus' restatement an analysis of his metaphor. Columbus' restatement is a clarification of the *meaning* of his original metaphor.

Poetic metaphor is similar in that the metaphorical vehicle is like the metaphorical tenor in *some* but not *all* senses. Thus, a critical analysis of the metaphor, like Columbus' restatement, lists the *relevant* senses in which the vehicle is seen as the tenor. These relevant senses clarify metaphor's *meaning*. Seeing as, I shall argue in Chapter III, is the act by which the relevant sense of a metaphor is found. I shall also argue that seeing as, the act which leads to the discovery [38] of the metaphor's meaning, essentially involves imagery. In other words, the meaning of poetic metaphor involves imagery. Further, it follows that if metaphorical meaning involves imagery then the critics' clarification of the metaphor's meaning refers to this imagery excited while reading. I shall argue in Chapter IV that the critic justifies his analysis on the basis of the metaphor as that metaphor is realized in its imagistic fullness while being read. I shall then claim that meaning with regard to language *in* the metaphor involves imagery and that clarification of this meaning by language *about* the metaphor involves reference to this imagery in order to justify the adequacy of the critics' understanding of the metaphor's meaning.

---

[38] I shall speak throughout this book of "discovering" or "finding" metaphorical meaning. The word "discovery" is appropriate to metaphorical meaning because the implicatively-full, image-laden language of metaphor calls for a stance of active openness or sensitivity to the imagery and implicative suggestiveness of that language. As Wimsatt and Brooks argue metaphorical meaning is discovered through a process of exploration (*Literary Criticism: A Short History*, New York, Alfred A. Knopf, 1957, p. 644). The stance for discovering metaphorical meaning is *reading*. Reading will be analyzed in Chapter III.

Wittgenstein's theory then is relevant on two important counts. His attack on the inner meaning theory denies both that meaning is an inner experience and that meaning involves inner experience. This attack is relevant to the claim that metaphorical meaning involves imagery. Second, the same attack and his positive analysis of meaning as use state that the correctness of one's understanding of an expression is established by reference to "criteria". "Criteria", as I shall show, mean for Wittgenstein observable features selected by convention. Wittgenstein's understanding of "criteria" then will not allow that the critic justify his understanding of a metaphor as read because such an appeal is not solely an appeal to observable features selected by convention. The literary critic does not justify the adequacy of his understanding of the metaphor by reference to criteria in the strict sense understood by Wittgenstein. Wittgenstein's analysis then is relevant to language in the metaphor and language about the metaphor.

In summary, I have: (1) clarified in a preliminary way what I mean by "theory of meaning"; (2) shown that Wittgenstein's later philosophy develops a theory of meaning in this sense; (3) sketched the relevance of his theory to metaphorical meaning. Now at least part of my intention in saying my procedure will be to present a dialogue between theories of meaning and examples of poetic metaphor is clearer. However, the second problem mentioned earlier (namely, how examples can be selected without first having a definition) is still pressing.

2. Preliminary Definition for Selecting Examples

The solution to this problem becomes apparent if one attends closely to the nature of the disagreement over definitions of metaphor. All the theorists agree that the metaphor has two elements related in some way. The "some way" is the problem. Is it analogical, ornate, interactive, or tensional? I propose to avoid at present the question of how the elements are related by appealing to the modicum of agreement, namely, that two elements are involved and that these elements are related in some way. Everyone can be satisfied if a particular type of metaphor is chosen, namely, an explicit metaphor or simile.[39] Surely the gramma-

---

[39] I am following Aristotle (Ross, XI, 1406b 20) in classifying the simile as a type of metaphor. There is no essential difference between a simile and an implicit metaphor except for the ease with which the former is recognizable due to its having a grammatical "red flag" in the words "like", "as", etc.

tical red flag, the "like" or "as" in an explicit metaphor, gives evidence that the poet is making a metaphorical comparison. Certainly this grammatical cue indicates that the parts of the example are to be taken as related in some significant way. For example, in the following lines

> Our two souls therefore, which are one
>   Though I must go, endure not yet
> A breach, but an expansion,
>   Like gold to airy thinness beat.
> (John Donne, "A Valediction: Forbidding Mourning", ll. 21-24)

the separation of lovers' souls stands in a clear metaphorical relation to gold beat "to airy thinness". The various theorists cited previously then could agree that this explicit metaphor is a metaphor because it has two parts somehow related although they could not agree on the nature of this relation. The thought behind my point here is that parties to a dispute over a definition can often agree that a particular case falls under the class being debated though the extension of that class is still in dispute.

However, this clear way of selecting examples is unsatisfactory. Any literary critic would be offended at the suggestion that explicit metaphors or similes were the only or the main type of poetic metaphor. This objection is just. Similes constitute only a fraction of poetic metaphor. To see the other fundamental type we need to consider the following example.

> O the mind, mind has mountains; cliffs of fall
> Frightful, sheer, no-man-fathomed. Hold them cheap
> May who ne'er hung there.
> (Gerard Manley Hopkins, "Carrion Comfort", ll. 23-26)

One will immediately notice that this example differs from the first type in a very important way. The grammatical red flags, "like" or "as", are missing. These types of metaphor will prove to be very tricky and complex for the very important reason that *the sheer grammatical form of the examples is that of a literal assertion.* There is no internal clue that a metaphorical statement is being made. I will call this most important type of metaphor *implicit* metaphor.

I shall consider it more closely. Hopkins states that the "mind has mountains". The reader's immediate reaction is almost certain to be: "Surely Hopkins knew that the mind doesn't have mountains in it. At best it has only creases." This reaction stems from a very important insight. We want to say: "Surely the poet is here using a *conscious* metaphor. Hopkins is certainly comparing the mind to mountainous terrain; he is not identifying the two." We believe that Hopkins certainly sensed the conscious tension or difference between the *content* of his stanza and our body of scientific knowledge. The problems raised by our example of implicit metaphor vastly complicate the analysis because we cannot even know *a metaphor has occurred without going outside the poem.* Implicit metaphor is recognized by its literal falseness.[40] Implicit metaphor by being literally false forces itself, so to speak, away from our body of literal knowledge. This step back from our natural knowledge will be very significant in my analysis of reading in Chapter III.

A second, less basic, way of recognizing implicit metaphors is that they startle our literal language sense. Implicit metaphors are odd ways of speaking.

By contrast, explicit metaphors are much easier to detect. We can say, figuratively speaking, that explicit metaphors are horizontally detectable. By looking across the page *in* the poem we discover evidence of the metaphor in the grammatical signals "like" or "as". To recognize an explicit metaphor we have only to know that these grammatical conventions mean a metaphor is being stated. Implicit metaphor requires a looking beyond the poem on the page. That an implicit metaphor has occurred cannot be known within the poem. Such a metaphor is recognized by its tension with our body of knowledge.

Implicit metaphor becomes even more problematical because of its resemblance, in fact, its grammatical identity with its two first cousins, metaphor in myth and "dead" metaphor in literal language. Consider the following mythical example:

> We have carried away Death,
> And brought Life back.
> He has taken up his quarters in the village,
> Therefore sing joyous songs.

("Bohemian Chant", quoted by Frazer in *The Golden Bough,* Chapter xxviii)

Certainly we feel a tension between this metaphor and our body of

---

[40] Of course, not all literally false statements are implicit metaphors. The predicate of one type of false statement is wrongly asserted of the subject of that statement while the predicate of a metaphor is asserted in some *relevant* sense of the subject of that metaphor. Another species of false statement applies its subject incorrectly to some observational context. Implicit metaphor differs from this type of false statement in that it is not the purpose of metaphorical statements in poetry to apply its subject to an observational context.

scientific knowledge, but the question can be asked: When this *myth was taken as myth*, instead of aesthetically, was there a tension with literal knowledge? Barfield argues that mythical thought has not yet reached the distinction between the self and objects, between words and their referents. Therefore, no self consciousness has emerged.[41] Metaphor in myth does not express a conscious separation yet relatedness of its parts. For *poetic* metaphor to emerge a level of consciousness must arise. Poetic metaphor presupposes a body of prose knowledge because such metaphor represents a *deliberate* yoking of unlikes by an individual artificer.[42] To recall Berggren's thought, the conscious tension of metaphor is not present in myth. Mythical statements are direct assertions in intent. As Morris argues, they are informative in purpose.[43] Reinhold Niebuhr argues similarly that the essential difference between myth and poetry is that myth is poetry believed.[44] The fact that metaphor in myth differs from implicit metaphor in poetry, as noted by Barfield, Morris, and Niebuhr, only in being taken as true or assertive in intent complicates the selection of examples of poetic metaphor. Belief or assertive intent is not evident from the statements themselves. Thus, there seems to be no grammatical signal to distinguish implicit metaphor in poetry from metaphor in myth. The close relation between poetic metaphor and mythical metaphor makes more difficult the selection of examples of poetic metaphor.

This problem is further complicated by the fact that implicit metaphor has another first cousin. Examples of this relative, namely, "dead" literal metaphors, are not hard to find. Consider: "the *leg* of a table", "the *arm* of a chair", "the *neck* of a bottle". In fact, the present writer suspects that one would have great difficulty in finding any literal statement which does not contain "dead" metaphors. A tracing of the origin of our most abstract terms, often requiring pursuit through several languages, usually reveals an original metaphor. From this fact the present writer in no way intends to claim that poets created all our language and their metaphors have simply died. Study of the origins of language is the linguist's domain. One such excellent scholar, Leo-

---

[41] Owen Barfield, *Poetic Diction: A Study in Meaning* (London, Faber & Faber, 1952), p. 103.
[42] *Ibid.*, p. 81.
[43] Morris, p. 134.
[44] Eugene Garett Bewkes *et al.*, *The Nature of Religious Experience: Essays in Honor of Douglas Clyde Macintosh* (New York, Harper & Brothers, 1937), pp. 119-20.

nard Bloomfield, tells us that the poet-created-the-language theory has the cart before the horse. In fact, metaphor is a common principle of transference of ordinary language. The poet merely taps these natural tendencies. "The picturesque saying that 'language is a book of faded metaphors' is the reverse of the truth, for poetry is rather a blazoned book of language." [45] I have presented this cousin of poetic metaphor in order to point out that the grammatical similarity between implicit poetic metaphor and "dead" metaphor in literal statements makes selection of examples of poetic metaphor more difficult.[46]

Since an easy grammatical way of discovering implicit metaphors has failed, the writer suggests that a tentative definition of poetic metaphor be accepted. This definition will include the following conditions. First, the examples selected will be from verbal vehicles which are clearly recognized as poems. Second, the parts of the metaphor must be in conscious *tension* with each other; which is to say, the metaphorical predicate is not literally asserted of the subject. As Berggren saw it, the parts must be related but not absorbed into each other. The tension between parts is noticed because of some contrast with our body of knowledge or usual way of speaking. The first condition will assure that the example is "poetic" as contrasted to "mythical" or "dead" metaphors. This condition will limit examples to those taken from poems. Certainly there are instances of verbal forms which some critics call "poetry" while other critics withhold this partially honorific word. The present writer will avoid such debates by choosing examples only from recognized poems. The second condition indicates that only certain elements in the poem will be called metaphor. Poetry certainly has devices other than metaphors. These two conditions are as of yet only *procedural* points. Later, when more concepts have been clarified, more essential conditions can replace these procedural ways of selecting examples. In Chapter III where the most essential nature of metaphor emerges (namely, that metaphor is a seeing as between elements of an imagistic description) this procedural means of selecting examples can be replaced by that more adequate understanding. At present I suggest

[45]   Leonard Bloomfield, *Language* (New York, H. Holt & Co., 1933), p. 443.
[46]   In Chapter III I shall distinguish "dead" literal metaphors from poetic metaphors on the grounds that the tenor and vehicle of the latter are related by seeing as not by recognition. We are correctly said to "recognize" instances of "the leg of a table" or "the neck of a bottle" because such phrases are now taken literally. Only with regard to degenerate poetic metaphors is it correct to use the term "recognition". With regard to Hopkins' metaphor we do not "recognize" that the mind has mountains in it; we "see" the mind "as" having mountains in it.

that the following definition is procedurally adequate to justify examples selected of implicit and explicit metaphor. The examples must be from recognized poems and the examples must have two parts (tenor and vehicle) which are in conscious tension with each other and with our body of literal knowledge. The first part of my definition restricts my examples to certain verbal forms, poems; and the second part, to particular parts of the poem. If you will, these are procedural criteria for selecting examples.

However, the special problems raised by implicit metaphor must not be allowed to over stress its difference from explicit metaphor. Implicit metaphor differs from explicit metaphor only in that recognition of an instance of an implicit metaphor – the first step to discovering metaphorical meaning – is more difficult than recognition of an explicit metaphor. To recognize an explicit metaphor one has only to know a language, to know that these conventions mean a metaphor is being stated. To recognize an implicit metaphor requires in addition a body of literal knowledge with which the metaphor is in tension. However, here the difference ends. The result of recognizing either an implicit or explicit metaphor is the same. In both cases one is forced, so to speak, to stand off from literal knowledge. In both cases this distance demands that the metaphorical tenor and vehicle are related in some but not all senses. The vehicle is not literally predicated of the tenor. This enforced distance assists one in the second and third conditions (the first condition being recognizing that the metaphor is a metaphor) for discovering, and thus conditions for being said to "understand", a metaphor's meaning. These conditions will be *reading* the metaphor and *analyzing* the relevant senses in which the vehicle is like the tenor. With regard to these latter two conditions, explicit and implicit metaphor are identical. Thus, in my analysis of reading in Chapter III and in my treatment of how an analysis of a metaphor is justified in Chapter IV, I shall not distinguish implicit and explicit metaphor.

Further, it is worth noting here that these three conditions for understanding a metaphor's meaning are distinguished somewhat artificially here. In an actual case of trying to discover a metaphor's meaning, we do not first recognize the metaphor, then read it, then analyze its meaning. In actual cases the three are interwoven. For example, the more adequate definition of metaphor in Chapter III, a definition which will replace this procedural means of *recognizing* examples of metaphor, is very much bound up with the type of *reading* appropriate to metaphor. Further, reading, as the mode in which the imagistic fullness of metaphor is realized, is not an entirely passive state but borders on active analysis in what I shall analyze as the experience-act of seeing as. Thus, in trying to understand a particular metaphor, one does not switch on his recognizing capacity, then switch it off and activate his reading mechanism, and then finally stop reading and start analyzing. All three are closely related and bound up with each other. One cannot draw a line where recognition stops and reading starts or where reading ceases and analysis begins. Reading, as I shall understand it, is an active openness.

In conclusion, a statement of the intended accomplishments of this Introduction may clarify my arguments. First, a preliminary justification of my procedural methodology has been established. Now examples of implicit and explicit metaphor can be selected and treated "scientifically". Second, certain urgent problems inevitably arise. Implicit metaphor forces a consideration of the problematic relation between poetic and literal statements. A theory of meaning of poetic metaphor can most adequately answer these problems. Some hint of the theory here being developed has been given in my remarks clarifying my understanding of the phrase "theory of meaning" and in the sketch of the necessary conditions for discovering metaphorical meaning.

Now, having given a tentative defense of my general procedure and suggested some of the problems and significance of my subject, I can be more specific as to chapter order. In Chapter I I shall analyze Wittgenstein's attack on the inner meaning theory and his positive formulation of meaning as use. I shall adumbrate the relevance of his analysis for poetic metaphor. In Chapter II I shall analyze four theories of poetic language and generalize from these to conclusions about poetic language. In Chapter III I shall show how metaphor fits the general conclusions of Chapter II, while having its own unique features. Thus, I shall reach a theory of meaning of poetic metaphor. I shall also look back to Chapter I and give metaphor's answers to the problems raised by Wittgenstein. Finally, in Chapter IV I shall show how the critic justifies his understanding of the meaning of a particular metaphor. These conclusions will be drawn mainly on the basis of Chapter III.

I. WITTGENSTEIN'S THEORY OF MEANING

The purpose of this chapter is to analyze Wittgenstein's thought in so far as it is relevant to poetic metaphor. However, this relevance is not at all clear. His remarks on metaphor are almost non-existent. He does say a metaphorical sense is not a secondary sense. By secondary sense he means the application of a term such as "calculate", which is primarily an act done on paper, to another context such as calculating in one's head.[1] These remarks are helpful only in a negative sense.

More positively helpful is his brief remark on understanding a poem. He says: "We speak of understanding a sentence in the sense in which it can be replaced by another which says the same; but also in the sense in which it cannot be replaced by another." [2] This latter sense, that is, attending to these words in these positions, is related to understanding a poem. This fruitful insight that a poem cannot be stated in an alternate way is left with the suggestion that we should ask ourselves how we lead someone to comprehend a poem.[3]

Wittgenstein's remarks on general aesthetics are almost as rare. He suggests that ethical and aesthetic terms are open class terms,[4] a point elaborated by Morris Weitz.[5] An open class term is a term which, though useful, has no precisely defined extension. Moore cites another interesting tidbit on general aesthetics from Wittgenstein's 1930-33 lectures. He says Wittgenstein stated that aesthetic questions were not psychological because they were not causal explanations. The aesthetic question is not "do you like" but "why do you like this". Aesthetic arguments are like a law court in that they try to clear up circumstances

---

[1] *Investigations*, p. 216.
[2] *Ibid.*, # 531.
[3] *Ibid.*, # 533.
[4] *Ibid.*, # 77.
[5] Morris Weitz, "The Role of Theory in Aesthetics", *The Journal of Aesthetics & Art Criticism*, XV (Sept., 1956), pp. 27-35.

before submitting to the judge.[6] In an even earlier work Wittgenstein said: "Art is a kind of expression. Good art is complete expression." [7] None of these remarks are amplified. One could collect these aphorisms and speculate as to Wittgenstein's views on poetry and general aesthetics, but such a method would be pure speculation.

I suggest this procedure as more fruitful. I shall analyze Wittgenstein's attack on the inner meaning theory. I shall ask in what sense the attitudes of the poet and the critic toward poetic language fall under this specific attack. I shall ask if the conflict between the poetic view of language and Wittgenstein's attack on the inner meaning theory is significant and, if so, can the poet and critic provide answers to the difficulties cited by Wittgenstein with regard to the particular theory attacked. In other words, are the offenses which one commits in analyzing the meaning of a poetic metaphor indications that an odd language-game is being played or are they indications that no game at all, in Wittgenstein's sense, is being played? Does Wittgenstein's understanding of rules or criteria fundamentally exclude an adequate treatment of the meaning of metaphor or can a more amiable relation between his analysis and the theory here being developed be established? To answer these questions, I shall follow this procedure. First, I shall analyze Wittgenstein's attack on the theory that meaning is a mental parallel to our actual words. At various places I shall state the relevance of specific parts of this attack to poetic metaphor. Second, I shall analyze his positive answer to the difficulties of this theory. Finally, I shall show how the poet's language and the critic's language are related to both the attack and the positive answer.

A. ATTACK ON INNER MEANING THEORY

Pole accurately points out that Wittgenstein's attack on the inner experience theory is an attack on the private world of the dualist.[8] However, it is quite essential to emphasize that this attack is not made for the sake of a theoretical monism. Wittgenstein does not deny that

[6]   G. E. Moore, "Wittgenstein's Lectures in 1930-33", Pt. III, *Mind*, LXIV (Jan., 1955), pp. 18-19.
[7]   Ludwig Wittgenstein, *Notebooks: 1914-1916*, ed. G. H. von Wright and G. E. M. Anscombe, trans. G. E. M. Anscombe (Oxford, Basil Blackwell, 1961), p. 83.
[8]   David Pole, *The Later Philosophy of Wittgenstein* (London, The Athlon Press, 1958), p. 64.

mental processes occur but rather says that when they are interpreted as a mental something then they are a *"grammatical* fiction".[9]
The question becomes: What is a grammatical fiction? This question
can be answered by seeing what he meant by saying his method was
grammatical.[10] A grammatical analysis is a description, not an explanation. Philosophy gives no explanations. Explanations are empirical and
scientific. "Philosophy really *is* 'purely descriptive'." [11] Philosophers
simply look at the workings of our language. A grammatical analysis

---

[9] *Investigations,* # 293, 307.

[10] *Ibid.,* # 90.

[11] *Blue Book,* p. 18. Wittgenstein says philosophy is purely descriptive. Yet later
he says "we are handicapped in ordinary language. . . . This, of course, does not
mean that ordinary language is insufficient for our special purposes, but that it
is slightly cumbrous and sometimes misleading" (*Blue Book,* p. 52). This last
sentence seems simply to be confused. If ordinary language is sufficient for our
purposes then how can it be cumbrous and misleading? If philosophy is purely
descriptive, how can we speak of being handicapped by ordinary language? We
can make the latter statement only if there are some rules or standards which
stand above ordinary language and by which ordinary language can be criticized.
Philosophy might be purely descriptive; but, if so, it doesn't describe ordinary
language. Only the lexicographer should be worried if the man on the street does
not agree with his analysis. I am quite aware of Wittgenstein's objections to holding a calculus up to ordinary language and declaring the latter inadequate. The
present writer agrees that such a comparison is misleading. However, if philosophy has any formative function, if the sample language-games do clear up mud-
dles because we have been bewitched by our language, then some principles
which have some distance from the flux of ordinary language must be used. If
we do not hold language up to a calculus, we must hold it up to some standard.
Fortunately, Wittgenstein does have normative elements despite his talk of pure
description and despite his calling his method of philosophy grammatical. His
further grounds of appeal can be seen in any of his numerous examples. Consider
this one: "A gun is fired in my presence and I say: 'This crash wasn't as loud as
I had expected.' Someone asks me: 'How is this possible? Was there a crash,
louder than that of a gun, in your imagination?' I must confess that there was
nothing of the sort" (*Blue Book,* p. 40). I agree with Wittgenstein that there is
nothing of this sort when a sound is not as loud as expected. But what is Wittgenstein's ground of appeal here? Do we agree that his example is illuminating because a vote would reveal that the ordinary man said this example was true?
I rather suspect that the grounds for accepting the example as significant are that
when we say "the crash wasn't as loud as expected" we *in fact* did not hear a
louder noise in our imagination. We must confess with Wittgenstein that there
was *nothing* of this sort. Wittgenstein here is appealing to what must honestly be
called good old fashion introspection. In many other places he appeals to extra-
grammatical grounds. Many of his language-games function in a loose argument.
Stanley Cavell has even suggested (Cavell, p. 89) that Wittgenstein's real method
involves an appeal to self-knowledge. The present method is an appeal to self-
knowledge not in the sense of knowledge *of* the self, but as knowledge of what
the self is doing when reading poetry. However, I call this method not introspection, but phenomenology,

does not explain, but describes the use of signs.[12] "The problems are solved, not by giving new information, but by arranging what we have always known." [13] Thus, Wittgenstein is not making an empirical claim about mental events in saying that such inner occurrences interpreted as objects are a "grammatical fiction". He means images are inessential to using language.

Wittgenstein's use of sample language-games further clarifies his basic grammatical method and thus clarifies what it means to be a "grammatical fiction". Seeing language in its primitive form in the simple language-games reminds us that speaking language is an activity, a form of life.[14] Language-games help us see how we have learned language.[15] Language-games are not intended to show us the essence of language. Various games have no common essence, but rather "we see a complicated network of similarities overlapping and criss-crossing: sometimes overall similarities, sometimes similarities of detail".[16] The traditional philosophical error of searching for essences has arisen from the mistaken notion that only sharply defined concepts are complete or useful.[17] A study of various language-games underlines the fact that we learn and use language. Language-games are to be compared to our language. They throw light on our language, our grammar and the way we use words. Language-games show us which factors function in operating with or using language and, by negative implication, which factors are inessential "grammatical fictions".

Inner images are a "grammatical fiction" in the sense that they have no role in the learning and using of our language. Wittgenstein does not deny that inner images exist or occur, but only that they are *necessary* to our ordinary use of language.[18] Wittgenstein then is never a theoretical behaviorist but a type of operational behaviorist. In saying Wittgenstein is never a theoretical behaviorist, I mean that he never denies that mental events exist or occur. He only denies the relevance of such events to our operation with language. A theoretical behaviorist would have to make an empirical claim about the nonexistence of mental happenings. For Wittgenstein, empirical information is not relevant to

---

[12]   *Investigations*, # 496.
[13]   *Ibid.*, # 109.
[14]   *Ibid.*, # 23.
[15]   *Ibid.*, # 5.
[16]   *Ibid.*, # 66.
[17]   *Blue Book*, pp. 18-19.
[18]   *Ibid.*, p. 42.

distinguishing the mind from a machine.[19] Therefore, nothing factual is being asserted or denied by his operational behaviorism. "Grammar tells what kind of object anything is." [20] The soul is distinguished from a machine on grammatical grounds. Wittgenstein does not deny that the soul exists, but insists that the body is the best picture of the soul.[21] These introductory remarks are an important warning not to overextend Wittgenstein's attack. In conclusion, images are a grammatical fiction in the sense that they play no role in the use of our language.

The force of Wittgenstein's attack on the inner experience theory lies largely in his success in showing that words for the most intangible mental acts have public, not private, criteria. The specific mental words treated here will be "meaning", "intending", "thinking", and "understanding".

1. *"Meaning"*

The internal experience view holds that meaning a sentence or statement is two acts; one a verbal act and the other a parallel internal act. Wittgenstein counters by saying that reading a sentence aloud is like singing from a musical score, but meaning the sentence is not like reading from a score.[22] The dualist seems to think that meaning a sequence of words requires an effort to insure that the right meanings are paraded *in* one's mind *while* the words are being said.[23] I have emphasized the words "in" and "while" which are used by the dualist because they are words usually used to refer to location in physical space or time. Pole accurately says: "Wittgenstein's general thesis [is] that philosophical perplexities arise when, deceived by similarities of form and neglectful of differences of function, we interpret one part of our linguistic system on the false analogy of some other." [24] Wittgenstein would say that the "in" and "while" of the dualist indicate precisely such a misleading analogy. It is a typical metaphysical answer because it expresses in these words an unclarity about grammar in the form of a scientific question.[25] The dualist thinks that if physical objects have a spatio-temporal location so must mental activities. Meaning then must exist somewhere at

19   *Investigations,* # 360.
20   *Ibid.,* # 373.
21   *Ibid.,* p. 178.
22   *Ibid.,* # 22.
23   *Ibid.,* p. 176.
24   Pole, p. 65.
25   *Blue Book,* p. 35.

some time. A pseudo-physical sphere parallel to our actual words is posited. Wittgenstein does not say that "in" or "while" cannot be used in different senses; but when extended to a new sense, a new game, we must not expect this game to be like the original game in having spatio-temporal co-ordinates. For example, we must not expect "having a toothache" to have a location in the same sense that "having a gold tooth" does. We must beware of the misleading grammatical similarity.[26] Applied specifically to "meaning", this means that if we use "in" and "while" with regard to it we must not expect this new use to have the same significance that the words had in their original spatio-temporal context. We must not look for a scientific place and time in which meaning is situated while our words are being said.

However, forcing the dualist to see that "in" and "while" are being used in a new context is not enough. One could now more accurately ask someone what was going on in his mind while meaning such and such a sentence; but his answer still would not tell us what he was meaning when he said the particular sentence.[27] To substantiate this point Wittgenstein uses an example involving the use of nonsense syllables. Suppose someone points to his cheek and says "abracadabra". We might ask what he meant. He responds: "I meant toothache." When asked what he meant, the speaker responds not by describing what went on in his mind when he said the syllables but by giving us a definition, an application of these syllables.[28] The subject's words, his definition, not his images, give his first sign meaning. The subject's verbal behavior has given his nonsense syllables an application, a meaning in a language-game. Signs do not intrinsically have meaning but are given meaning by an application, a use. Use is the life of the sign.[29] "Look at the sentence as an instrument, and at its sense as its employment."[30] The explanatory definition of the nonsense syllables establishes a use, gives the syllables employment.

Wittgenstein's attack on the dualistic view that meaning is an inner performance has a double prong. He denies both the relevance of inner images and inner verbal translations to meaning. Both can really be considered as translations of the overt sentence.

[26]   *Ibid.*, p. 49.
[27]   *Investigations*, # 675.
[28]   *Ibid.*, # 665.
[29]   *Blue Book*, p. 4.
[30]   *Investigations*, # 421.

a. *Inner Images*

The attack on the inner images is very clearly stated in "The Blue Book". The inner image is really a shadow of the objective application, an inner picture which represents by means of its similarity to its outward counterpart. Such an intervening shadow between the words and the physical context becomes useless if the spoken sentence can serve as the shadow, a shadow which does not picture by similarity. The sentence then can be applied directly.

If we were doubtful about how the sentence "King's College is on fire" can be a picture of King's College on fire, we need only ask ourselves: "How should we explain what the sentence means?" Such an explanation might consist of ostensive definitions. We should say, e.g., "this is King's College" (pointing to the building), "this is a fire" (pointing to a fire). This shews you the way in which words and things may be connected.[31]

We give our sentence a use by our ostensive definitions. That "use" is quite similar to the "manner of verification" is born out by Moore's notes on those lectures in which Wittgenstein attacked the inner image theory. Wittgenstein is quoted as saying that the meaning of a "proposition is the way in which it is verified".[32]

This example is quite similar to the abracadabra example. In both cases the subject has responded to a question of meaning not by telling what images he had while saying the sentence, but by applying the sentence, giving it a place in a language-game.

The significance of this point is that images are not related to the overt or original statement in the same way that the definitions in the abracadabra and King's College examples are related to their original statements. Definitions give a statement application, while images do not. Further, images are private and thus not justifiable by reference to criteria. There is no independent source of appeal which can assure the correctness of an image translation.

Let us imagine a table (something like a dictionary) that exists only in our imagination. A dictionary can be used to justify the translation of a word X by a word Y. But are we also to call it a justification if such a table is to be looked up only in the imagination?[33]

There are conventions which justify the relation between the definition and the original statement in our two examples, but there is no con-

---

[31]   *Blue Book*, p. 37.
[32]   Moore, Pt. I, LXIII, p. 14.
[33]   *Investigations*, # 265.

vention which justifies the relation of an image translation to its original statement. Our examples show that if we want to understand a person's meaning we do not ask for a report on images. We look for what are called "explanations of meaning".[34] Explanations of meaning clarify the place or use of the original statement in a language. Explanations of meaning are susceptible to criteria.

Explanations of meaning can be divided roughly into verbal and ostensive definitions.[35] The King's College example illustrates the ostensive explanation. The continuing a series example which follows in the section on "Understanding" illustrates the verbal type. These two types of explanation exhaust the class of explanations. There is no further type of explanation which consists in pointing to inner images. As the above quote indicates, such an explanation referring to an inner image can have no independent source of justification. We cannot look up images in a dictionary. There would be no criteria for this type of explanation.

Wittgenstein has a quite important reason for emphasizing that we should ask for "explanations of meaning" rather than "meanings". If we ask "what is meaning" instead of "what is an explanation of meaning" we are apt to look for images or objects.[36] The dualist here being criticized made this very mistake and was led to postulate meaning as an inner object.

b. *Inner Translations*

Wittgenstein clearly attacks the inner translation theory in the *Philosophical Investigations*. In the simple language of section 2 the builder orders his assistant to get a slab simply by saying "slab". When a more complex language is developed someone may ask: Is the word "slab" really an elliptical form of "bring me a slab"? Wittgenstein simply asks if the builder needs to say the unshortened form to himself when he means bring me a slab. The answer is an obvious no. It would be equally valid to argue that "bring me a slab" is a long word for "slab". A more complex game certainly has alternate forms, but the question is: Do these forms all occur at one time in the speaker's mind while he is saying the shortened form? The answer is an emphatic no. "Slab" in the simple game functions perfectly well to express bring me a slab.

[34]   *Ibid.*, # 560.
[35]   *Blue Book*, p. 1.
[36]   *Ibid.*

Neither the helper nor the builder has to say the longer form in his mind.[37] To say a sentence and mean it does not mean to accompany the sentence with an internal translation.[38]

Wittgenstein then in attacking the inner meaning theory intends to oppose both the view that meaning is an inner image and the view that meaning is an inner verbal translation. The same dual-pronged objection is relevant to the analysis of "intending", "thinking", and "understanding" which follows.

Wittgenstein's attack on the inner meaning theory will be seen to be relevant to poetic metaphor because I shall argue that the meaning of such metaphors involves imagery. However, three very significant differences between metaphorical imagery and the mental pictures of the dualist can profitably be adumbrated here. First, the dualist is accused of thinking that meaning a sequence of words is a dual act requiring an effort to parade the right picture before one's mind's eye while the words are being said. I shall argue that even though metaphor involves imagery reading a metaphor does not involve such a dual act. In reading a poem we do not try to keep one eye focused on the words on the page while the other eye watches a mental movie screen. In reading, the metaphor is a unity. Second, the images of the dualist, as clearly shown by the King's College example, are *intervening*, shadowy images. I shall argue that metaphorical imagery is not an intervening image. Metaphorical imagery is not some sort of negative transparency which is supposed to be aligned or correspond with the physical world. Third, the dualist being attacked holds that meaning is equivalent to an inner experience. I shall argue that metaphorical imagery is involved in metaphorical meaning but is by no means equivalent to such meaning.

2. *"Intending"*

Very closely related to "meaning" a sentence or combination of signs is "intending", the dualist's *second* refuge. The similarity of these two words is shown by the fact that we are often able to substitute "I intended..." for "I meant...". Wittgenstein points out that intending is to some extent what one actually does.[39] "Then the 'inner experience' of intending seems to vanish again. Instead one remembers thoughts,

37 *Investigations*, # 19-20.
38 *Blue Book*, p. 34.
39 *Investigations*, # 644.

feelings, movements, and also connexions with earlier situations." [40]
"An intention is embedded in its situation, in human customs and institutions." [41] In other words, intention is not internal but is shown by the many subtle ways of behavioral expression, verbal and nonverbal, and by the context in which the expression occurs. To intend or to mean something is to say it in a certain way.

The significance of Wittgenstein's analysis of "intending" to poetic metaphor is that the literary critic in an important sense agrees that the poet's intention must be "embedded in its situation, in human customs and institutions".[42] The school of "new criticism", which the methodology of this book (as developed in Chapter III in my analysis of reading) favors, emphasizes that the only intention relevant to poetic meaning is embedded in the poem. The poem itself, the way the poet spoke, is definitive of intention. The purpose of literary analysis is not to speculate about spooky events or intentions in the poet's mind while he was writing the poem. To write the poet about his intention or to speculate about such an intention is to deserve this answer: "Only two people know what I was intending when I wrote the poem; myself at that time and God. I have since forgotten and God won't tell."

3. *"Thinking"*

The third dualistic stronghold which Wittgenstein invades is "thinking". An important point at stake here is the question: Is language the vehicle of thought or is thought internal? Wittgenstein's answer is unequivocal. "The language is itself the vehicle of thought." [43] Thinking is not an incorporeal shadow taking place on a mental back-stage.[44] Wittgenstein clearly states:

It is misleading then to talk of thinking as a "mental activity". We may say that thinking is essentially the activity of operating with signs. This activity is performed by the hand, when we think by writing; by the mouth and larynx, when we think by speaking; and if we think by imagining signs or pictures, I can give you no agent that thinks.[45]

---

[40]   *Ibid.*, # 645.
[41]   *Ibid.*, # 337.
[42]   *Ibid.*, # 337.
[43]   *Ibid.*, # 329.
[44]   *Ibid.*, # 339.
[45]   *Blue Book*, p. 6.

This last phrase about an agent is a warning not to hypostatize the mind. We have postulated a substantial mind because of a misleading analogy between thinking and writing. We think: The hand is the agent of writing. The mind must have a similar agent. Thoughts have to exist somewhere. Therefore, we postulate a mental substance which is the agent of thinking and which gives thought a location. A physical analogy has mislead us.[46]

However, there is still a point needing clarification in Wittgenstein's analysis. Why has he said language is the *vehicle* of thought? If he had wished to stress the inseparability of thought from language, a stronger word could have been used. Wittgenstein early in the *Investigations* says thinking is something like talking to oneself.[47] However, the translator, Anscombe, in a comment on this passage says Wittgenstein requested that she add a note referring the reader to a later correction. On this indicated page Wittgenstein says: " 'Talking' (whether out loud or silently) and 'thinking' are not concepts of the same kind; even though they are in closest connexion." [48] If by "talking out loud" Wittgenstein means talking in public with an audience then his distinction between this type of talking and "thinking" seems well founded. If one talks before an audience others can report what one said, while others cannot report one's thoughts. However, I cannot see Wittgenstein's reason for distinguishing "talking silently" from "thinking". There seem to be no grounds which he could consistently cite for this distinction. This passage simply remains a mystery. He evidently wants to remind us that the grammar of "thought" is different from that of "sentence".

4. *"Understanding"*

Finally, Wittgenstein is able persuasively to clarify the evasive nature of "understanding". In the Introduction to this book a sketch of two senses of understanding, one of analytic signs and the other of synthetic signs, was presented. How does one show that he knows or understands how to give an analytic performance such as continuing a series, for example, the series 1, 5, 11, 19, 29?

Wittgenstein says *several* things may happen in displaying one's knowledge. The subject may cite the formula and apply it; or he may

---

[46]   *Ibid.*, pp. 6-7.
[47]   *Investigations*, # 32.
[48]   *Ibid.*, p. 217.

feel the relief of a mental tension and then continue the series; or he may say: "Yes, I know that series", and then continue it; or he may say nothing but simply continue the series.[49] Emphasis should be placed on the "ors" because they indicate that there is no one process of understanding which has exclusive claim to being *the* process. And even if we discovered that all the subjects used the same method to reach their conclusion "why should *it* be understanding?"[50] To show understanding is quite simply to be able to execute a technique,[51] and even a constant mental accompaniment is not proof of understanding if the technique is not performed. The grammar of the word "knows" is closely related to that of "can".[52]

And hence also 'obeying a rule' is a practice. And to *think* one is obeying a rule is not to obey a rule. Hence it is not possible to obey a rule 'privately': otherwise thinking one was obeying a rule would be the same thing as obeying it.[53]

A language with private rules would not be a language but an impression of a language. [54] A justification, a claim that one has followed a rule, must consist in an appeal to something independent of one's memory.[55] "Following a rule is analogous to obeying an order." [56] Malcolm here points out that Wittgenstein means private definitions are valid only if they lead to correct use. Thus the private picture or definition is irrelevant to actually following the rule.[57] Further, if memory is most basic, how is a true memory distinguished from a false memory? Are they included in another memory, ad infinitum? [58] A private language could not distinguish seeming from being correct.[59] Wittgenstein here is probably objecting to Russell's view of the primacy of memory.

In summary, all the subjects might report that they followed the same inner process to get an answer, but if they could not continue the series they would have only thought they understood. "Understanding" is

---

49   *Ibid.*, # 151.
50   *Ibid.*, # 153.
51   *Ibid.*, # 199.
52   *Ibid.*, # 150.
53   *Ibid.*, # 202.
54   Norman Malcolm, "Wittgenstein's *Philosophical Investigations*", *The Philosophical Review*, LXIII (Oct., 1954), p. 537.
55   *Investigations*, # 265.
56   *Ibid.*, # 206.
57   Malcolm, pp. 530-33.
58   *Ibid.*, p. 533.
59   Leonard Linsky, "Wittgenstein on Language and Some Problems of Philosophy", *The Journal of Philosophy*, LIV (May 9, 1957), p. 287.

shown by an overt act, not by a mental feeling. If we say we know how to continue the series but cannot continue it, then we did not really know how or "understand" in the first case.

Understanding the meaning of "red" is given a similar treatment. We may test a person's understanding of the word "red" by ordering him to fetch a red flower. The person ordered may carry a color chart, may conjure up a mental image of red and compare it to the flower, or may simply pick a red flower. There is no *one* process of understanding. Any of these alternate ways would show understanding if a flower called "red" were *actually* picked. We must not yield to the temptation to postulate an inorganic inner act which is somehow *the* understanding. We must remember "that no adding of inorganic signs can make the proposition live".[60]

Understanding the meaning of "pain" is very much more complex than the previous senses of understanding. To move into these problems it will be helpful to see how understanding "pain" is similar to understanding "red". There are many clues indicating that Wittgenstein thought them similar. If asked how we know this color is red, we could reply by saying I have learned English.[61] Also, we learn the concept "pain" when we learn language.[62] Further, we exhibit pain like we exhibit red.[63] We shall then temporarily say "pain" is a sensation word for Wittgenstein.

Wittgenstein analyzes sensation words in the calendar example. Suppose we wanted to keep a diary in which we record a certain sensation by the letter "E". The question is: Is there a type of internal ostensive definition, inward criteria, which can justify our writing the "E"? The important point at stake here is: Is there such an act as internal naming or pointing? Is there some internal ceremony which somehow christens a sensation with a name? Is there a way the mind can focus its eyes on an internal sensation? Wittgenstein's readers disagree on this point. Strawson says Wittgenstein denied that "sensations can be recognized and bear names".[64] Malcolm says Strawson is quite wrong on this point. "Wittgenstein does not deny that we *name* sensations." [65]

[60] *Blue Book*, p. 4.
[61] *Investigations*, # 381. Wittgenstein no doubt omitted the quotes around the word "red" in this passage through an oversight.
[62] *Ibid.*, # 384.
[63] *Ibid.*, # 313.
[64] P. F. Strawson, "*Philosophical Investigations*", *Mind*, LXIII (Jan., 1954), p. 87.
[65] Malcolm, p. 551.

Malcolm cites section 244 in the *Investigations* as evidence for his interpretation. However, attention to this section will show it to be quite inconclusive. Further, it is a beginning paragraph of the treatment of this very problem and is thus a stage setting paragraph. A later paragraph in the same series quite clearly states that we do not point to sensations, which is to say we do not name them. "Can I point to the sensation? Not in the ordinary sense." [66] Wittgenstein never examines any figurative sense of pointing. Thus, it seems that Strawson is without a doubt correct on this point. This point is very important for this reason. If there were some internal act of naming of which we were conscious, then we could justify our use of a word by recalling this metaphorical christening. There could be internal criteria for use. Strawson is quite right in saying Wittgenstein would deny such internal justifications.[67] Our example shows that the only way we can say we impressed "E" on ourselves is if we remember how to use "E" correctly in the future.[68] This is to say that justification, in this case justification of using "E" for the sensation, must appeal to something independent like a dictionary or an existing state of affairs. Justification is the association of a sign and a context in a way which is actually correct.[69] In our experiment we use public words such as "sensation", "has", and "something". We said that we had some sensation when we wrote "E". If we use public words we need a justification which everybody understands.[70] Public language needs public criteria. These are the same objections Wittgenstein used against the primacy of memory over criteria. "Red" and "pain" then are alike in that both are sensation words justified by independent criteria.

However, here the similarity abruptly ends. There are two senses in which it is relevant to speak of knowing or understanding the word "pain". The first sense of knowing "pain" will be seen to be meaningless. The second sense, which is a meaningful sense, will be seen to have quite a different sort of justification from one's justification of his understanding of "red".

First, we can ask in what sense one knows one's own pain. This sense of knowing is nonsense. We do not say we know our pain except perhaps as a joke. We *have* our own pains.[71] My relation to the

---

[66] *Investigations*, # 258.
[67] Strawson, pp. 87-88.
[68] *Investigations*, # 258.
[69] *Ibid.*, # 265.
[70] *Ibid.*, # 261.
[71] *Ibid.*, # 246.

statement "I am in pain" is different from my relation to the statement "he is in pain". I can doubt his pain but not my own. Thus, we can say "I know he is in pain" while we do not say "I know I am in pain".[72] We do not speak of knowing what we are having.

We do not report our own pain on the basis of criteria, since there are no criteria in the introspective dimension. Use of "know" with first person pain expressions is senseless because there are no private criteria. "Know" makes sense only where we could give a justification.

Wittgenstein is here trying to emphasize the fact that a person's statement about his pain is incorrigible. By "incorrigible" I mean that there is no mode of verification which would be relevant to determining if the sensory quality I call "pain" is the same sensory quality others call "pain". One is logically excluded from direct access to the pains of another. If we could have another's pain it would no longer be his pain but ours.[73] A person's statements about his pain are not hypotheses. Now the important question here is why are one's own pain statements not questionable. The reason seems to be that we cannot meaningfully doubt a use established by convention. The reason "know" is not proper to one's own pain is a grammatical reason. The solipsist in insisting that, on the contrary, "know" applies only to his sensations is simply arguing over a notation.[74] Neither realism, idealism, nor solipsism changes our practical relation to a person in pain.[75] In short, "by a new notation no facts of geography are changed".[76] If we do not speak of knowing our pains but do speak of knowing the pain of another, then this is a grammatical difference, a difference established by a convention. This point is crucial. It is meaningless to speak of "knowing my pain" *not* because the characteristics of the sensation are so distinct and unmistakable, the internal criteria so marked that we are certain we have in the past called this sensation "pain". Rather, it is meaningless to speak of "knowing my pain" because of a grammatical use. The logic of first person pain expressions will not tolerate the word "know". Wittgenstein here again bends over backward to avoid any internal sense of pointing or identification, thus further substantiating Strawson's interpretation. In summary, it is senseless to speak of knowing pain with regard to our own pain.

[72]   *Ibid.*
[73]   *Blue Book*, pp. 53-54.
[74]   *Investigations*, # 403.
[75]   *Blue Book*, p. 48.
[76]   *Ibid.*, p. 57.

The second sense, the legitimate sense of speaking of "knowing pain" is in reference to another's pain. Quite often we know a person is in pain in this sense. In fact, it is difficult to doubt the pain of another in an actual context.[77] Wittgenstein quite clearly means that we know another's pain by his behavior. The question then becomes: Does the sensation of pain play any role in the language-game with regard to another's pain? This question brings us to the beetle in the box example. Suppose each person has a box with something in it called a "beetle". No one can look into anyone else's box. Each claims he knows what a beetle is only by looking at his own beetle. Does the beetle enter the language-game? "The thing in the box has no place in the language-game at all; not even as a *something*: for the box might even be empty." [78] Wittgenstein says the absurdity of the beetle in the box results from thinking of sensations on the model of object and name. In such cases the object drops out.[79] Wittgenstein says that pain "is not a *something*, but not a *nothing* either!" [80] One wonders what to do with such paradoxical remarks. Evidently Wittgenstein means that we should stop thinking of pain as similar to a physical object. He could not say pain is nothing because this would be a denial of information. His arguments are grammatical, not scientific assertions. In other words, pain conceived of as an object is a "*grammatical* fiction".[81] Wittgenstein does not deal with the question whether pain properly understood as a sensation (instead of as a queer object) functions in the pain language-game. He suggests that it does not. Only pain behavior is relevant to the game. Use of the word "pain" is only a sophisticated form of behavior that replaces crying.[82]

The sensation of pain then is irrelevant to knowing that another person is in pain. We know their pain by their behavior. This point indicates how "pain" differs from "red". If we want a person to justify his use of "red" we get him to use signs, verbal, ostensive, etc., to indicate a physical context. Then we decide if this context is what we call "red". "Pain" is quite different in this sense. It is justified by coordinating one set of signs, for example, words about pain, with other signs, pain behavior. We justify our use of "red" by using signs,

---

[77] *Investigations*, # 303.
[78] *Ibid.*, # 293.
[79] *Ibid.*
[80] *Ibid.*, # 304.
[81] *Ibid.*, # 304-307.
[82] *Ibid.*, # 244.

verbal and behavioral, to indicate a context. We justify our use of "pain" by co-ordinating one set of signs with another. This is a very queer type of justification for a sensation word. In fact, it is precisely the same type of justification that one gives in showing one knows how "to continue a series". We believe another is in pain if there is a co-ordination between his verbal reports and his behavior. Basic to any of Wittgenstein's arguments is the premise that speech is a form of behavior and behavior a form of speech. Thus to explain one by the other is to give a verbal explanation. Verbal explanations appeal only to conventions, while an ostensive explanation, and thus an ostensive justification, appeals to conventionally selected aspects of a physical context. Wittgenstein seems to have been basically confused as to whether a correct understanding of the use of "pain" is justified like one justifies his understanding of "red" or like one justifies his understanding of "continuing a series". He says we exhibit pain like we exhibit red. But the point of his analysis of understanding "red" is that a public context called "red" is indicated. Do we indicate a public context called "pain"? Wittgenstein wants to have his cake and eat it too. He claims that we exhibit an understanding of "pain" like an understanding of any sensation word, but then his analysis argues that we show an understanding of "pain" like we show that we understand "how to continue a series".

Some of the strangeness of Wittgenstein's analysis of pain statements could be removed by taking seriously one of his remarks on pain. He says: "To use a word without a justification does not mean to use it without right." [83] This would mean we use the word "pain" with a right but without a justification, which means without public criteria. To accept this answer of right without justification would mean Wittgenstein would have to allow that we use certain words meaningfully which do not have criteria as he defines them. This consequence would seem inconsistent with the *Investigations* as a whole. Thus this remark should probably be ignored. In my critical summary I shall argue that Wittgenstein's treatment of "pain" would be more adequate if developed along the lines of this fragment.

The significance of Wittgenstein's analysis of "understanding" is that the critic in analyzing the meaning of a metaphor has to *justify* his understanding of that metaphor. Some analyses are better or worse than others indicating, respectively, the critic's understanding or lack of

[83] *Ibid.*, # 289.

understanding of the metaphor. In a particular case we may choose Richards over Winters, claiming that the former's analysis shows more of an understanding or grasp of the metaphor. The question is: On what grounds are such choices made? How is one's analysis of a metaphor justified? I shall only sketch here the answer which is developed in Chapter IV. I agree with Wittgenstein that justifying the correctness of one's understanding of a metaphor involves, as does justifying one's understanding of "red" or "how to continue a series", appeal to an independent source. This independent source for Wittgenstein is "criteria". I agree with Wittgenstein that a necessary condition of being said to "understand" a metaphor is knowledge of the criteria for the words in the metaphor. However, appeal to criteria is not a sufficient condition. We do not choose Richards over Winters in a particular case solely on the basis of criteria. One justifies his understanding of a metaphor by appealing to *the metaphor as read*. We choose Richards over Winters because the explanation of the metaphor of the former seems more adequate to the *metaphor as read*. The metaphor as read is an independent source of appeal, but not independent or sharable in the strict sense in which criteria as physically observable features selected by convention are sharable. This wider sense of accessibility will imply a criticism of Wittgenstein's criteria.

A summary paragraph is now needed to point out the underlying significance of the specific attacks on the inner experience theory. All four of the specific applications, "meaning", "intending", "thinking", and "understanding", would be included under Wittgenstein's theory of meaning.[84] All four words are defined as ways of operating with signs, ways of meaning. Here I am emphasizing that a theory of meaning would not be limited to the specific section above on "meaning" but would equally include "intending", "thinking", and "understanding".

Having made this point we can ask: What is the most significant result, in this case negative, of Wittgenstein's attacks? The conclusion is really quite simple but quite important in its implications. It is: "The meaning of a word is not the experience one has in hearing or saying it, and the sense of a sentence is not a complex of such experiences." [85] This section shows that meaning is not an inner experience; nor does meaning *involve* inner experience. Wittgenstein's treatment of "pain"

---

[84]　Of course, many other speech acts not examined here would also fall under his theory of meaning.

[85]　*Investigations*, p. 181.

statements makes this stronger claim. A word is never explained by pointing to an inner image or inner sensation. Meaning is predicated only of actual signs, written or spoken, and their application. The King's College example implies that even the application is included as a type of sign. Ostensive pointing, facial expression and all the other subtleties of expression are actually signs in Wittgenstein's sense. Language for Wittgenstein includes the subtle, nonverbal behavior which accompanies speech. Meaning then is predicated of language in this broad sense. Wittgenstein's basic reason for rejecting a dualism which predicates meaning of an inner experience can be summarized by his statement: "An 'inner process' stands in need of outward criteria." [86] A great part of Wittgenstein's analysis consists in citing these outward criteria for inner processes. Wittgenstein is successful in citing such criteria because, as Hudson argues, the giving and getting of results with regard to mental acts are logically independent of each other. The full dress performance, including images, thus is dispensable because there are achievement criteria for evaluating the results.[87] Wittgenstein is able to present a convincing analysis because there do seem to be overt, behavioral achievement criteria for our use of the mental words "meaning", "intending", "thinking", and "understanding". The critical question which will arise shortly is: Are there areas of meaningful discourse where there are no conventional achievement criteria as defined by Wittgenstein?

B. RELEVANCE OF ATTACK ON NAMING THEORY TO ATTACK ON INNER MEANING THEORY

Some further understanding of Wittgenstein's attack on the inner meaning theory will result from a consideration of an aspect of his attack on the naming theory, though a full consideration of this latter attack is irrelevant here. The naming theory is that theory which assumes that all words are names. Thus, since a proper name seems to have meaning in terms of its bearer this theory assumes that all words mean in terms of their bearers. The naming theory assumes that for a word to have meaning there must be some corresponding object which gives the word meaning. Wittgenstein does not explicitly mention Plato as one

---

[86] *Ibid.*, # 580.
[87] H. Hudson, "Why We Cannot Witness or Observe what Goes on 'In Our Heads' ", *Mind*, LXV (April, 1956), pp. 225-30.

holding such a theory, although the Platonic correspondence between universal words and ideal forms would be a likely candidate for this type of criticism. Wittgenstein does have in mind explicitly Russell's and his own early logical atomism. In the *Tractatus* Wittgenstein quite clearly states: "A name means an object. The object is its meaning." [88] One can quite easily see in this quote from Wittgenstein's early philosophy the correspondence between a name and its bearer.

In the *Philosophical Investigations* Wittgenstein clearly rejects this name theory. He asks: If Mr. N. N., the bearer of a name, dies do sentences which contain his name now have no meaning? [89] The answer is obvious. There is no escaping the conclusion that this answer is a direct rebuttal of the *Tractatus* 3.203, quoted above, where it is explicitly stated that the object is a meaning of a name. Wittgenstein argues that this confusion of the meaning with its bearer is apt to lead to hypostatized bearers or entities for all types of grammatical elements. We are inclined to hypostatize negative facts and universals in order to give these parts of our sentence meaning. Wittgenstein's corrected view is that though the meaning is not the bearer "the meaning of a name is sometimes explained by pointing to its *bearer*".[90]

The relevance of this specific attack to the inner meaning theory is that though the inner meaning theory and the naming theory appear to be quite different they are similar in that both hypostatize entities which are the meaning of words. The inner meaning theory posits an inner image or translation which is the meaning of the word, while the naming theory posits an independently existing object which is the meaning of the word. Both identify meaning with a corresponding bearer, one a mental image and the other a physical object. The essential differences between the naming theory and the inner meaning theory are, first, that the former involves two terms, the name and its bearer, while the latter, as the King's College example shows, involves three terms, word, intervening image, and bearer. Second, Wittgenstein recognizes that the meaning of a name is sometimes explained by pointing to its bearer, while he never stated that the meaning of a word is explained by pointing to an inner image or inner sensation. Even with these important differences there is a significant similarity between the two attacks.

---

[88] Ludwig Wittgenstein, *Tractatus Logico-Philosophicus*, trans. D. F. Pears and B. F. McGuinness (London, Routledge & Kegan Paul, 1961), sec. 3.203.
[89] *Investigations*, # 40.
[90] *Ibid.*, # 43.

C. MEANING AS USE

The attack on the inner meaning theory and the attack on the naming theory, which I have stated only as it clarifies the former attack, form a major part of the context against which Wittgenstein formulates his positive statement of meaning. The attacks have denied that meaning is an inner object or experience and a physical object. Wittgenstein rejects all approaches which presuppose that meaning is some one thing or process (mental or physical). Instead he stressed the plurality of ways in which language forms may mean. The only generalization about meaning that we can make is the very limited one: "For a *large* class of cases – though not for all – in which we employ the word 'meaning' it can be defined thus: the meaning of a word is its use in the language." [91]

1. *Senses of "Use"*

Meaning as use is developed in great breadth and subtlety by Wittgenstein. His understanding of "use" has the following three senses.

a. *Individual Sense*

First, there are individual uses. If we want to know what a particular person means we get him to use the expression in question. The continuing the series example, the King's College example, the fetching the flower example and the abracadabra example are all instances in which an individual specified or displayed what he meant by a term or sentence. We could perhaps teach a child what pain is by pricking it with a pin and saying "that is pain". Since ostensive defining is a complex game which the child does not yet know how to play, he could take the explanation in many ways. The point is that we could discover how he understood it by his later use of the word.[92] One discovers how a word is functioning for an individual by looking at the way that individual uses the word.[93] Use tells us what an individual means.

---

[91] *Ibid.*, # 43.
[92] *Ibid.*, # 288.
[93] *Ibid.*, # 340.

b. *Instrumental Sense*

Second, "use" means for Wittgenstein that language is an instrument. "Language is an instrument. Its concepts are instruments." [94] As long as language is used no difficulty results. Philosophy is born when language goes on a holiday. [95] Wittgenstein's comparison of words to tools, such as a hammer, pliers, a saw, etc., unmistakably emphasizes their instrumental nature. [96] This analogy also emphasizes, as does the analogy to games, that words, like tools, have many diverse functions. We should not look for one function common to all types of words. This sense of "use" for Wittgenstein is closely related to pragmatism's understanding of meaning.

c. *Social Sense*

Third, and most significant, meaning as use emphasizes the social nature of language. "And to imagine a language means to imagine a form of life." [97] "The *speaking* of language is part of an activity, or of a form of life." [98] The existence of a language being spoken is the most basic condition of meaning. Language as a form of life, of activity, is presupposed by all meaning. The existence of a language in the social sense is the *sine qua non* of meaning. Saying that language is a social activity means basically three things.

1. *Involves public actions*

First, it emphasizes that a meaningful use of language is an *activity* which is socially accessible. The examples used in the attack on dualism clearly show that meaning is not a hidden phenomena. When we asked for meaning in the abracadabra example, in the King's College example and in the fetching the red flower example, we were given definitions; verbal and bodily acts. Wittgenstein argues that "meaning", "intending", "thinking", and "understanding" are defined by verbal and subtle bodily behavior. Wittgenstein's attack on the naming theory argues that meaning is no more an object than a private experience. Meaningful speaking is a publicly accessible activity, not an object. "The common behavior of mankind is the system of reference by means

---

[94] *Ibid.*, # 569.
[95] *Ibid.*, # 38.
[96] *Ibid.*, # 11.
[97] *Ibid.*, #19.
[98] *Ibid.*, # 23.

of which we interpret an unknown language." [99]   Using language meaningfully is practicing a technique, an activity. The first sense in which
meaning is social is that it is an *act*, verbal and behavioral.

2. *Involves public objects*

The social sense of meaning as use emphasizes that publically accessible objects, a common physical environment, are presupposed.
This does not mean that objects are meanings, as the *Tractatus* argued,
but rather that an object may be involved in clarifying a meaning. The
King's College example shows the relation of a public context to ostensive explanations. "Meaning" presupposes *public acts* and *public objects*.

3. *Involves body of accepted conventions*

The third sense in which language is a form of social activity is that
there exists a body of cultural conventions which defines the form of the
signs and their application. These conventions determine the sounds
and visual shapes of the signs, the grammar and behavioral accompaniments such as pointing. Convention determines that we call red
"red", that we speak in a subject-predicate form and that we look off
the end of a pointer's finger rather than off his elbow. A grasp of the
way Wittgenstein understands "convention" is no doubt the key to
understanding what he means by saying meaning is use. A great step
toward this understanding is taken by seeing in what ways conventions
in a language are like rules in a game.

Comparison of conventions to rules in a game. – The first question
is how did Wittgenstein mean for the comparison between languages
and games to be taken. He speaks in places of "the analogy between
language and games. . .".[100] Speaking of analogy implies that language
is not literally a game. Wittgenstein does seem to want to keep some
distance or separation between language and games because he says the
games are used as "*objects of comparison* which are meant to throw light
on the facts of our language by way not only of similarities, but also of
dissimilarities".[101] But, on the other hand, he speaks of "noting a
language-game" [102] and says *"this language-game is played"*.[103] Wittgenstein claimed his method, which includes presenting language-games,

[99]   *Ibid.,* # 206.
[100]   *Ibid.,* # 83.
[101]   *Ibid.,* # 130.
[102]   *Ibid.,* # 655.
[103]   *Ibid.,* # 654.

was purely descriptive. Statements such as these would imply a more literal relation between language and games. Wittgenstein certainly seemed to think that a complex language differed only in degree from his simple language-games. He says he will call "the whole, consisting of language and the actions into which it is woven, the 'language-game' ".[104] Wittgenstein never sharply clarifies the relation between language and games.

However, even in view of this lack of explicit statement there are several clear similarities for Wittgenstein between conventions in a language and rules in a game.

First, the basic synonymity between rules and conventions begins to emerge with the statement that it is impossible to obey a rule only once. A rule is a custom.

> It is not possible that there should have been only one occasion on which someone obeyed a rule. ... To obey a rule, to make a report, to give an order, to play a game of chess, are *customs* (uses, institutions).[105]

Wittgenstein considered this statement an assertion of a grammatical point. Rules are by definition customs or institutions.[106]

> What do I call 'the rule by which he proceeds'?—The hypothesis that satis-factorily describes his use of words, which we observe; or the rule which he looks up when he uses signs; or the one which he gives us in reply if we ask him what his rule is?—But what if observation does not enable us to see any clear rule, and the question brings none to light?—For he did indeed give me a definition when I asked him what he understood by "N", but he was prepared to withdraw and alter it.—So how am I to determine the rule according to which he is playing? He does not know it himself.—Or, to ask a better question: What meaning is the expression: "the rule by which he proceeds" supposed to have left to it here? [107]

The answer to this last rhetorical question is none. We would not apply the phrase "rule by which he proceeds" to random behavior. Wittgen-stein does say we could play a game in which we constantly changed the rules.[108] He must mean either that we change the rules in accord-ance with a rule or we formalize our changes of the rules. If he does not mean either of these alternatives his remark is totally inconsistent with his view of a rule.

Conventions in a language also must have this regularity of custom.

---

[104] *Ibid.*, # 7.
[105] *Ibid.*, # 199.
[106] *Ibid.*
[107] *Ibid.*, # 82.
[108] *Ibid.*, # 83.

If we came upon a strange people whose utterances had no regular connection with their actions we would say that not enough regularity exists for their utterances to be called "language".[109]

Second, rules in a game and conventions in a language both must function *overtly* in the game or language. The passage just quoted also implies this point in the question "but what if observation does not enable us to see any clear rule...".[110] Rules of a game must appear in the game. The rule may appear as an aid in teaching the game, or be an instrument of the game, or be revealed by watching how others play. In other words, "there are characteristic signs of it in the players' behaviour".[111] In short, the rule must be revealed in operating with it. If the rule does not affect the game, if no verbal or overt behavior expressing it is displayed, then the rule is quite inessential. In draughts the fact that a king is marked by putting one piece on top of another is quite inessential to the game.[112] "So I am inclined to distinguish between the essential and the inessential in a game too." [113]

Wittgenstein in his attack on the dualist has argued quite similarly that private or non-overt rules are inessential to the game in which words mean. Observation of this game brings no images of rules to light. Inner processes do not function in a public language game. "An 'inner process' stands in need of outward criteria." [114] There must be criteria, overt verbal and behavioral indications of conventions in a language. Inner processes do not function in a public language-game. A rule then is a stable custom which functions overtly in the game.

Third, rules in a game and conventions in a language are similar in that both allow freedom within limitations. Wittgenstein means every move in a game is not dictated by a rule. In tennis rules do not tell one how high to throw the ball while serving.[115] Rules in a game allow freedom within limitations. The same can be said of conventions in a language.

Fourth, rules of a game and conventions of a language are arbitrary bedrock. With regard to baseball it would be senseless to ask why one plays with a small round horsehide instead of an oval pigskin. Wittgen-

109   *Ibid.*, # 207.
110   *Ibid.*, # 82.
111   *Ibid.*, # 54.
112   *Ibid.*, # 562.
113   *Ibid.*, # 564.
114   *Ibid.*, # 580.
115   *Ibid.*, # 68.

stein emphasizes that conventions in a language also cannot sensibly be questioned. When in questioning or being questioned we reach such rules or customs we have reached "bedrock" and our "spade is turned".[116] "When I obey a rule, I do not choose. I obey the rule *blindly*." [117] Wittgenstein's meaning here can be clarified by considering his arrow example. The meaning of an arrow sign is not self-evident. In order to make clear the direction one is to follow, that is, in order to clarify that one goes in the direction from the shaft through the point instead of vice versa, we might add an interpretation to the arrow symbol. Such an interpretation "is a new symbol added to the old one".[118] The question is: Is there an interpretation of this interpretation ad infinitum? Wittgenstein's answer, of course, is no. "But adopt whatever model or scheme you may, it will have a bottom level, and there will be no such thing as an interpretation of that." [119] Wittgenstein means that if, for example, a foreigner asks us why we follow the line from the shaft of the arrow through its point we would give some such interpretation as in our culture the arrow is to be taken in this way. If asked for an interpretation of this interpretation we would not know what to say. We can give no further reason why we follow the direction from shaft to point. We have reached "bedrock". We blindly take the arrow in this way. In fact, this bottom level is so basic that Wittgenstein suggests that we *not* call it an interpretation. "What this shews is that there is a way of grasping a rule which is *not* an *interpretation*, but which is exhibited in what we call 'obeying the rule' and 'going against it' in actual cases." [120] Rules in a game and conventions in a language are bedrock.

Pole remarks here that Wittgenstein's understanding of rules or conventions is the same as his view of mathematical rules. Wittgenstein held that mathematics is an arbitrary construction by fiat. Nothing is discovered in doing mathematics.[121] Wittgenstein's 1930-33 lectures clearly substantiate this point. Rules of grammar and rules of mathematics are arbitrary and treat only of symbolism. Only this view of conventions can avoid an infinite regression.[122] The problem here is the

[116]   *Ibid.*, # 217.
[117]   *Ibid.*, # 219.
[118]   *Blue Book*, p. 33.
[119]   *Ibid.*, p. 34.
[120]   *Investigations*, # 201.
[121]   Pole, pp. 38-39.
[122]   Moore, Pt. II, LXIII, pp. 298-316.

same one which led Wittgenstein to say that every interpretation must have a bottom level and that conventions are bedrock. The only significant difference between mathematical or logical and conventional rules is that we construct the former and inherit the latter.[123] Wittgenstein then extended his formalism to the conventions of language. Wittgenstein's treatment of games then clarifies his understanding of conventions in language. Both rules in a game and conventions in a language are arbitrary but stable patterns which are essential and thus are displayed overtly in the game or language.

Conventions and criteria. – Fifth, and here the comparison to games is left behind, conventions select the defining characteristics or criteria of an object or act. Thus one appeals to conventions to justify that one correctly understands an expression. Appeal to the conventionally selected, defining characteristic of an act or object is appeal to what Wittgenstein calls "criteria".

In an excellent article Carl Wellman shows that criteria are conventionally selected features of an object and thus that one appeals to criteria to justify one's *understanding* of an expression, but not to justify the *empirical* correctness of an expression.

An expression fits an object when it is linguistically, rather than factually, correct to apply it to that object. There is a difference between saying "It is an X" on the grounds that this is what we mean by the term "X" and on the grounds that there is empirical evidence for its being an X.[124]

To confuse a justification by reference to criteria with a justification on the basis of empirical generalization is to confuse criteria with symptoms, a distinction which is clearly made in "The Blue Book".[125] Wellman generalizes on this passage in "The Blue Book":

Criteria are observable features which are directly connected to an expression by its meaning; symptoms are features which are indirectly connected to the expression by being associated with criteria in our experience. To justify one's use of a description by giving criteria is to appeal to a convention; to justify one's use of a description by giving symptoms is to appeal to an empirical generalization.[126]

Wellman does correctly recognize that for Wittgenstein the line between criteria and symptoms is usually fluid. Criteria and symptoms are

---

[123] Pole, p. 32.
[124] Carl Wellman, "Wittgenstein's Conception of a Criterion", *The Philosophical Review*, LXXI (Oct., 1962), p. 434.
[125] *Blue Book*, pp. 24-25.
[126] Wellman, pp. 437-38.

often not sharply delineated. Convention does not clearly select from
the observable features of an object *the* criterion, or *the* essential definition. Wellman correctly sees that for Wittgenstein "a term is usually
applied on the basis of many overlapping characteristics which form
a family likeness".[127]

Even in view of the fluid line between criteria and symptoms it is
quite essential that the distinction be preserved. Criteria are observable
features selected by convention. Criteria involve empirical features of
the object although they are not empirical generalizations. One appeals
to criteria either to show that one's expression correctly fits an object
or that an object fits or is an example of one's expression. The correctness shown by such an appeal to criteria is a *linguistic* correctness
because "a criterion is a purely linguistic ground for judging that it is or
is not correct to apply a given expression to some object".[128] To appeal
to criteria, that is, to try to determine linguistic correctness, is to appeal
to convention. Such conventions are, as the fourth point in the comparison of conventions to rules in a game argued, bedrock.

Such an appeal to criteria is a necessary and sufficient condition for
justifying one's *understanding* of an expression. One is said to "understand" an expression *only if* one shows knowledge of the criteria
involved in that expression. "Therefore, anyone who does not know
the criteria for the use of a descriptive expression literally does not understand its meaning." [129] *If* one shows knowledge of the criteria one is said
to "understand" an expression. "As a result, one can justify his use of a
descriptive expression by means of the criteria for its application." [130] It
is a necessary and sufficient condition for showing one's understanding
of the term "red" or the term "pain" that one is able to associate such
a term by his speech and behavior with the "observable features" in our
environment conventionally called "red" or the behavior conventionally
called "pain". The significance of this conclusion is that the first two of
what I have called the social aspects of Wittgenstein's meaning as use,
namely that use involves public actions and public objects, are defined
by the third social sense, namely convention. All justifications of one's
understanding come to rest on the "bedrock" of criteria. As my fourth
comparison of conventions to rules in a game shows, questions of
meaning come to an end when a convention is reached. The pivotal

[127]   *Ibid.*, p. 438.
[128]   *Ibid.*, p. 441.
[129]   *Ibid.*, p. 436.
[130]   *Ibid.*, pp. 436-37.

point of Wittgenstein's saying meaning is use is that meaning is social usage; that is, meaning is established by convention.

Albritton also correctly sees that for Wittgenstein criteria are not empirical generalizations but empirical features selected by convention.

A criterion for a given thing's being so is something that can show the thing to be so and show by its absence that the thing is not so; it is something by which one may be *justified in saying* that the thing is so and by whose absence one may be justified in saying that the thing is not so. And a criterion for a thing's being so has this relation to the thing's being so not as a matter of fact, like what Wittgenstein calls a "symptom" of its being so, but as a matter of "logical" necessity. That is, on Wittgenstein's account of such necessity, its relation to the thing's being so is "founded on a definition" or "founded on convention" or is a matter of "grammar".[131]

Both the remarks of Wellman and Albritton make sense in terms of Wittgenstein's remark: "Grammar tells what kind of object anything is." [132] I take Wittgenstein's remark here as meaning that grammar or convention selects the defining observable characteristics of an object. Convention selects criteria.

In summary, it is essential to see that for Wittgenstein criteria are (1) physically observable features (2) which are determined by convention. It is because of this emphasis on physically observable features that Wittgenstein insists: "An 'inner process' stands in need of outward criteria." [133] Wittgenstein is so intent on finding such outward criteria that a great portion of his remarks on criteria are on criteria for these inner experiences. In fact, Albritton states that sixty per cent of the passages treating criteria are in fact about criteria for psychological concepts.[134] Wittgenstein's understanding of criteria as *observable* features selected by convention leaves him no alternative but to define such psychological concepts in terms of behavior. It is on the basis of this first aspect of criteria that critics such as Hardin accuse Wittgenstein of physicalism.[135] It is this first aspect which leads Wellman to say "there is one fundamental point on which Wittgenstein is mistaken. One of his main theses is that our ultimate criteria are *publicly* observable

---

[131]   Roger Albritton, "On Wittgenstein's Use of the Term 'Criterion' ", *The Journal of Philosophy*, LVI (Oct. 22, 1959), p. 854.
[132]   *Investigations*, # 373.
[133]   *Ibid.*, # 580.
[134]   Albritton, p. 853.
[135]   Clyde Laurence Hardin, "Wittgenstein on Private Languages", *The Journal of Philosophy*, LVI (June 4, 1959), p. 519.

features of the situations in which we use the language." [136] Wellman
thinks Wittgenstein is mistaken because there do seem to be criteria
with regard to our sensations yet these sensations are not publicly observable.[137] Wellman argues elsewhere that Wittgenstein's understanding
of criteria is inadequate for pain statements.[138]

2. *Significance of Analysis of Meaning as Use*

The significance of Wittgenstein's positive analysis of meaning as use
is that it raises the question: In showing that one understands a metaphor is it a necessary and sufficient condition to show that one knows
the criteria involved in the words of the metaphor? I shall argue that a
necessary condition for understanding the meaning of a metaphor is
knowing the criteria involved. In the following chapter I shall analyze
certain theorists of poetic language whom I shall call "medium" theorists.
They will be so called because they emphasize that the "stuff" which the
poet shares with his reader, analogous to the stuff which the sculptor shares with his audience in his marble, is language having the
qualities of sense and sound. For this stuff to be truly shared the reader
must know the sound and sense of the words involved. Ignorance of
either quality is likely to lead to failure to understand the metaphor.
Thus in an important way the medium theorists, and the other theorists
analyzed in that chapter, could agree with Wittgenstein that a necessary
condition for understanding the meaning of a metaphor is understanding the criteria of the words involved. However, I shall argue in
Chapter III that understanding of such criteria is not a sufficient
condition for understanding a metaphor's meaning. For example,
with regard to Wordsworth's metaphor

> I wandered lonely as a cloud
> That floats on high o'er vales and hills,
> (William Wordsworth, "I Wandered Lonely as a Cloud", ll. 1-2)

one might well know the criteria for the words "cloud" and "wandered"
but still not be able to see the *relevant* senses in which wandering is
like a cloud's travelings. In order to grasp the relevant sense of this

---

[136]   Wellman, p. 444.
[137]   *Ibid.*, pp. 445-46.
[138]   Carl Wellman, "Our Criteria for Third Person Psychological Sentences", *The
Journal of Philosophy*, LVIII (May 25, 1961), p. 290.

metaphor it is necessary that one *see* the poet's wandering *as* a cloud's journey. In Chapter III I shall analyze seeing as beginning with Wittgenstein's understanding of the concept of "seeing as". I shall agree with Wittgenstein that "seeing as" involves a technique in a way which a case of normal "seeing" does not. Thus, one might well be able to "see" but not be able to "see as". Wittgenstein calls this latter failure "aspect-blindness".[139] The equivalent in the act of reading metaphors to aspect-blindness is a case where one knows the criteria for the metaphorical subject and predicate, for "wandering" and "clouds", but still cannot *see* the poet's wandering *as* a cloud's journey. Conversely one not aspect-blind, one who can see human wandering as a cloud's wandering, is one who understands or grasps the metaphor's meaning. Thus to justify one's understanding of a metaphor requires that one give indication that one has seen the metaphorical subject as the metaphorical predicate. This sense of justification I shall argue involves reference to the metaphor as read. The metaphor as read involves features which are not "observable features" in the strict sense of that phrase. It involves these additional features in its imagery. Thus I shall argue that metaphorical meaning involves imagery and thus that one's justification of his understanding of this meaning involves reference to this imagery. Justification of an understanding of meaning in this game then does not refer only to criteria in the strict sense understood by Wittgenstein. That justification in this game involves reference to the metaphor as read implies some inadequacy in Wittgenstein's criteria with respect to this particular language-game. In this game criteria will not be a sufficient condition for showing one's understanding of an expression.

D. CRITICISM

My criticism of Wittgenstein's analysis of meaning has been implied above where I argued that he never decides whether "pain" is a sensation word or is analytically related to behavior. Wittgenstein clearly recognizes two senses of explanation, one verbal and the other ostensive.[140] Two senses of explanation call for two senses of justification. Showing that one knows the meaning of the phrase "continuing a series" is a verbal justification. When questioned as to meaning one

---

[139] *Investigations*, p. 213.
[140] *Blue Book*, p. 1.

gives other signs in accordance with a rule. The King's College example is one involving ostensive justification. One uses signs, verbal and behavioral gestures, to indicate a physical context. My analysis tried to force Wittgenstein to say whether one's understanding of the meaning of "pain" is justified in the former or latter sense.[141] Do we mean by "pain" that the person is behaving in accordance with culturally defined patterns of pain behavior; which is to say, one is giving signs (behavior) in accordance with a rule? Or do we mean by "pain" that the person is indicating by his behavior a context of pain sensation? Does one justify his understanding of the term "pain" like he justifies his understanding of the phrase "continue a series" or like he justifies his understanding of the word "red"? I shall argue that if Wittgenstein chooses the former answer he would have to advocate the absurd doctrine that "pain" is analytically defined by pain behavior and if the latter he would have to rework his definition of criteria. The following example will clarify the absurdities of saying pain is defined by pain behavior.

Showing that one understands how to "play chess" is clearly like showing one knows how to "continue a series". It is conceivable that we would be able to say someone was playing chess on purely verbal grounds. The physical men and board could be eliminated for the purely verbal game which very advanced players often play, imagining the board and men in their heads. Imagine this experiment. I know how to "play chess", meaning that I am familiar with the rules, know how to apply them, etc. I call two subjects to determine if they know how to "play chess". The subjects confront each other over their imagined board and men and then proceed. It is conceivable that a very complex game ensues, a game so complex that both subjects display knowledge of all the rules. I would need to know none of the subjects' past histories for truthfulness to determine if "chess" were being played. There are purely verbal or conventional grounds for determining if "chess" is being played. There are sufficient conditions in the period from the first move to the checkmate to unquestionably justify their understanding of the words "playing chess". That each knows the meaning of the phrase "playing chess" is shown by their playing this verbal chess. It would be inconceivable that one of the players would later report that he was lying and was not really playing the game. As long as there is

---

[141] Of course he could have shown that "pain" functions in its own unique game. I have tried to show that he did not develop this alternative.

conventional agreement on the rules, the events prior to the game and the events after the game are irrelevant to a correct application of the words "playing chess". If the rules were displayed what sense would it make to ask if perhaps one of the subjects were lying? I simply ask is pain behavior related to the word "pain" in the same sense in which chess behavior is related to the word "chess"? The answer seems to be an obvious no. I may be an excellent actor and put on a perfect example of pain behavior, yet would others not always keep open the possibility that I was lying or deceiving them? If one denies the relevance of the sensation of pain to the language-game in which "pain" is used, as Wittgenstein does, then one must say that pain behavior is related to "pain" as playing chess is related to "chess". Performances whose correctness is analytically justified involve no question of sensation. For example, you either "continue the series" or you do not "continue the series". There is a clear conventional standard of correctness. We can say that someone is unquestionably playing chess or continuing a series, but we cannot be as certain that a person is in pain.

The counter to my point here is that the criteria for the application of the word "pain" are simply not as clearly defined as those for "chess". My reply is that questions as to whether one is or is not in pain are not necessarily over the clearness of the conventional signs. An actor on the stage may unmistakably display the correct signs. In a case where we suspect that we are being deceived we are not trying to determine if the conventional indications have been displayed but if the person is having the sensation of pain. I argue that we do in fact take pain behavior as an indication, a pointing to the sensation of pain. In case of doubt we are not concerned over the clearness of the pointing, over the indicating signs, but want to know if the sensation is there. If we want to know if someone uses the word "red" for what we call "red" we cannot answer this question by examining the correctness of his pointing posture. We cannot answer our question by deciding if the person is pointing in a correct form, if he has his finger extended, etc. Rather we have to see if the pointing indicates a context which we call "red". I argue that we understand "pain" the same way. Of course, I realize that "pain" introduces the problem of pointing to an internal sensation whereas red seems to be public. Pain statements raise the problem of other minds. Wittgenstein's treatment of pain as a "grammatical fiction" means that he precisely intends to skirt the problem. Pain as a "grammatical fiction" means that the sensation is as irrelevant to the game as are images in the mind while continuing a series. If this is the case why not call "pain" a word with a verbal justification since behavior is a type of language? If pain is irrelevant to the game why not say pain behavior is the game? Why not identify "pain" with a pain performance in the same way that we identify "chess" with a chess performance? I see no way Wittgenstein can avoid this identification. Fundamental to his thought that the meaning of a word is its use is that the meaning is the application, is the justification of a word. The only sense of justification Wittgenstein allows with regard to "pain" is in regard to another's pain. This type of justification differs in no essential way from justification that one knows how to "continue the series" or how "to play chess". All three are instances of a verbal justification. Pain behavior is related to "pain" in the same way that writing signs is related to "continuing a series". In both cases one justifies his understanding of the meaning of a word or phrase by producing other signs in accordance with a rule.

The real crux of the reason why Wittgenstein is led to make "pain" a verbally justified word instead of an ostensively justified word is that he formulates his definition of criteria in such a stringent way as to leave himself no other alternative. We seem to be pointing to a public, external red when we use the word "red" but pain does not exist publicly. "Pain" thus might call for a figurative internal pointing. Such an internal pointing, an inward criterion, is absolutely *verboten* for Wittgenstein. His view is summarized in his statement: "An 'inner process' stands in need of outward criteria." [142] Wittgenstein simply will allow no internal criteria. Wittgenstein's conception of criteria, if held to rigorously, denies the validity of any justification of first person psychological statements by the person making them because there are no criteria, in his sense, by which the user can determine if he is using the word correctly. It seems to me that in a different sense we do have "criteria" for our pain, and use these criteria in some situations (for example, in a doctor's office when we are asked to describe our pain). The meaning of "pain" involves these "internal criteria" just as it certainly involves the external criteria noted by Wittgenstein. To be consistent Wittgenstein would have to hold the position that there are criteria for determining if another is in pain but none by which we can determine if we are in pain, unless we happen to be seeing ourselves in a mirror. He has denied internal pointing in the case of pain and validity in the case of memory. The following critical analyses of Witt-

[142]   *Investigations,* # 580.

genstein's thought on precisely these two points lend valuable support to my arguments.

Rhees argues that Wittgenstein is involved in this confusion because he confused the way we would teach a child arithmetic and the way we would teach a child how to speak. The point of speech is not to get the child to imitate sounds which he has memorized, but to get him to be able to tell us something. "If he can speak, he has got something to tell you. In arithmetic it is different. Telling you things is not part of his achievement when he learns to multiply." [143] Applied to pain statements and pain behavior, Rhees' point means that such language tells you something about the speaker. Such language indicates or points to pain. A person using such language would have, as Rhees argues, "something to tell you".[144] In the difference between the games in sections 2 and 8 Wittgenstein provided himself with distinctions by which he could recognize this difference which Rhees points out. The game of section 2 had only four terms used to order building material. Section 8 expands this primitive game to include numbers, "this" and "that". Numbers introduce a significant difference between sections 8 and 2 because they are first learned by memorization.[145] As Feyerabend notes, Wittgenstein distinguishes learning numbers from learning names.[146] The basic reason Wittgenstein distinguished these two ways of learning is to distinguish between ostensive and verbal explanations. Wittgenstein notes "that for many words in our language there do not seem to be ostensive definitions; e.g. for such words as 'one', 'number', 'not', etc.".[147] Such words must be learned by verbal explanations; by memorization. Wittgenstein could have said we learn "pain" like we learn "slab" instead of like we learn "two".[148] "Pain" then would be an indicating or pointing word, like "slab", not a word defined by pain behavior, like "chess" is defined by chess behavior. We would not memorize that "pain" means certain behavior like "chess" means certain behavior. Wittgenstein refused to admit that "pain" is a word with

---

[143]   R. Rhees, "Wittgenstein's Builders", *Proceedings of the Aristotelian Society, New Series*, LX (March 14, 1960), p. 182.

[144]   *Ibid.*

[145]   *Investigations*, # 9.

[146]   Paul Feyerabend, "Wittgenstein's *Philosophical Investigations*", *The Philosophical Review*, LXIV (July, 1955), p. 461.

[147]   *Blue Book*, p. 1.

[148]   Wittgenstein even suggests that we might teach a child the meaning of "pain" in a sort of ostensive way by pricking him with a pin and saying "see, that's what pain is" (*Investigations*, # 288). However, he does not develop his suggestion.

ostensive meaning, in some figurative sense, because he refused to allow any internal sense of pointing. Wittgenstein could agree with Rhees that the purpose of multiplication is not to tell you anything. The difficulty is that in making "pain" defined by pain behavior he would have to deny that the purpose of pain words and behavior is to point you to something, that is, to indicate pain sensations. He seems forced to deny that pain has ostensive meaning.

Strawson, who certainly is a sympathetic student of Wittgenstein, finds similar difficulties. Wittgenstein erred in not seeing that we can internally name and recognize sensations. Thus we sometimes do apply a word on the strength of a non-sharable experience while still publicly reporting or describing the experience. Here experience is shared in a weaker sense. Here fully sharable experiences are relevant to non-sharable experiences

either by the existence of shared experiences which count as signs (criteria in the weaker sense) of the occurrence of the unshared experiences (the case of 'I am in pain'), or by the adoption or invention of analogical modes of description, where the analogy is with shareable experiences (e.g. reporting the words that pass through my mind).[149]

Hervey continues a similar line of objection to Wittgenstein's treatment of pain. She attacks Wittgenstein's restrictions on pain criteria. She cites Robinson Crusoe as an example. Even if Crusoe knew no language is it not conceivable, even likely, that he could localize and remember pains without language? We do seem to have ability to localize pain and also have a type of physiological memory. Both would be types of internal criteria. Crusoe it seems could use signs to establish a private but regular use. Why not allow pain a similar role in our public use of the word "pain"? [150]

Wellman raises strong objections to Wittgenstein's treatment of memory. Wellman argues that Wittgenstein has the cart before the horse.

One cannot claim that credibility of the indentification depends entirely on the possibility of corroboration, for of what value is checking one identification against another unless each has some independent credibility? Actually, corroboration is a test of correctness only because the identifications which support one another each have some antecedent claim to correctness. Thus it is the corroboration which depends upon the identification and not vice versa.[151]

---

[149]   Strawson, p. 99.
[150]   Helen Hervey, "The Private Language Problem", *The Philosophical Quarterly*, VII (Jan., 1957), pp. 73-77.
[151]   Wellman, *The Philosophical Review*, LXXI, pp. 446-47.

In other words, if each memory does not have some validity of its own what sense does it make for one memory to appeal to another for confirmation? [152] Wellman argues that Wittgenstein failed to see that there can be public language with private criteria. Then our justification of pain statements by other minds is indirect, that is, on the basis of our own experience. "My reason for saying 'He is in pain' is that he has hit his finger with a hammer, but this is a reason only because hitting and hurting have been associated in my own experience." [153] "To insist that one have direct justification for every statement is to make indirect justification under any circumstances either impossible or unnecessary." [154] Wellman's remarks are quite incisive.[155]

All of the critics of Wittgenstein cited have criticized him on what is generally called the problem of other minds. These critics predominantly hold an analogical view of statements about other minds. My agreement with their criticism has not been because I necessarily hold such a view of other minds. The present work does not intend in any way to make such a general epistemological claim. I have cited these critics because their critical discussions further help to clarify Wittgenstein's understanding of criteria. At certain critical junctures, namely in his treatment of pain statements and memory, Wittgenstein most clearly reveals the basic physicalism of his theory of criteria. However, my reason for criticizing this aspect of Wittgenstein's criteria will not hinge on a view of statements about other minds but on the inadequacy of criteria to the game in which metaphorical meaning is analyzed, namely the game of literary criticism.

---

[152] Carl Wellman, "Wittgenstein and the Egocentric Predicament", *Mind*, LXVIII (April, 1959), p. 225.
[153] Wellman, *The Journal of Philosophy*, LVIII, p. 290.
[154] *Ibid.*, p. 293.
[155] For further critical evaluations of Wittgenstein's treatment of inner processes or inner criteria I refer the reader to the following articles: W. W. Mellor, "Three Problems about Other Minds" (*Mind*, LXV, April, 1956, pp. 200-17); and Clyde Laurence Hardin, "Wittgenstein on Private Languages" (Hardin, pp. 517-28).

II. POETIC LANGUAGE

Wittgenstein has posed basic problems with which a theory of meaning of poetic metaphor must come to terms. He has argued that meaning is predicated neither of inner processes, inner experiences, nor of things in the world, physical bearers. Rather, the meaning of a word is its use. Signs have no intrinsic meaning, but are given meaning by being linked to public contexts by use. The sign in no way is to be confused with its bearer. Thus, there is a gap between the sign and its signified bearer. It is precisely here that a contrast between poetic language and literal language begins to emerge. In this chapter it will be seen that the poet presents us with a deliberate confusion, or rather a deliberate fusion of sign and signified, sense and sensa, language and experience. Of course, poetic language does not bodily present its signified object, but presents a fusion of sign and experience as defined below. The language in the poem is not so much a reference to experience as it is an experience when such language is read. To read a poem is to have an experience in the sense to be analyzed. Poetic language does not so much refer us *to* an experience as it presents us *with* an experience. The gap between a word and its context, which, according to Wittgenstein, is bridged by use, is overcome by the poem in a different way.

In the preceding paragraph I have spoken indiscriminately of the language in the poem and the language in the metaphor as though the two were synonymous. This is not at all the case. Language in the poem is a much more inclusive category. There are many elements in a poem, such as rhythm, rhyme, and alliteration, which are not strictly speaking metaphorical elements. Thus, the question becomes: Have I not made some type of part-whole assumption? Have I not assumed that speaking of the whole, the language in the poem, is also speaking of the part, the language in the metaphor? Yes, I have at present assumed this relation, but substantiation follows. This substantiation will be in the following order. First, I shall analyze several general theories of language in the poem and generalize from these to conclusions about poetic language. I shall compare this result with the thought of Wittgenstein and Cassirer. Second, in the following chapter I shall show how metaphorical language fits these general conclusions while still having certain characteristics unique to it. This general conclusion will be that language in the poem functions iconically through its sense and sound. The most significant way in which metaphor fits this general conclusion is through its two essential aspects, imagery and seeing as. These two aspects will be discussed in the following chapter. The concern of this chapter is to establish general conclusions about poetic language. In order to do this I shall discuss four theories, which are: that the poem is a presentational symbol; that the poem is a concrete universal; that the poem is an icon; that the poem is a fusion of sense and sensa achieved by exploiting language as a medium.

A. THE POEM AS A PRESENTATIONAL SYMBOL

Susanne Langer is the foremost exponent of the view that the poem is a presentational symbol. To understand her meaning one must begin with her basic distinction between sign and symbol. A sign function involves three parts: the subject using the sign, the sign, and the object. A symbol, on the other hand, involves subject, symbol, *conception* and object.[1] The addition of the conception which the symbol introduces allows a more remote relation between symbol and signified. The sign can only announce its object while the symbol leads to a conception of an object which may be absent.[2] Symbols are subdivided into discursive and presentional symbols. The discursive symbol has: a vocabulary and a syntax; single words definable by other words making dictionaries possible; and alternate words for the same meaning.[3] A presentational symbol has none of these, rather it is "a direct *presentation* of an individual object".[4] An example of a presentational object in the *Philosophy in a New Key* is a painting.[5]

In her later work *Feeling and Form*, which is a conscious continua-

---

[1]   Susanne K. Langer, *Philosophy in a New Key: A Study in the Symbolism of Reason, Rite, and Art* (New York, A Mentor Book, 1959), pp. 63-64.
[2]   *Ibid.*, p. 61.
[3]   *Ibid.*, p. 87.
[4]   *Ibid.*, p. 89.
[5]   *Ibid.*, pp. 90-91.

tion of *Philosophy in a New Key*, Langer includes poetry as a type of presentational symbol. In this later work she refines her definition of an art form. An art form is one which is abstracted from material existence; it has a remoteness from practical life.[6] Thus, the art form becomes an image; an object of sensuous contemplation which is abstracted from the physical and causal order.[7]

In poetry there is the particular problem of transforming the normal, practical function of language into a presentational symbol. Thus, in a poem discursive language or propositions are material to be transformed.[8] Into what are they transformed? They are transformed into an *appearance* of life, an image of life, not actual life.

The poet's business is to create the appearance of "experiences", the semblance of events lived and felt, and to organize them as they constitute a purely and completely experienced reality, a piece of *virtual life*.[9]

The phrase "a piece of *virtual life*" shows that the poet is presenting an appearance of life, not representing life. In poetry propositions are no longer discursive but presentational. In reading a poem one has the illusion that one is directly experiencing life.[10] The question of illusion in poetry, whether poetry refers to the natural world, will be analyzed in the following chapter in the section on "Imagery and Reference". Langer has here clearly stated the position that the poem is a presentational object.

Ogden and Richards also hold that the poem in some sense presents an experience. They say that the difference between an art object and a photograph

is the difference between the *presentation* of an object which makes use of the direct emotional disturbances produced by certain arrangements, *to reinstate the whole situation* of seeing, or hearing, the object, together with the emotions felt towards it, and on the other hand, a presentation which is purely scientific, *i.e.*, symbolic.[11] (Italicizing mine, except for "*i.e.*")

A poem, using language emotively or evocatively, is precisely a "pre-

---

[6] Susanne K. Langer, *Feeling and Form: A Theory of Art* (New York, Charles Scribner's Sons, 1953), pp. 50-51.
[7] *Ibid.*, p. 47.
[8] *Ibid.*, pp. 227-28.
[9] *Ibid.*, p. 212.
[10] *Ibid.*, p. 234.
[11] Ogden and Richards, p. 237.

sentation of an object"; it reinstates "the whole situation of seeing, or hearing..." in its reader.[12]

However, the fact that Langer and Ogden and Richards all interpret a poem as a presentational object should not lead us to overlook the essential divergence of their views. Langer clearly intends to include poetry as a type of symbolism. As a type of symbolism it is cognitively significant. Discursive thought must not *be regarded as our only intellectual activity*.[13] A presentational form, the poem, is still a symbolic form and thus is rooted in human rationality just as basically as are the discursive forms of thought.[14] To place art beyond reason would be to misunderstand her thought in a fundamental way. Ogden and Richards, on the other hand, intend precisely such a dichotomy between the symbolic and emotive use of words.[15] For Ogden and Richards symbolic language is concerned with correctness and truth while emotive language is concerned with "the character of the attitude aroused".[16]

Philip Wheelwright also holds a version of the presentation theory. He states:

Poetry's first urgency is, in Richard Hovey's words, to "have business with the grass"; it presents as well as represents, it evokes something of the very quality, tone, and flavor of the concrete qua concrete with a directness and a full experiential relevance that steno-symbols cannot do.[17]

Wheelwright's position shortly will be analyzed more fully. Here it suffices to merely *state* his position.

The three theorists cited here, despite the differences noted, agree in emphasizing that the poem is a presentation of an experience. The significance of this position is that it argues that in reading a poem one has an experience; thus reading a poem differs significantly from reading discursive or literal language. The poem as a presentational object tends to reinstate itself, in some form, in the act of being read. The theory that the poem is a concrete universal will be seen to agree in a significant way with this theory.

---

12 *Ibid.*, p. 235.
13 Langer, *Philosophy in a New Key*, p. 82.
14 *Ibid.*, pp. 82-87.
15 Ogden and Richards, p. 149.
16 *Ibid.*, p. 239.
17 Philip Wheelwright, *The Burning Fountain: A Study in the Language of Symbolism* (Bloomington, Ind., Indiana University Press, 1959), p. 79.

B. THE POEM AS A CONCRETE UNIVERSAL

The view that the poem is a concrete universal is clearly stated by W. K. Wimsatt, Jr. It will be seen that this doctrine is similar to the presentational view of the poem, but differs in that it also calls attention to the universal or general nature of poetic language. For Langer universality is achieved because the symbol forming activity, which produces poetry, is a form of consciousness. For Wimsatt the universality is due to the nature of language common to all men.

Generality and particularity seem to oppose or repulse each other. This tension is expressed in the phrase "concrete universal". Wimsatt is quite aware of this seeming conflict. One way to solve this conflict is to argue as Johnson and Reynolds do that the universal is somehow immanent in the particular. Wimsatt refuses this, as he sees it, Neo-Aristotelian position because it "leads to platitude and to a standard of material objectivity, the average tulip, the average human form, some sort of average".[18] Yet Wimsatt is convinced that the venerable phrase "concrete universal" describes something of the nature of poetry. He suggests that this universality can be noted by seeing that: "Every description in words, so far as it is a direct description (the barn is red and square) is a generalization. That is the nature of words." [19] The semanticists are likely to choke over the phrase "the nature of words" as an explanation of generality, but nevertheless Wimsatt's general meaning is clear.

Still poetry is not universal and abstract like scientific discourse. We must go on to see "that what distinguishes poetry from scientific or logical discourse is a degree of irrelevant concreteness in descriptive details".[20] Wimsatt's concreteness is acknowledgedly similar to Ransom's local irrelevance. Ransom says poetry "is a loose logical structure with an irrelevant local texture".[21] Wimsatt, however, disagrees with Ransom's calling such description "irrelevant". In answer to Ransom he states:

Poetry achieves concreteness, particularity, and something like sensuous shape not by irrelevance of local texture, in its meter or in its images (as in one currently sophisticated literary theory), but by extra relevance or hyper-

---

[18] W. K. Wimsatt, Jr., *The Verbal Icon: Studies in the Meaning of Poetry* (New York, The Noonday Press, 1958), p. 74.
[19] *Ibid.*, p. 75.
[20] *Ibid.*, p. 76.
[21] John Crowe Ransom, *The New Criticism* (Norfolk, Conn., New Directions, 1941), p. 280.

relevance, the interrelational density of words taken in their fullest, most inclusive and symbolic character.[22]

Wimsatt means that poetry becomes concrete not by somehow escaping from language but by immersing itself in language. Poetry becomes concrete through its descriptive detail. Such a concrete form of language has the sensuous fullness emphasized by the presentational theorists. A concrete form of language is experienced as the presentational theories argued. This fullness of description gives poetry its concreteness. The nature of all words to be universal gives poetry its universality.

Wimsatt's reconciliation of the apparently mutually exclusive tendencies expressed in the phrase "concrete universal" can be further clarified by considering his examples. One example of what he means by a concrete universal is a character in a drama. A great character such as Falstaff has a certain roundness (!) or fullness of detail and at the same time a more universal significance.[23] A second example of a concrete universal is metaphor. Wimsatt here anticipates my analysis of the nature of metaphor. Wimsatt argues: "Even the simplest form of metaphor or simile ('My love is like a red, red rose') presents us with a special and creative, in fact a concrete, kind of abstraction different from that of science." [24] In Chapter III I shall show how metaphor is a concrete universal.

Wimsatt quite perceptively sees that if a poem has any meaning or universality at all, if a critic has a job which "is by approximate descriptions of poems, or multiple restatements of their meaning, to aid other readers to come to an intuitive and full realization of poems themselves . . .",[25] then some type of concrete universal position must be true. If the poem were merely particular there could be no mediation between the poem and analyses of it. Particulars do not mean. If we correctly see the poem as a concrete universal, its concreteness means that the critics' analysis, using universal or abstract words, is never equivalent to the poem; but, at the same time, the poem's universality allows some relation between the critics' language and the poets' language. Wimsatt makes the very incisive remark that:

The situation is something like this: In each poem there is something (an individual intuition—or a concept) which can never be expressed in other terms. It is like the square root of two or like pi, which cannot be expressed

[22] Wimsatt, p. 231.
[23] *Ibid.*, pp. 78-79.
[24] *Ibid.*, p. 79.
[25] *Ibid.*, p. 83.

by rational numbers, but only as their *limit*. Criticism of poetry is like 1.414 ... or 3.1416..., not all it would be, yet all that can be had and very useful.[26]

Critical analysis only approaches poetic meaning; it is never an equivalent in other words.

If Wimsatt's remark here is correct then the critic is denied an *analytical* justification of the correctness of his understanding of a metaphor. One of the possible relations (I shall argue that there are two other possible relations) between language in the metaphor and language about the metaphor is eliminated. If the poem is a concrete universal, an experience in some sense, then a critical analysis or explanation of poetic meaning only *approaches* or *approximates* such meaning. The critic cannot claim that he has logically derived his analysis from the metaphor and thus that his analysis is equivalent to the meaning of the metaphor. If the poem is in some important sense a concrete thing, an experience, then the critic's analysis can no more be analytically related or derived from it than the scientist's analysis of natural phenomena is analytically related or derived from such phenomena. To recall Wittgenstein's example, the critic could not show his correct understanding of the poem in the same way as his understanding of how to "continue the series". The way in which the critic does justify his analysis will be examined in Chapter IV.

Wheelwright further supports Wimsatt's argument that the poem is a concrete universal. Poetic language is concrete for Wheelwright because it has iconic self reference. It is universal because it points beyond itself. Wheelwright's meaning here is best clarified by citing the first way in which literal and expressive language, of which poetry is a form, contrast. The first assumption of literal language is that "*of semantic discreteness*: that a linguistic symbol is always distinct, or at least distinguishable, from its referend. Symbol and referend are, so to speak, non-interchangeable".[27] On the other hand, the first principle of expressive language is that "*of iconic signification*: that there are symbols which, although they may point beyond themselves, have a largely self-intentive reference as well".[28] Wheelwright means that poetic language becomes an end in itself; it becomes iconic, while yet referring beyond itself. In becoming an icon the poem overcomes partially the gap between sign and signified. Mysticism is the ultimate way to overcome this

---

26   *Ibid.*
27   Wheelwright, *The Burning Fountain*, p. 55.
28   *Ibid.*, p. 60.

gap, and aesthetic contemplation is "but a halfway house to mysticism, keeping the self-identification and discrimination in fairly even balance".[29] Thus, poetry evokes some of the very quality of the concrete, while still pointing beyond. In referring beyond, however, the poem does not refer to the natural world. Poetic statements, in contrast to literal statements, assert "lightly" about the world.[30] What then do poetic statements refer to if not to the physical world? Wheelwright's answer is reality. "Poetry has its deepest roots in metaphysics." [31] This argument that poetic statements do not refer to the natural world but do refer to reality, that poetic statements express "deep" instead of "surface" truth, will be analyzed in the next chapter under the section "Imagery and Reference".

Thus far Wheelwright's meaning is very close to Wimsatt's. He goes beyond Wimsatt in arguing that poetic language, being expressive language rather than literal language, has the quality of coalescence. By this Wheelwright means that, for example, the poet's rose is both objective and subjective. "The *I* who am aware and the *that* of which I am aware are but two aspects of a single sure actuality, as inseparable as the convex and concave aspects of a single geometrical curve." [32] The coalescence of the self and the not self involves a second coalescence between the particular and universal.[33] Thus Wheelwright's understanding is that expressive language involves a coalescence of the particular and universal and also a coalescence of the self and the not self. This particular emphasis differs from Wimsatt's analysis which saw the concrete universal as only a tension between the descriptive particularity of poetic language and more universal meanings.[34] Given

---

[29] *Ibid.*, p. 61. Wheelwright's relating poetry to mysticism has some grounds as Cassirer's analysis, relating such language to myth, will shortly show.

[30] *Ibid.*, p. 66.

[31] *Ibid.*, p. 269.

[32] Wheelwright, *Metaphor and Reality*, p. 166.

[33] *Ibid.*, p. 167.

[34] Wheelwright's contention that poetic language represents a fusion of the self and not self, the poet and nature, will receive support from Pongs' argument (below, p. 148) that the two processes operating in the metaphor are *Beseelung* and *Gleichnis*, animation and comparison. The arguments of Wheelwright and Pongs receive support from the large number of metaphors which involve personification. Such personification, of course, raises the question of subjectivity in metaphorical language since personification opposes objectification, animated nature opposes objective nature. The problem of subjectivism is inevitably raised by metaphor because poetic description is never the depersonalized description of scientific or literal language. Metaphorical descriptions always bear the mark of the poet.

this difference, namely that Wheelwright argues poetic language implicates the wider problem of the self and not self, still Wimsatt and Wheelwright agree that poetic language as a concrete universal both *is* and *means*; that is, poetic language is a concrete object and yet has universal meaning.

The significance of the position that the poem is a concrete universal is that it raises the question: How can a particular object still be said to have universal significance? Is there any ground for the mediation between the critic's analysis which must use universal terms and the particularity of the poetic description? Implicit in these questions are really two questions raised by the concrete universal theorists: How is the poem related to larger systems of meaning such as our body of natural knowledge? And: How is the poem related to "reality"?

C. THE POEM AS ICON

Wimsatt also says the poem is an icon. Since he argued that the poem is a concrete universal, one would suspect that he understands these words as synonyms. This will in fact turn out to be the case. Not only is there a similarity between these two, but also a similarity between these two and the view that the poem is a presentational symbol. The following fourth view, that the poem is a fusion of sense and sensa, is also basically similar to the other three. Thus, it is beginning to appear that all four views treated here have very significant similarities. This basic agreement, which will be specified shortly, will play an essential part in the theory of metaphor here being developed. Having noted this emerging similarity we can proceed to analyze what is meant by saying the poem is an "icon".

Daitz has analyzed the difference between an icon and a sign. Thus, even though she does not apply this distinction to poetic language, her categories will clarify what it means to say a poem is an icon. Daitz's article is essentially an attack on Wittgenstein's early picture theory which held that elements in the sign stand for and are in a one to one correspondence with elements in the signified. Her basic argument is that Wittgenstein confused signs with icons. She argues that the two are in fact quite distinct. In the first place, an icon shows while words or signs state.[35] We can say of an icon of a tree "this is a tree", but we

[35] Edna Daitz, "The Picture Theory of Meaning", *Mind*, LXII (April, 1953), p. 189.

cannot say the same of the word "tree". The word "tree" is not related to its object in the same way that a drawing is related to its object. Sentences refer and describe while icons show, represent and arrange.[36] Second, the difference is emphasized by the fact that a sentence states while its elements do not, while an icon *and* its elements show. Elements which refer do not state, but elements which represent also show.[37] Daitz here means that the parts of a sentence do not function as does the whole sentence, while the parts of an icon do function as does the whole icon. A part of a picture is also a picture. Third, the order in a sentence is arbitrary; but in an icon it must be representational. A picture demands a certain arrangement, while the grammatical structure of a language is conventional.[38] Finally, elements in a sentence are part of a vocabulary, while elements in an icon are not. An iconic element pictures this and no other object, while words in a vocabulary can be applied to many objects. In fact, iconicity and vocabulary formulation are in an inverse relationship. "As iconicity decreases so the possibility of a vocabulary increases." [39] An icon thus has a very limited range. Language gains range of application and use by its conventionality. There are certain intermediate forms between icons and signs, such as maps and picture languages using hieroglyphs; but the basic difference between icon and sign must not be overlooked.[40]

Wittgenstein's later philosophy shows at least a partial agreement with Daitz's criticisms. Wittgenstein's King's College example analyzed in Chapter I is a clear refutation of his early view that language pictures *by similarity*. Language rather indicates its object by use. Here Wittgenstein would agree with Daitz's criticism. However, here Daitz's accuracy in interpreting the *Tractatus* is not as important as is her definition of an icon. The significance of Daitz's understanding of the word "icon" is twofold. First, in recognizing that an icon, unlike a sign, shares certain qualities with its object, like a picture shares certain qualities with the pictured object, Daitz sees that an icon has a sensuous form or structure; an icon shows. This quality of an icon, that it pictures, will prove to be very significant with regard to poetic language in general and metaphorical language in particular. Second, Daitz's

---

[36]   *Ibid.*, pp. 190-91.
[37]   *Ibid.*, p. 191.
[38]   *Ibid.*, p. 192.
[39]   *Ibid.*, p. 193.
[40]   *Ibid.*, pp. 193-200.

argument that iconicity and signification are inversely related can probably be supported by the history of the evolution of language, as Cassirer will shortly show. The arbitrariness of signs gives them range of application at the expense of particularity.

Wimsatt develops the meaning of iconicity as specifically applied to the poem. The very title of his book, *The Verbal Icon*, emphasizes that the poem as an icon is essential to his thought. In a note to the title of his book he says:

The term icon is used today by semeiotic writers to refer to a verbal sign which somehow *shares the properties of, or resembles, the object which it denotes. The same term in its more usual meaning refers to a visual image and especially to one which is a religious symbol. The verbal image which most fully realizes its verbal capacities is that which is not merely a bright picture (in the usual modern meaning of the term* image) *but also an interpretation of reality in its metaphoric and symbolic dimensions.*[41]

One of the "semeiotic writers" referred to might be Daitz. Daitz has emphasized that an icon is a type of picture; it has a sensuous structure. Wimsatt seems to agree in comparing the poem to more sensuous art forms.

For poetry approximates the intuitive sensuous condition of paint and music not by being less verbal, less characteristic of verbal expression, but actually by being more than usually verbal, by being hyperverbal. ... Through its meaning or meanings the poem *is*. It has an iconic solidity.[42]

Yet even in this passage, which agrees with Daitz in seeing an icon as having concrete qualities of a picture, a note of discord seems to be sounded. Wimsatt says through its *meaning* the poem achieves iconic solidity. The point of Daitz's argument is that normal language is not iconic. However, Wimsatt qualifies his statement by saying that *in a poem* the logical and iconic are not in tension with each other. Thus, Wimsatt does not necessarily hold that meaning outside the poem in literal language is iconic. In fact, he recognizes that literal language does not function iconically. "It seems worth reiterating that both the logical and the counterlogical qualities of style are iconic. In an abstract and relational way they *present* the things which language is otherwise occupied in designating." [43] By counterlogical Wimsatt means certain homophonic elements such as puns, rhymes, agnominations, allitera-

---

[41]   Wimsatt, p. x.
[42]   *Ibid.*, p. 231.
[43]   *Ibid.*, p. 217.

tions, and turns.[44] Both the logical and the counterlogical are iconic in the poem. They are not inversely related as Daitz argues they are for literal language. Thus, the apparent disagreement between Daitz and Wimsatt vanishes because the former is speaking of literal meaning and the latter poetic meaning. Wimsatt recognizes that in ordinary language things are designated while in poetic language they are presented. Wimsatt's point is that in a poem the logical and counterlogical coalesce in the icon. Daitz could agree to this point with regard to poetic language. Logical qualities of style function differently in a poem. The new function which logical or meaningful language plays in the poem is clarified by Wimsatt in this very significant passage.

Poetic symbols—largely through their iconicity at various levels—call attention to themselves as symbols and in themselves invite evaluation. What may seem stranger is that the verbal symbol in calling attention to itself must also call attention to the difference between itself and the reality which it resembles and symbolizes. ... In most discourse we look right through this disparity. There is one-way transparent intellectual reference. But poetry by thickening the medium increases the disparity between itself and its referents. Iconicity enforces disparity. The symbol has more substance than a noniconic symbol and hence is more clearly realized as a thing separate from its referents and as one of the productions of our own spirit. ... And all this has one further important corollary, the enhancement of the symbol as metaphor. For metaphor proceeds from likeness and disparity. (I refer not to the metaphors which a poem contains, but to the total metaphoric relation between a good poem and the reality or the many circles of reality to which it refers.) As a stone sculpture of a human head in a sense *means* a human head but in another sense *is* a carved mass of stone and a metaphor of a head (one would rather have one's head carved in stone than in cheese), so a poem in its various levels and relations of meaning has a kind of rounded being or substance and a metaphoric relation to reality.[45]

Wimsatt's arguments in this passage and the previous ones can be summarized thus: The logical and counterlogical elements in the poem function to make the poem an icon. Iconic language is "thick" and presents its object in a manner similar to a painting's presentation of its object. This means that iconic language, the thick language of the poem, is not transparent. Like a painting it is looked at and not through. The poem has become "thingy". As such, it forces us to recognize that it is related to reality in the same way in which a sculptured object is related to reality, that is, metaphorically. Wimsatt sees the whole poem

[44]   *Ibid.*, p. 213.
[45]   *Ibid.*, p. 217.

as a metaphor in his reference "to the total metaphoric relation between
a good poem and the reality or the many circles of reality to which it
refers".[46] In his analysis of the poem as an icon Wimsatt has touched on
practically all the problems which metaphor raises in relation to literal
language. His insight is relevant to the larger argument of this book in
the following three ways.

First, Wimsatt's seeing the whole poem as a metaphor is reminiscent
of my analysis of implicit metaphor. Merely to recognize implicit
metaphor necessitates a looking through or beyond the page to our body
of scientific knowledge. We cannot look horizontally across the page
in the poem for "grammatical red flags". Such metaphors are recognized by being in tension with what we know to be the case. Implicit
metaphors force the poem, if you will, away from our body of scientific
knowledge. This distance means that ultimately poetry is not read like
literal language. An analysis of the type of reading appropriate to poetic
metaphor follows in Chapter III. Wimsatt sees the same problem and
further sees that the relation of the poem to our body of knowledge is
not a literal relation. The poem as an icon is in some ways related to
normal meanings in our natural knowledge, but is also different in some
ways. In short, it is a metaphor. The whole poem has metaphoric distance from reality. Wimsatt sees here the problem which led Langer
to say the poem presents "virtual life" not real life. In reading a poem
one has only an apparent experience of life.

Second, Wimsatt anticipates my analysis of the answer metaphor
gives to Wittgenstein's attack on the inner meaning theory. Wittgenstein in the King's College example attacks the view that *intervening*
images, the images of the *Tractatus* and of the inner meaning theorists,
are necessary to meaning. Wittgenstein's whole point is that meaning as
use makes these intervening images unnecessary. Notice, however, the
twist that Wimsatt's understanding of icon would give to the image
theory. The poem as an image, an icon, a picture, is thick. It is looked
at, not through. The poem is a picture; but it is a picture in the sense
that a painting is a picture, not in the sense that a photograph is a picture. This is to say the poem is a picture (noun), but it does not picture
(verb) literally or correspond. The poem is a concrete object not a
transparent image. Wimsatt could quite easily agree with Wittgenstein
that no *intervening* images or pictures are necessary in literal language,
yet quite consistently say the poem is a picture, is an icon. The impor-

[46] *Ibid.*

tant word "intervening" or "corresponding" drops out. The poem is looked at, not through. Below, in Chapter III in the section on "Imagery and Reference", it will be argued that the images associated with metaphor have precisely this "thick" opaque character. Thus, many of the problems of the inner image theory can be avoided.

Third, Wimsatt's argument that *both* the logical and counter-logical function iconically is quite significant. It means that not only is the poem iconic in its auditory exploitations, in its pun, rhythm, rhyme, meter, in words whose *sound* mimics its object, but it is iconic through its *meaning* also. The poem then *presents* its object through sound and sense. In Chapter III it will be argued that metaphor is iconic in both ways. Metaphor exploits sound qualities which Wimsatt calls counterlogical elements. Metaphor also exploits iconicity through the sense, the meaning of its words. The specific way in which metaphor is iconic through its sense is in exciting imagery. Imagery, as the section in Chapter III on "Imagery and Sense Impressions" will show, shares certain traits with sense impressions, though it also differs in quite significant ways. Imagery will thus properly deserve the name "iconic" because of this similarity to a perceptual image. "Iconic" means, as Daitz and Wimsatt argue, that the icon shares certain sensuous qualities with its object. The language in the metaphor in being iconic becomes, in the words of C. Day Lewis, "a picture made out of words".[47] The most essential metaphorical element, namely seeing as, functions through the iconicity of the meaning of the words. Metaphor will prove to be iconic in both its logical and counterlogical elements, its sense and sensa.

D. THE POEM AS A FUSION OF SENSE AND SENSA ACHIEVED BY EXPLOITING LANGUAGE AS A MEDIUM

The above three theories agree that a poem is in important senses both particular and universal. By particular they respectively mean: (a) reading the poem is an experience; (b) poetic language has particularity of detail; and (c) counterlogical elements function iconically in the poem. By universal they respectively mean: (a) the poem as a presentational symbol is cognitively significant; (b) poetic language by its nature is related to wider contexts; and (c) logical elements function iconically

[47] C. Day Lewis, *The Poetic Image* (London, Jonathan Cape, 1947), p. 18.

in the poem. The fourth theory, that the poem is a form which has language as its medium, a medium having the qualities of sense and sensa, will support the emphasis that the poem is in some important sense particular and universal. The quality of sensa will emphasize particularity; the quality of sense, universality. The more general significance then of the medium theorists for my overall argument is that they support the three theories thus far dealt with, which theories, in turn, support my analysis of metaphor in Chapter III. The more specific significance of the medium theorists is that they will establish these conclusions in this order. Language is the medium or "stuff" of the poet. As a "stuff" it has qualities shared by poet and reader. It has the qualities of sense, sound, and perhaps imagery. I say "perhaps imagery" because all the theorists here are not *explicit* in citing this quality, though it is implicit in the thought of them all, and explicit in the statements of some. Further, these theorists will argue that the qualities of this medium are *fused*. The main testimony to this fusion is the fact that poetry is untranslatable in a very significant sense. Emphasis on this fusion leads to a very significant conclusion. If in fact it is true that one of the qualities which the poet has at his disposal in his medium is imagery, and if the word fusion is taken seriously, then it is implied that imagery and sound affect sense. This implication is very significant with regard to Wittgenstein because he has argued precisely that imagery does not affect the sense or meaning of words. The medium theorists presage a disagreement with Wittgenstein which reaches its climax in Chapter III. However, this is enough anticipation. Now I shall present the particular arguments of the medium theorists.

1. *Language is the Poet's "Stuff"*

The term "medium" as used here will designate the "stuff" the poet *shares* with his readers in the sense in which marble is the stuff the sculptor shares with his audience. That the poet views language as a medium in this sense, in the sense that the poem is a full-fledged sensuous object, has already emerged in the above three views of poetic language. Wimsatt's analysis of the iconicity of poetry especially implies that language is to the poet thick, opaque and full like a painted or sculptured object. Bosanquet argues:

Poetry, like the other arts, has a physical or at least a sensuous medium, and this medium is sound. It is, however, significant sound, uniting inseparably in itself the factors of formal expression through an immediate pattern, and of representation through the meanings of language, exactly as sculpture and painting deal at once and in the same vision both with formal patterns and with significant shapes.[48]

Nor is the view that the poet sees language as a medium as defined here peculiar to philosophers of art or literary critics. An excellent linguist, Edward Sapir, states:

Language is the medium of literature as marble or bronze or clay are the materials of the sculptor. Since every language has its distinctive peculiarities, the innate formal limitations—and possibilities—of one literature are never quite the same as those of another.[49]

Sapir's last sentence, noting the peculiarities of each language, raises the whole question of the translatability of poetry. In further commenting on this question Sapir notes that a language has two levels, the content of a language and the particular conformation of a given language. If a particular poem exploits the former intuitive record of experience then it is translatable without too much loss, for example, a work of Shakespeare; while if the poem exploits the peculiarities of a particular language it can be translated only very poorly, for example, a lyric by Swinburne.[50]

2. *Qualities of Medium or "Stuff"*

The poet's medium has qualities which are shared by poet and reader. Bosanquet and Sapir have already anticipated the statement of the qualities, but now a more extensive treatment is needed. The sculptor is prepared to cite the qualities of his medium. Can the poet also oblige us? A great poet has obliged us. Probably the most elegant statement of the qualities of the poet's medium is Pope's passage on sound and sense.

> True ease in writing comes from art, not chance,
> As those move easiest who have learned to dance.
> 'Tis not enough no harshness gives offence,
> The sound must seem an echo to the sense:
> Soft is the strain when Zephyr gently blows,

[48] Bernard Bosanquet, *Three Lectures on Aesthetics* (London, Macmillan and Co., Ltd., 1923), p. 65.
[49] Edward Sapir, *Language: An Introduction to the Study of Speech* (New York, A Harvest Book, 1949), p. 222.
[50] *Ibid.*, p. 223.

> And the smooth stream in smoother numbers flows:
> But when loud surges lash the sounding shore,
> The hoarse, rough verse should like the torrent roar:
> When Ajax strives some rock's vast weight to throw,
> The line too labors, and the words move slow;
> Not so, when swift Camilla scours the plain,
> Flies o'er th'unbending corn, and skims along the main.
>> (Alexander Pope, "An Essay on Criticism", ll. 362-373)

In this passage, as has often been noted, Pope not only states the theory of sound and sense as qualities of the poet's medium but practices it. The sibilant sound in lines five and six gives the subdued sound of a whisper, thus matching the sense of those two lines, while the cacophonous effect of lines seven and eight matches the violence of their sense.

An equally elegant statement by another poet, this time in prose, is given by Paul Valéry. Valéry combines the qualities, rarely united, of being a fine poet and a first-rate theorist of poetry. Thus, he is in an incomparable position for describing the qualities of the poet's medium. Valéry in his pendulum metaphor cites the same two qualities of the poet's medium recognized by Pope, that is, sound and sense.

Now observe the effect of poetry on yourselves. You will find that at each line the meaning produced within you, far from destroying the musical form communicated to you, recalls it. The living pendulum that has swung from *sound* to *sense* swings back to its felt point of departure, as though the very sense which is present to your mind can find no other outlet or expression, no other answer, than the very music which gave it birth.[51]

It is very important to emphasize that Valéry never forgot either quality of the poet's medium. To forget either quality is to fall off the narrow ridge which the poet is called to tread between music and algebra. In either case the poet would be deserting his medium, language. "One might say that the bounds of language are, on the one side, *music* and, on the other, *algebra*."[52] Very shortly I shall present one of Valéry's own disciples who falls off into music, and another theorist who falls off into the normal propositional function of language symbolized in the quote by algebra.

Valéry especially emphasized this latter danger; namely, the danger that poetry will degenerate into prose. The poet has a special problem

---

[51] Paul Valéry, *The Art of Poetry*, trans. Denise Folliot (New York, Vintage Books, 1961), p. 72.
[52] *Ibid.*, p. 205.

in that he has to wrench the ordinary function of language from its practical end of communicating only sense. "Poetry implies a decision to change the function of language . . .",[53] to change the walking of prose to the dancing of poetry. Valéry's metaphor here is brilliant.

Walking, like prose, has a definite aim. It is an act directed at something we wish to reach. Actual circumstances, such as the need for some object, the impulse of my desire, the state of my body, my sight, the terrain, etc., which order the manner of walking, prescribe its direction and its speed, and give it a *definite end*. All the characteristics of walking derive from these instantaneous conditions, which combine *in a novel way* each time. There are no movements in walking that are not special adaptations, but, each time, they are abolished and, as it were, absorbed by the accomplishment of the act, by the attainment of the goal.

The dance is quite another matter. It is, of course, a system of actions; but of actions whose end is in themselves. It goes nowhere. If it pursues an object, it is only an ideal object, a state, an enchantment, the phantom of a flower, an extreme of life, a smile—which forms at last on the face of the one who summoned it from empty space.[54]

Wittgenstein could quite easily agree, as my analysis of the pragmatic aspect of "use" has shown, to this emphasis on the functional end of language. Language as a dance, however, is quite transformed. Instead of passing away, vanishing when understanding is accomplished, the language of poetry becomes an end in itself. "The poem . . . does not die for having lived: it is expressly designed to be born again from its ashes and to become endlessly what it has just been."[55] The poem recreates itself because it is a harmonious exchange between expression and impression. "This harmonious exchange between impression and expression is in my eyes the essential principle of the mechanics of poetry, that is, of the production of the poetic state through speech."[56] The poem then becomes an experience through its sound, image, sentiment and thought.[57] The relation between the word as sound and its meaning or thought, which relation is arbitrary in prose, is made into an intimate union of word and meaning in poetry.[58] Poetic thought then can be expressed in this way and no other.[59]

The significance of this transformation of the function of language

---

[53] *Ibid.*, p. 208.
[54] *Ibid.*, p. 70.
[55] *Ibid.*, p. 72.
[56] *Ibid.*, p. 210.
[57] *Ibid.*, p. 73.
[58] *Ibid.*, p. 74.
[59] *Ibid.*, p. 98.

to an end in itself that tends to endlessly re-create itself is that it agrees significantly with Langer's conclusion that the poem becomes an image abstracted from the practical world and that to read the poem is to have an experience of virtual life. The emphasis of Valéry and Langer that the poem is somehow an image-ladened form of language which tends to re-create itself when read contrasts again with Wittgenstein's argument that literal language is unconcerned about imagery. Whether Wittgenstein's clear recognition of a plurality of language-games can include a game with this particular purpose depends on whether it is claimed that such images affect or are involved in the *meaning* of such a form of language. I shall argue that metaphor makes precisely such a claim, thus implying some divergence from Wittgenstein's analysis of meaning.

Northrop Frye's thought presents a significant broadening of the qualities recognized explicitly by Pope and Valéry. They emphasize, as their noun "sound" indicates, the auditory quality of the poem. Frye recognized that the sensuous nature of literature appeals not only to the ear but also to the inner eye; it is related to music *and* the plastic arts.[60] "The lyric is an internal mimesis of sound and imagery, and stands opposite the external mimesis, or outward representation of sound and imagery, which is drama." [61] The two elements in a lyric thus are *melos* and *orsis*.[62] The poem thus becomes a more "rounded" sensuous object in having "sound-links, ambiguous sense-links, and memory-links very like that of the dream".[63] Frye further points out that in the lyric this sensuous form is fused with more reflective, cognitive elements.[64]

Frye's point that the lyric is a mimesis of sound and imagery is problematical. Mimesis always reintroduces the problem of a correspondence between a picture and a fact, thus becoming susceptible to Wittgenstein's criticisms. In the section on the iconicity of poetic language it was argued that Wimsatt's solution enables one to see the poem as a picture but not necessarily as picturing. Frye's analysis would be more powerful with a similar solution. It may be the case that the artist imitates nature or reality; but, if so, knowledge of this fact tells us more about the act of creating than it does about the finished product.

[60] Northrop Frye, *Anatomy of Criticism: Four Essays* (Princeton, Princeton University Press, 1957), p. 244.
[61] *Ibid.*, p. 250.
[62] *Ibid.*, p. 275.
[63] *Ibid.*, p. 272.
[64] *Ibid.*, pp. 280-81.

The significance of Frye's recognition that a list of the qualities of the poet's medium includes imagery, a recognition that is only implicit in Pope and Valéry, is that it suggests that the poem is a sensuous object in a more "rounded" sense. The poem is sensuous not just in an auditory sense, but also includes imagery. This conclusion agrees with Wimsatt's comparing the sensuous fullness of a poem to painted and sculptured art forms. Metaphor will demand that such imagery be recognized. Frye's broader understanding of the qualities of the poet's medium calls for a new phrase. I shall use *"sense* and *sensa"* when I intend to include not only sense and sound, but sense, sound and imagery.[65]

3. *Absurdity of Forgetting Any of the Qualities*

A perverse view of the nature of poetic language results if either of the qualities, sense or sensa, is forgotten. Each has in fact been ignored by theorists of poetry. Sense has been forgotten by the theorists of pure poetry; sensa, by the theorists of intellectual poetry.

Henri Brémond clearly formulates an extreme doctrine of pure poetry.

---

[65] A note is needed here on the phrase "sense and sensa". When I use this phrase instead of "sense and sound" it is for this reason. "Sensa" is a broader term and includes not only sound, that is, auditory sensations, but sensations relevant to all the senses. With regard to metaphor this broader understanding of the sensuous elements in the poem is essential. Metaphors will prove to be sensory in senses *in addition to* auditory sensations. I have in mind the ability of metaphors to arouse imagery. Imagery may appeal to any of the senses. Metaphor will be seen to involve imagery which appeals to each of the senses and often to several senses at once in the phenomena of synesthesia. Imagery, however, will turn out to be not a full-fledged sensation but only a quasi-sensation. Onomatopoetic words such as "murmuring" involve true sensations since the sound of the words is actually an impression in the full sense of the word. An auditory *image*, on the other hand, is only quasi-sensuous. This metaphor

> At the violet hour, when the eyes and back
> Turn upward from the desk, when the human engine waits
> Like a taxi throbbing waiting, . . .
> (T. S. Eliot, "The Waste Land", ll. 215-17)

involves auditory images in the comparison of the "human engine" to the taxi, and perhaps also involves auditory impressions in the sound of "throbbing". My use of the phrase "sense and sensa" then includes the sense and sound of Pope and Valéry and other quasi-sensory elements such as metaphorical imagery and metaphorical seeing as. Very shortly it will be seen that in fact Valéry and Wimsatt see the poem as a sensuous object in this broader sense, although their language does not explicitly emphasize this fullness as does the phrase "sense and sensa".

He begins by arguing that in order to read a poem properly or to listen properly it is not necessary to understand the poem's sense. His examples are a peasant hearing a Latin liturgy and a child hearing speech before it understands.[66] In both cases all that is important is the sheer beauty of the sound of language. Likewise, poetry loves meaningless sentences. Brémond is convinced that the supreme summits of poetic beauty have very rarely been achieved. One can recognize such summits of verbal music by finding one in which the least change of syllable or letter would destroy its beauty.[67] As an example of supreme height Brémond cites this line by Malherbe:

<blockquote>Et les fruits passeront la promesse des fleurs</blockquote>

Brémond admits that this verse has not exactly the strongest idea. In fact, this lack of a striking sense is a positive quality. The true poet expurgates his lines of all logic of ideas, all progression of narrative, all sense in each phrase, all details of description and even the emotions directly excited.[68] What could be left by such a purge? The answer is pure sound: "Poésie, musique, c'est même chose." [69] All poetry is verbal music, though the converse is not so.[70] Brémond then moves toward mysticism by saying that the degree to which a work is poetical is the degree in which it is inexpressible.[71] His final step toward mysticism is taken when he argues that some type of mystical essence is transmitted by the poem.

Nous nous offrons à ces vibrations fugitives, si exquises d'ailleurs que soient leurs caresses, non pour goûter le plaisir qu'elle donnent, mais pour recevoir le fluide mystérieux qu'elles transmettent: simples conducteurs, plus ou moins précieux ou sonores, il importe peu; ou plutôt, conducteurs qui doivent leur sonorité même et leur splendeur éphémère au courant qui les traverse.[72]

Decker is correct in stating that for Brémond verbal music is important only because of this magic essence which passes through it. Thus, the surface of the poem, its pure sound, is for the purpose of freeing us to a world of mystical fulfillment.[73]

---

[66] Henri Brémond, *La poésie pure: avec un débat sur la poésie par Robert de Souza* (Paris, Bernard Grasset, 1926), p. 18.
[67] *Ibid.*, p. 24.
[68] *Ibid.*, p. 22.
[69] *Ibid.*, p. 23.
[70] *Ibid.*, p. 24.
[71] *Ibid.*, pp. 22-23.
[72] *Ibid.*, p. 26.
[73] Henry W. Decker, *Pure Poetry, 1920-1930: Theory and Debate in France* (Berkeley and Los Angeles, University of California Press, 1962), pp. 50-51.

Critics of Brémond's extreme position are numerous. Robert Penn Warren argues that the dross of ideas is purposely included in a poem. Nor is such structure merely a background on which images are projected, a frame in which they are shown, nor a string on which they are strung. All such views are versions of the sugar-coated pill theory which sees structure as a device to sell "a well arranged showcase".[74] A more correct view sees that we can object to theory no more than to words. Nothing in human experience is legislated out of poetry.[75]

Kaplan argues that a formalism such as the pure poetry theory arises from taking the emotive-cognitive dichotomy too seriously. This dichotomy leaves the choice of literalism, in which art states emotional truths known by psychology and sociology and differs from these only in having a more developed vehicle, or emotivism. Formalism is really a flight from literalism into emotivism. Kaplan argues that a happier solution is to see that the reference in a verbal art form, such as a poem, is embedded in its expression. "Meaning in the arts is basically expressive; the semeiotical approach to arts is not committed to more than an insistance that the art object is not only sensed as an item in a perceptual field but is also interpreted." [76] Emotions in art are embedded in complex structures and thus result only from taking thought.[77]

My own version of these criticisms is that a pure poetry poet is essentially one who has been called to the wrong medium. Should one work in marble if he does not like volumes or oils if he does not like color? Should one work in language if he dislikes one of the two essential qualities of language, namely sense? In Brémond's words the poet is a musician. But I would add that his poet is essentially a miscalled musician.[78]

However, one further difficulty threatens this account. Valéry also used the term "pure poetry". Thus, this criticism of Brémond might seem also directed against Valéry and thus vitiate his doctrine of sense

[74] Robert Penn Warren, "Pure and Impure Poetry", *The Kenyon Review*, V (Spring, 1943), p. 245.
[75] *Ibid.*, p. 250.
[76] Abraham Kaplan, "Referential Meaning in the Arts", *The Journal of Aesthetics & Art Criticism*, XII (June, 1954), p. 461.
[77] Abraham Kaplan and Ernst Kris, "Esthetic Ambiguity", *Philosophy and Phenomenological Research*, VIII (March, 1948), p. 423.
[78] For further criticism of the pure poetry position the reader may consult the following articles: Charles Lalo, "The Aesthetic Analysis of a Work of Art: An Essay on the Structure and Superstructure of Poetry" (*The Journal of Aesthetics & Art Criticism*, VII, June, 1949, pp. 275-86); and W. K. Wimsatt, "Poetic Tension: A Summary" (*The New Scholasticism*, XXXII, Jan., 1958, pp. 73-88).

and sound which will be essential to my own arguments. The problem is even further complicated by the fact that Brémond claimed he formulated his ideas of poetry under Valéry's influence and further claimed he was using the phrase "pure poetry" in the same sense as Valéry.[79] However, as Decker indicates, Valéry was quite shocked at Brémond's understanding of "pure poetry" and quickly tried to dissociate himself from Brémond's extremes. For Valéry pure poetry was an *idée limité* which was a practical guide to help remove prose elements from poetry.[80] Valéry is quite explicit in stating that the problem of pure poetry is whether or not "one can give the impression of a complete system of *reciprocal* relations between our ideas and images on the one hand and our means of expression on the other . . .".[81] I ask the reader to note Valéry's own emphasis on the *reciprocity* between ideas, images, and expression. It is quite evident from this statement and my account above that Valéry did not intend to exclude ideas but merely to transform them, to change their pedestrian function into the dance. Brémond differs on this fundamental point in excluding ideas and ultimately concluding that the essence of poetry is non-linguistic. Decker is quite correct in emphasizing the wide divergence in their understanding of the term "pure poetry". Thus Valéry, never forgetting that sense is a quality of the medium of language, is not guilty of Brémond's extravagance.

Ruth Herschberger, in intentionally leaving emotivism or formalism for literalism, commits the opposite error from Brémond. She says that metaphor is fundamentally expository and is thus reducible to a multiplicity of prose arguments. The poet and scientist are no longer on separate planes. Poetry may, since poetic possibility is wider than what we now believe, discover truth or facts which psychology only later discovers. The poet differs from the scientist because he aims at a different audience. We must no longer call poetry merely emotive, but must see that it has usefulness, logical necessity and truth.[82]

John Crowe Ransom replies to Herschberger. He says that the possibility of a conversion of poetry into prose implies that departure from prose in the first place is pure illusion. He accuses Herschberger of practicing "wishful positivism" in her belief in one and only one way

[79] Decker, pp. 41-42.
[80] *Ibid.*, pp. 44-46.
[81] Valéry, p. 185.
[82] Ruth Herschberger, "The Structure of Metaphor", *The Kenyon Review*, V (Summer, 1943), pp. 433-43.

of knowing. He contends that poetry densifies; it is about the dense actual world which often escapes science. Positivism fails to see that there are modes of human behavior which go beyond function, for example, religion, art, manners, and sentiments. Poetry precisely explores this "reality beyond the possibility of usefulness".[83]

I sympathize with Herschberger's point that poetry is not merely emotive, but cannot agree with her literalism. Ransom is correct in seeing that poetry would be superfluous if completely reducible to prose. Herschberger, quite to the opposite of Brémond, forgets that meaning in poetry undergoes a sensuous transformation. Thus, her poet would be essentially a miscalled philosopher or scientist. She holds a clear version of the sugar-coated pill theory. Kaplan's argument above is correct in that a tacit acceptance of the emotive-cognitive dichotomy leads either to formalism on the emotive side or literalism on the cognitive side, to Brémond or Herschberger. Literalism and formalism despite their apparent animosity to each other are bed-fellows in that both naively accept the emotive-cognitive distinction. Both think that sense can function in only one way. Thus, one is led to embrace this understanding of sense while the other rejects it. These two perverted views have been presented because they consitute a *reductio ad absurdum*. The absurdity substantiates the point that language for the poet has the qualities of sound and sense. A position which forgets that imagery is also a quality associated with language as a medium is equally as absurd as the two above positions, a point substantiated more fully in Chapter III.

The conclusions of the medium theorists thus far are that language is the poet's medium, a medium sharing the qualities of sense, sound and imagery with the reader. That imagery is one of the qualities is explicit in Frye, implicit in Valéry's argument that the poem recreates itself in a full sense, implicit in Langer's arguments that to read the poem is to experience an image of life, and implicit in Wimsatt's comparison of poetry to the sensuous forms of painting and sculpture. Also strongly implied by the theorists is the argument that the qualities are not just thrown together, but are in an important sense *fused*. Pope has said: "The sound must seem an echo to the sense." Valéry has argued that a particular thought in a poem can be expressed in this and no other vehicle. There is an intimate union between the physical words

---

[83]   John Crowe Ransom, "Positive and Near Positive Aesthetics", *The Kenyon Review*, V (Summer, 1943), p. 445.

and meaning in poetry.[84] There is a harmonious exchange between expression and impression.[85] Wimsatt speaks of "the wedding" of these elements and of "an amalgam of the sensory and the logical . . .".[86] An emphasis on this fusion is significant because if sense, sound and imagery are interwoven, as these theorists imply, then it is suggested that meaning and imagery, Wittgenstein not withstanding, are mutually involved with each other. That in fact poetic meaning is involved in its sensuous vehicle is convincingly argued by the phenomenon of the untranslatability of poetry.

4. Fusion of Qualities makes Poetry Untranslatable

O. K. Bouwsma argues explicitly that poetic meaning is in some special sense in its sensuous vehicle and thus is untranslatable. His point emerges in attacking the expression theory of art. Such a theory would argue that the statement "the poem is sad" really means "the poem expresses sadness". The expressionist holds that the poem's expression is precisely analogous to a person's expressing sadness by tears. The expressionist, however, becomes embarrassed by his analogy between the poem's expression and the person's expression when it is pointed out that (a) the person has a soul and the poem does not, and (b) the emotion expressed in the former case is Wordsworth's emotion recollected in tranquillity while in the latter case the emotion expressed is a real emotion. One quite often reads a sad poem with dry eyes. The poem then is not like the person nor is its emotion like the person's emotion.

On being confronted with these difficulties the expressionist decides to change his analogy. Now he says music (or poetry) expresses sadness in the same sense that a sentence expresses an idea.[87] Bouwsma argues this analogy will not do either. An idea is not *in* a sentence.

Where is the idea of the elephant eating a jumbo peanut? Suppose we say, 'It's in the very words you hear.' Have you ever seen, in your mind's eye, that is, an elephant eating a peanut in the very words you hear? [88]

---

[84]   Valéry, p. 74.
[85]   *Ibid.*, p. 210.
[86]   Wimsatt, *The Verbal Icon*, p. 165.
[87]   William Elton (ed.), *Aesthetics and Language* (Oxford, Basil Blackwell, 1959), p. 90.
[88]   *Ibid.*, p. 93.

Bouwsma's remarks here border on unintelligibility. He seems to be making two points which are quite evidently similar to Wittgenstein's argument.

First, the expressionist has first conceived of this analogy between ideas and emotions because of misunderstanding ideas. The expressionist seems to think that an idea is a type of image that pops into one's head when a word is said. An emotion is evoked in the same way.[89] His elephant example is intended to show that ideas do not pop into the mind like this. What he seems to have in mind is Wittgenstein's thought that a meaning is not an inner image. Thus, the analogy between a sentence expressing an idea and a poem expressing an emotion vanishes because the nature of ideas has been misunderstood.

Second, even if the expressionist corrected his understanding of ideas, he still seems to want to deny the analogy between sentences and poem. Bouwsma wants to say here that the meaning of a sentence is not literally *in* the sentence. If the meaning were in the sentence we would never ask what a sentence meant because we would have already been given the meaning *in* the sentence.[90] Here again he badly expresses Wittgenstein's thought that in being questioned about a meaning one gives an *explanation* of the first meaning. One would not simply repeat the sentence in question as if the meaning were in it. Looking for meaning in a sentence would be like looking for life in a part of a squirrel.[91]

However, the foolish theory that meaning is in a sentence is not foolish with respect to poetry.

And now notice that what was admittedly a foolish theory in respect to sentences is not a foolish theory in respect to poems or music. Do you get the poem? Do you get the music? If you do not, pointing, gestures, translations will not help. (Understanding the words is presupposed.) There will be only one thing to do; namely, read the verses again, play the music once more. ... The meaning of sentences is translatable, but the 'meaning' of poems, of music, is not.[92]

Bouwsma emerges with the point that the meaning of a poem or music is in the words or notes respectively as sadness is on a face. He has arrived at this conclusion by taking seriously the thought of this section that language is the medium of the poet, like marble is the medium of

---

89   *Ibid.*, p. 91.
90   *Ibid.*, p. 94.
91   *Ibid.*, pp. 94-95.
92   *Ibid.*, p. 95.

the sculptor. By taking seriously this thought he emerges with these two conclusions. First, meaning is in a poem in a way in which meaning is not in a sentence. This fundamental point will be born out by the summary of these four sections which will yield a semantic of poetic language. Poetic meaning is fused with its sensuous vehicle. A fundamental contrast with literal language is already emerging. Second, since meaning is in a poem in a different sense from meaning in a sentence, a different stance is required to grasp their respective meanings. If you are in question about the meaning of a poem you reread it. If you are in question about the meaning of a sentence you request an explanation, a restatement in *other* words. A sentence is translatable, but a poem is not.

Bouwsma's point is reminiscent of Wimsatt's argument that the critic's analysis only in an imperfect way expresses the poem's meaning. However, Wimsatt's view is more balanced because he does not by any means rule out *some* function for critical explanation as does Bouwsma's statement that pointing, gestures, and translations will not help. I shall argue in Chapter IV that critical analysis is relevant to the meaning of a metaphor, thus helping to understand the metaphor, and that such analysis can be in some sense justified as correct, although the method of justification is not in the same way that one justifies the correctness of his understanding of "red" nor in the same way that one justifies the correctness of his understanding how "to continue a series". It does not follow from Bouwsma's point that a different stance is required by poetic meaning that no stance of any type is appropriate. I agree with Wimsatt that if a poem has meaning then there must be some mediation between it and explanations of its meaning.

John Hospers has similar reasons for his argument that poetry is untranslatable. He says poetic meaning is untranslatable because it is not purely logical meaning. A poem can be translated only to the extent that referential meaning is dominant, that is, only to the extent that the poem is poor or bad.[93] Nor can the poem be changed into other words in the same language. Such a prose restatement of a poem is nothing but an empty shell. To assume that a poem is translatable or restatable is to assume that the poem is a sugar-coated message, a sugar-coated pill. Translatability assumes that the poem expresses in pretty words what could be expressed with less beauty in prose.[94] Hospers' criticism

[93]   John Hospers, *Meaning and Truth in the Arts* (Chapel Hill, N.C., The University of North Carolina Press, 1948), pp. 130-32.
[94]   *Ibid.*, p. 133.

here is quite effective against the sugar-coated pill theory which is really Aristotle's ornamental theory. The ornamental theory sees metaphor as a device to give "clearness, charm and distinction..." to speech.[95] His argument is also effective against Herschberger's version of the ornamental theory where she argues that metaphor is reducible to a multiplicity of prose arguments.[96] The "sugar-coated pill" theory is absurd because of thinking that poetry is just literal language with an embellishment here and there.

The significance of the view of the medium theorists is, first, that it supports the first three theories in seeing the poem as particular and "thingy" while yet having sense, that is, meaning. Second, in noting the relative untranslatability of poetry the medium theorists detect a very significant contrast with literal language. Literal language is translatable because, as Hospers implies, it is interested only in sense or what is said. As Valéry clearly expressed it, literal language is happy to die after its sense has been transmitted. Literal language is not concerned with the sensuous envelope in which it is expressed. Literal language sees signs as *flatus vocis*. For such language there is nothing especially suitable about one sensory form of words over another so long as meaning is communicated. Here it is helpful to recall Wittgenstein's arguments that convention is bedrock. If asked why we follow the arrow in a certain way we can give no answer. We simply take the arrow in this way. Our questioning comes to an end here. Wittgenstein, of course, would extend this argument to the sounds or shapes of words. There is no reason why we use the particular shape and sound of the word "murmuring" instead of *"Gemurmel"* to express "a low, confused, and indistinct sound, like that of running water...".[97]

The poet, however, as the medium theorists so clearly note, insists on a fusion of sense and sensa. The sensuous envelope is important. As Pope so gracefully put it: "The sound must seem an echo to the sense." "Murmuring" when used in a phrase such as "the murmuring Winde" (Spenser, "The Faerie Queene", 1. 139) is precisely such an "echo to the sense". The sound of the word "murmuring" is in an important sense "a low, confused, and indistinct sound, like that of running water...". The auditory sound of "murmuring" matches its sense. The poet is not interested in just *what* is said, in sense, but *how* it is

---

[95]   Ross, 1405ᵃ 8-9.
[96]   Herschberger, p. 433.
[97]   *Webster's New Collegiate Dictionary* (Springfield, Mass., G. & C. Merriam Co., 1956), p. 555.

said, in the sensuous quality of language. Poetic meaning can be said in this and no other way, as Valéry argues. Of course, no poet or literary theorist would want to say that English words, by some magical reason, are somehow better able to express their referent than German words. The medium theorists would argue both that English is untranslatable into German and that German is untranslatable into English. Each language has its own subtilties and nuances. The medium theorists would say that within a given language, given that the poet shares a common stuff with the reader in that all have access to the sense and sound of the words, then the poet does try to fuse or weld together the sensuous vehicle and the meaning of words. The poet could agree with Wittgenstein that convention does establish the form or sound of the words, but then the poet would go on to say that *poetry* is a language-game in which words are selected so as to make their form appear as nonconventionally related to their meaning. Nor does it just appear that the sensuous envelope in this particular game is especially related to its meaning. The medium theorists have been arguing that in fact the form does affect the meaning. This is why poetic meaning is untranslatable; it does not just seem to be untranslatable.

Further, it was stated explicitly by Frye and implicitly by Valéry, Wimsatt, and Langer, that the poem is not just a fusion of sound and sense, but sense, sound and imagery. The contrast with Wittgenstein's understanding of literal language becomes even sharper here. Now not only does the poet have a queer obsession to use certain sounds with certain meanings but to weigh the image evoking quality of his words. And even more radically, the word "fusion" suggests that there is a two-way influence between meanings and imagery. If metaphor demands this conclusion it will become quite unpalatable to Wittgenstein.

E.   GENERALIZATIONS ON POETIC LANGUAGE

Now I shall generalize from the four theories of language in the poem to conclusions about the function and nature of poetic language. *Poetic language is that language in which both sense and sound function iconically, thus yielding a fusion of sense and sensa.* An icon, as Daitz notes, shares certain qualities with its object. An icon in being like its object becomes itself an object in its own right. Thus *poetic language attains the concreteness of an icon.* Of course, poetic language is never able to become as concrete, as "thingy" as a painting or a sculptured object. *The poem's concreteness is experiential. Thus to read a poem is to have an experience. Still this concreteness is in some incomplete sense amenable to analysis. The poem is not only a sensuous form, but a sensuous form having meaning.*

The theorists presented agree with these generalizations in significant ways. Langer clearly argues that in poetry the normal discursive function of language is transformed into a vehicle which has the appearance of experienced life. In reading a poem one has the illusion that he is directly experiencing life.[98] Still this particular concrete experience has more universal validity because the poem, as a presentational symbolic form, is based in human rationality just as basically as are discursive forms.[99] Wimsatt argues explicitly that both the logical and counter-logical elements of poetry function iconically. The poem in becoming an icon becomes "thick" or "thingy". He explicitly compares the poem as an icon to sculptured and painted art forms. In achieving concreteness, in reaching iconicity, the poem increases its disparity with regard to its referent. It becomes an opaque picture, not an image transparent to its referent. The poem, like other forms of art, has metaphorical distance from reality.[100] Yet the sensuous roundness or fullness which the poem develops by its descriptive detail does not rob it of more universal significance or meaning.[101] Wheelwright recognizes that the poem in becoming an icon, in having self-referential qualities, in becoming of sensuous importance in itself, tries to overcome the split between sign and signified.[102] Still the poem points beyond itself to more universal meanings. Valéry argues that it is of the essence of poetic language to re-create the poetic state, the poetic experience, in the reader. For Valéry to read a poem is to have an experience.[103] Still the concrete experience is an experience having sense or meaning.

The above generalizations are the first focal point on the way to my theory of meaning of poetic metaphor. General conclusions as to a theory of meaning of poetic language have been reached. The most significant conclusion is that poetic language is not only a body of signs, but also its own context in a very significant sense. As an icon the poem

---

[98] Langer, *Feeling and Form*, p. 234.
[99] Langer, *Philosophy in a New Key*, pp. 88-91.
[100] Wimsatt, *The Verbal Icon*, p. 217.
[101] *Ibid.*, pp. 76-83.
[102] Wheelwright, *The Burning Fountain*, pp. 60-61.
[103] Valéry, pp. 72-73.

is a body of signs which becomes an object in its own right. The poem is in an important sense its own referent. All the theorists explicitly note that the poem is a self-referring icon at least in an auditory sense. The theorists strongly imply that the poem is further iconic through becoming an image-laden form of language. Wimsatt with insight suggests that the more iconic the poem becomes the more distance the language puts between itself and its former referent. The poem becomes like a painting, not like a photograph. It is a picture which does not picture. Valéry suggests similarly that poetic language tends to re-create the poetic state in the reader. Langer argues that to read the poem is to have an experience of virtual life. The poem becomes its own context in reading. Metaphor will substantiate these conclusions. Frye agrees with the above generalizations in his recognition that the lyric is related to music and the plastic arts; the lyric involves *melos* and *orsis*.[104] The sensuous form of the lyric is also fused with more reflective, cognitive elements.[105]

1. *Questions Unanswered by Theorists*

However, this analysis of the agreement of these theorists with my generalizations in no way intends to imply a unanimity of opinion. Quite to the contrary, there are some very significant questions still outstanding which my analysis of metaphor will attempt to answer.

These questions are: first, what precisely is the nature of the experience one has on reading poetry? No one can seriously deny that the poem exploits sensuous sound qualities of language. Thus, reading poetry is having an auditory experience even if the lines are read silently. In such cases one hears rhyme, rhythm, alliteration, etc., in the ear of one's mind. As Berry argues, poetry is essentially a phenomenon of sound "which is recreated in the 'reader's' inner ear when he experiences verse...".[106] The debate arises when one extends his understanding of experience, following Frye, Wimsatt, Valéry, and Langer, to impressions derived from senses other than the auditory sense. I shall argue that metaphor involves precisely such an extension, for example, in the experience of imagery and the experience-act of seeing as. Even this extension would not necessarily involve a serious conflict with Wittgen-

---

[104]   Frye, p. 275.
[105]   *Ibid.*, p. 280.
[106]   Francis Berry, *Poetry and the Physical Voice* (London, Routledge & Kegan Paul, 1962), p. 17.

stein's understanding of meaning as use. He clearly recognized that language has a plurality of functions and that it could be the purpose of a game to excite imagery.[107] Thus, it is conceivable that he would agree that the function of metaphorical language is to excite imagery and use such imagery to assist the experience of seeing as. However, the rub begins when the critic claims that such imagery *means* and further claims to *justify* his understanding of a metaphor's meaning by referring to the metaphor in a full sense including imagery. "The metaphor" includes the actual words and the quasi-sensuous experiences accompanying the words, such as imagery and seeing as. It is apparent that such *justification* cannot be made in the same way that one justifies his understanding of "red" or justifies his understanding of how "to continue a series". There are no criteria, in Wittgenstein's sense, for pointing, in the way which the critic does, to the metaphor as read. I shall argue that literary analysis is a language-game in which the experience of imagery and seeing as have a definite function. Admittedly this game will involve a stretching of Wittgenstein's conception of games. In fact, the *existence* of the game of literary analysis will imply an inadequacy in Wittgenstein's understanding of criteria. Chapters III and IV deal with these questions.

Second, a question outstanding with regard to the theorists analyzed is: How is the poem related to the natural world or "reality"? The natural world and "reality" are in fact distinguished by the theorists. Thus, there are really two questions involved: How is the poem related to the natural world, our scientific knowledge or literal truth; and how is it related to "reality"? These are really the truth questions. Langer's presentational symbol as *virtual* life with regard to the poem and Wimsatt's icon metaphorically related to literal knowledge both emphasize some divergence between natural and poetic knowledge, yet both maintain some ties between the poem and "deeper" levels of meaning. Wheelwright shows a similar tendency where he argues that poetic statements assert lightly, implying a different type of truth claim than that of literal statements. Yet he goes on to say poetry is rooted in metaphysics. Herschberger, on the other hand, is anxious to draw poetic and scientific truth together. Brémond is equally anxious to drive them apart. Thus, our theorists vary from Brémond's hard-line purism to Herschberger's literalism. My conclusions on this point will be argued in the next chapter, in the section "Imagery and Reference".

[107] *Investigations*, # 6.

Third, the theorists, although all agreeing that the poem is in some sense particular and universal, by no means agree as to *how* such a status is achieved. Wimsatt argues that it is the nature of all words to be universals. Poetic language partakes of this characteristic while differing from logical and scientific thought through its richness of descriptive detail. Wimsatt then seems content with the answer that poetry is universal because it is the nature of words to be universal and poetry uses words. The poem thus fits in wider contexts while being particular.[108] Langer is not content with such an answer. For her the poem achieves particularity by being an experience of virtual life, an experienced object. But even such particulars, since they are constructed by symbolic transformation (which is Langer's equivalent to Kant's understanding in accordance with the categories), are both particulars and types. Presentational symbolic forms, such as poetry, are based in human rationality just as much as are discursive forms.[109] Poetry then is a particular experience which is universal in that it has been formed by symbolic transformation which is based in the nature of rationality. Valéry holds a position somewhat between Langer and Wimsatt in arguing that a poem is a form of language which has the power to evoke the poetic state in the reader. In the next chapter I shall deal with the problem of how the metaphor is particular yet in some significant sense able to be analyzed.

F. POETIC LANGUAGE IN A LARGER FRAME OF REFERENCE

My semantical generalization that poetic language is that language in which sound and sense function iconically, achieving a fusion of sense and sensa, has as yet been associated with no comprehensive theory of meaning, with the possible exception of Sapir's linguistic theory. As of yet no complete theory of poetic *and* literal language has been presented. Ernst Cassirer offers one such theory set forth in *The Philosophy of Symbolic Forms*. Cassirer's thought will sound familiar, especially in its relation to the main presentational symbol theorist whom I have analyzed. It is quite significant that Langer dedicates her work, *Feeling and Form*, to Cassirer. This analysis will show that her interpretation of "symbol" is quite similar to Cassirer's understanding of "symbolic form". His use of this term is quite inclusive, perhaps too

---

[108] Wimsatt, *The Verbal Icon*, pp. 75-83.
[109] Langer, *Philosophy in a New Key*, pp. 83-91.

much so. As Hamburg indicates, Cassirer means by "symbolic form":
(1) symbol concepts; (2) various cultural forms, such as art, myth and
religion; (3) space, time, number, cause and effect; that is, the most
pervasive forms.[110] Cassirer considered his symbolic forms a broadening
of the Kantian categories of the understanding.[111] Hamburg's account
of these three meanings is essentially correct, but is somewhat misleading in not stating, explicitly, that *language* is a symbolic form. In
parenthetically remarking on his term Cassirer includes "the result of
language, myth, religion, art, and theoretical knowledge".[112] One immediately notices the continuity between natural knowledge and cultural
forms. As Hendel correctly argues, for Cassirer: "There is no gulf then
between Nature and Culture – in respect to forms." [113] Langer's thought
comes to mind at this point. For her also there is no gap between the
discursive and artistic forms. Art forms are not, as Ogden and Richards
argued, emotive, but have as their purpose "to articulate knowledge
that cannot be rendered discursively because it concerns experiences
that are not *formally* amenable to the discursive projection".[114]

However, since poetry is an art form of *language*, we are interested
mainly in what Cassirer says of language as a symbolic form. He
argues:

In general, language can be shown to have passed through three stages in
maturing to its specific form, in achieving its inner freedom. In calling these
the mimetic, the analogical, and the truly symbolical stage, we are for the
present merely setting up an abstract schema—but this schema will take on
concrete content when we see that it represents a functional law of linguistic
growth, which has its specific and characteristic counterpart in other fields
such as art and cognition.[115]

By mimetic Cassirer means the phenomena in primitive languages by
which the symbol imitates the symbolized. He is referring to the "type
of sound painting" which the onomatopoetic theory of language

---

[110]   Carl H. Hamburg, *Symbol and Reality: Studies in the Philosophy of Ernst
Cassirer* (The Hague, Martinus Nijhoff, 1956), p. 58.
[111]   Ernst Cassirer, *The Philosophy of Symbolic Forms*, Vol. II: *Mythical
Thought*, trans. Ralph Manheim (New Haven, Yale University Press, 1960), p. 29.
[112]   Ernst Cassirer, *The Philosophy of Symbolic Forms*, Vol. III: *The Phenomenology of Knowledge*, trans. Ralph Manheim (New Haven, Yale University Press,
1957), p. 276.
[113]   Ernst Cassirer, *The Philosophy of Symbolic Forms*, Vol. I: *Language*, trans.
Ralph Manheim (New Haven, Yale University Press, 1961), p. 29.
[114]   Langer, *Feeling and Form*, pp. 240-41.
[115]   Cassirer, I, p. 190.

stressed.[116] For example, in primitive forms of language a, o, w, almost always designated greater distances while e and i designated the more immediate.[117] Cassirer means that the "heavier" vowels a, o, w, literally imitated the greater distances which they symbolized, while conversely the sharper vowels of e and i imitated a close spatial location. The sounds in both cases actually resemble their referent. Cassirer is aware, as Sapir argues,[118] that the onomatopoetic theory of language is dead as a *general* explanation of all linguistic elements, but the theory does serve to explain *some* phenomena which have occurred in practically all primitive languages, such as the vowel imitation noted above, and further *some* phenomena which still exist in modern languages.[119]

However, the passage quoted above indicates that language in the mimetic stage has not achieved "its inner freedom". Cassirer means: "The more the sound resembles what it expresses; the more it continues to 'be' the other, the less it can 'signify' that other." [120] In striving toward its freedom language goes through the analogical stage. The analogical stage ceases to be purely mimetic and rather communicates its context "by a *formal* analogy between the phonetic sequence and the sequence of contents designated; this analogy makes possible a *coordination* of series entirely different in content".[121] An example of symbols in their analogical function is reduplication in both the morphology of words and the syntax of sentences. Reduplication means that phonetic repetitions are used to indicate "a repetition given in the sensuous reality or impression".[122]

Language, however, in the analogical stage is still bound to its referent. True freedom is achieved in the symbolic stage where a remoteness between the symbol and the symbolized is achieved. The symbol "precisely in and by virtue of its otherness, becomes the vehicle of a new and deeper spiritual content".[123] Language achieves symbolic powers at the expense of the sensuous and concrete.[124] Cassirer's argument recalls Daitz's point that iconicity and vocabulary formulation are inversely related. Daitz argued that language gains range of applica-

---

[116]   *Ibid.*, I, pp. 190-91.
[117]   *Ibid.*, I, p. 193.
[118]   Sapir, p. 7.
[119]   Cassirer, I, pp. 190-91.
[120]   *Ibid.*, I, p. 189.
[121]   *Ibid.*, I, p. 193.
[122]   *Ibid.*, I, p. 195.
[123]   *Ibid.*, I, p. 197.
[124]   *Ibid.*, I, p. 289.

tion and use by its conventionality. Cassirer concludes that symbolic freedom in language is achieved on the abstract end of the continuum which began with the mimetic through the analogical to the truly symbolic. Since language is a symbolic form one would expect the other symbolic forms to receive similar treatment. They do. Cassirer analyzes space, time, number, and inner intuition in a similar manner. All exhibit these same stages.[125]

It is important to emphasize that the evolution of language analyzed above is through stages. No leaps are taken. The truly symbolical is never divorced from the sensuous content of the imitative; nor is the imitative totally sensuous. Rather they are extremes of a continuum. Cassirer's point here is an extension of the Kantian maxim that: "Thoughts without content are empty, intuitions without concepts are blind." [126] Cassirer's reason for this continuity is also similar to Kant's reason.

Here consciousness does not passively confront the aggregate of sensory impressions, it permeates them and fills them with its own inner life. ... In language, the process of animation and the process of definition constantly merge to form a spiritual unity. And it is through this twofold movement, from the inside out and back again, through this ebb and flow of the spirit, that inner and outer reality take form and definition.[127]

Cassirer definitely acknowledges Kant as the predecessor of his symbolic forms. "*The Philosophy of Symbolic Forms* takes up this basic critical idea, this fundamental principle of Kant's 'Copernican revolution', and strives to broaden it." [128] Cassirer's claim to have broadened Kant's revolution means that he extends the argument that the self is constitutive in knowing to cultural forms such as myth and art. It is precisely these forms which are most relevant to this analysis. The question then becomes: Where on the continuum are the forms of myth and art to be classified?

The magical attitude of myth towards language is a form of the extreme mimetic type.

For language there is at first no sharp dividing line between the word and its signification, between the content of the representation and the content of the mere sign: the two merge immediately with each other. The nominal-

---

[125]   *Ibid.*, I, pp. 198-277.
[126]   Norman Kemp Smith (trans.), *Kant's Critique of Pure Reason* (London, Macmillan & Co., Ltd., 1958), p. 93.
[127]   Cassirer, I, pp. 288-89.
[128]   *Ibid.*, II, p. 29.

istic view, in which words are mere conventional signs, mere *flatus vocis,* is a product of late reflection, not an expression of the "natural," immediate linguistic consciousness, for which the essence of the thing is mediately designated in the word and at the same time in some way contained and present in it. This concrescence of name and thing in the linguistic consciousness of primitives and children might be illustrated by a number of striking examples (we need only think of the various forms of name taboo). But as language develops, the differentiation becomes sharper and more conscious. At first the world of language, like that of myth in which it seems as it were embedded, preserves a complete equivalence of word and thing, of "signifier" and "signified".[129]

As Langer correctly notes, Cassirer's thought on myth is precisely parallel to the thought of Owen Barfield,[130] whose theory was examined in the Introduction of this book. There (above, p. 21) Barfield argued that mythical thought does not distinguish self and objects, words and their referents. The language of myth is apprehended as an immediate reality. Cassirer's thought is exactly parallel to Barfield's on this point. Both are essentially correct in view of, as Cassirer noted, the massive body of information regarding primitive name taboos. One need only recall in our own western tradition examples such as the Hebraic strictures on the use of the name "Yahweh" to substantiate this point. These strictures imply that the name "Yahweh" somehow is Yahweh. Further, mythical thought, expressing this attitude toward language, would be a most extreme example of the confusion Wittgenstein attributes to the naming theorist, that is, confusing the meaning of a name with its bearer. Mythical thought goes beyond the naming theorist in that it confuses the name itself with its bearer, not just the meaning with its bearer. We can then expect poetry to run into the same objections to the degree that it has a magical view of words.

Now the question is: Where does Cassirer place poetic thought? How is the poetic view of language related to the magical view? He does not specifically mention poetry, but does analyze art.

The beginnings of creative art seem rather to partake of a sphere in which creative activity is still embedded in magical representations and directed toward specific magical *aims,* in which consequently the image itself still has no independent, purely aesthetic significance. And yet in the development of spiritual expression the very first stirrings of artistic activity provide an entirely new beginning, achieve a new principle. Here for the first time the image world acquires a purely *immanent* validity and truth. It does not

---

[129] *Ibid.,* II, p. 25.
[130] Langer, *Feeling and Form,* pp. 237-39.

aim at something else; it simply "is" and consists in itself. From the sphere of efficacy to which the mythical consciousness clings and the sphere of signification in which the linguistic sign perseveres we are transposed into a sphere where, as it were, only the pure reality, only the intrinsic and inherent essence, of the image is apprehended as such. Thus for the first time the world of the image becomes a self-contained cosmos with its own center of gravity. And only now can the spirit enter into a truly free relation with it. Measured by empirical, realistic criteria, the aesthetic world becomes a world of appearance; but in severing its bond with immediate reality, with the material existence and efficacy which constitute the world of magic and myth, it embodies a new step toward the truth. Thus, although myth, language, and art interpenetrate one another in their concrete historical manifestations, the relation between them reveals a definite systematic gradation, an ideal progression toward a point where the spirit not only is and lives in its own creations, its self-created symbols, but also knows them for what they are.[131]

For Cassirer art forms are a step from the mimetic toward the purely symbolical. Such forms have, so to speak, a foot in each. On the one hand, in its *"immanent* validity and truth" the art form overcomes the hiatus between sign and signified in a manner similar to myth. Myth overcomes the hiatus by identifying the sign with the signified. Thus mythical thought is quite foreign to the view that words are mere *flatus vocis*, mere conventions. My analysis above of the semantic of poetic language quite definitely indicates that the nominalist's *flatus vocis* is foreign to the poet also. The insistence that language is the poet's medium which fuses sense and sensa, that poetry is untranslatable and "unrephrasable", that poetic meaning can be expressed in this and no other way, that there is a necessary union between form and content leaves no doubt that the poet agrees with the mythical writer that words are not *flatus vocis*. However, the poet's reasons for this attitude to words will prove to be quite different from those of the mythical writers. Poetic language, it will be seen, presents a fusion of sense, sound and imagery, not a fusion of word and physical bearer. On the other hand, in its lack of reference to anything else, in existing in itself as a world of its own, the art form, the poem, establishes a gap between sign and signified similar to the gap established by the abstract symbol. In poetry and art the symbol is beginning to be recognized as a symbol. Art has the concreteness of a mimetic form but the detachment of a symbol.

I consider Cassirer's point here, that poetry has a foot in the magical and symbolical, a fruitful insight for poetic metaphor. His insight ties in with the above four theories of poetic language. As noted Langer's

[131]   Cassirer, II, pp. 25-26.

analysis is almost identical to Cassirer's. Her art form is a presentation of a sensuous image that at the same time is an image abstracted from the material world. Her argument that the world of the poet, in being freed from material reference, presents virtual life but not actual life is precisely intended to let "the world of the image" become "a self-contained cosmos with its own center of gravity".[132] Her world of the poet becomes precisely such an end in itself in being freed from practical life to become an object of contemplation. Her understanding of poetry is that it presents life, but this life is virtual, not real. Barfield also agrees with Cassirer that the poet is beginning, in contrast to the magician, to recognize the symbols of language for what they are. Poetic metaphor, in contrast to mythical metaphor, is a *conscious* or deliberate yoking of unlikes.[133] Wimsatt argues that the poem as icon has the "thick" sense of magical language. Yet in becoming self referential, in becoming an opaque icon like a painting it becomes detached from the natural world like a painting. It becomes a metaphor. The poem becomes a picture which does not picture literally. It has magical concreteness and magical reverence of words as things but symbolic abstraction. Valéry's metaphor, in which he sees the poet related to his medium as the surgeon to his patient,[134] reveals the magical attitude in which words are taken as things. He argues for the detachment of the abstract symbol in his metaphor in which poetic language is like the dance, an end in itself removed from practical affairs. Bouwsma argues a similar point in stating that in the poem meaning is in the language in a way which differs significantly from meaning in literal language. The poet is like the magician, as Walsh argues, in that he identifies words with reality. The poet avoids the bifurcation between things or events and the words which refer to them. There is no separation between what is said and how it is said.[135] Poetry is untranslatable because it tries, with magic, to overcome the form-content dichotomy. To forget either quality of the poetic medium is to drive poetry to the extremes of Cassirer's continuum. To forget that sense functions iconically in the poem is to follow Herschberger's literalism to the extreme symbolical end. To exclude sense altogether is to follow Brémond's purism to the extreme magical end. Cassirer's thought

[132] *Ibid.*, II, p. 26.
[133] Barfield, p. 81.
[134] Valéry, p. 54.
[135] Dorothy Walsh, "The Poetic Use of Language", *The Journal of Philosophy*, XXXV (Feb. 3, 1938), pp. 79-80.

serves to place the theories of poetic language in a larger context by clarifying how such language relates to mythical language and symbolical language.

However, my apparent enthusiasm in analyzing Cassirer's thought, implying my acceptance of his analysis as applied to poetic language, has very significant limitations. First, I reject Cassirer's implied progressionism from the mimetic to symbolic stages. If his analysis were merely intended to explain the historical fact that language seems to evolve from a more concrete stage to a more abstract one, then it could be accepted as accurate. However, Cassirer seems to think the progression is more than a historical fact. That he intended more is shown by his explicit comparison of his own version of the "spiritual development" of language to Hegel's analysis of development in the *Phenomenology of Spirit*.[136] Further, Cassirer's argument that freedom is reached at the symbolic stage again reminds us of Hegel's thought. Thus Cassirer would have to be responsible for the problems which Hegel's superhuman consciousness raises. How is the analogy between human consciousness and some superhuman consciousness working itself out in culture to be justified? The present study in no way denies that such an analysis is possible, perhaps even true, but does claim its intention to be dissociated from any such arguments. Further, if Cassirer's progressionism is taken seriously then it is implied that art, as a sort of form between myth and abstract symbolism, is an interim phenomena. What means does Cassirer have to prevent the conclusion that art will vanish when the truly free symbolic stage reaches fruition? He seems to be in no way able to avoid such a conclusion. Such a conclusion seems to the present writer no more than an unwarranted guess about the future.

One further qualification needs to be added, though this one is concerning scope rather than assertion. Cassirer's analysis of art and his implied analysis of poetry is based on his general theory of meaning which is Kantian. The present writer does not intend to generalize from the theory of meaning of metaphor being developed to a general theory of meaning, nor does he intend inversely to see metaphor as a species of a general theory of meaning. The present work claims adequacy only to metaphorical language. It does not make Cassirer's more general claims.

However, least these qualifications become too severe, a restatement

---

[136] Cassirer, II, p. 26.

of the positive value of Cassirer's thought is needed. His thought is
fruitful for two reasons. First, he supports the general semantical
conclusion that the language of poetry functions iconically achieving
a fusion of sense and sensa. He supports this conclusion in that poetry,
as an art form, is on the language continuum between the extreme
mimetical end of myth or magic and the abstract symbolic end. (It
shares with the magical view the belief that words are not mere *flatus
vocis* and with the symbolic view the knowledge that words have their
own immanent validity as detached from the signified.) Since poetry
is on the continuum, as are all symbolic forms, thought and sensation
cannot be radically separated. The four theories of poetic language
already examined reach a similar conclusion not on the basis of the
general epistemological considerations of Cassirer but by analyzing
poetic language. Second, he suggests an answer to the second question
still outstanding from my above generalizations on the semantic of
poetry. That question is how is the poem related to the natural world.
Cassirer's answer, developed by Langer, is that the poem does not
refer to the natural world, in the rigorous sense of the term "refer". The
art object has its own immanent validity.

G.   WITTGENSTEIN AND POETIC LANGUAGE

A point raised by Cassirer's analysis has implied a conflict between
Wittgenstein's theory and the theory of meaning of metaphor being here
developed. Cassirer noted that the primitive language of magic and myth
expresses a view toward language which stands in sharp contrast with
the nominalistic view that a word is a *flatus vocis*. I stated, following
the lead of Cassirer and the theorists examined, that the poet has a
similar attitude toward words, but for a different reason. This similarity
between metaphorical and mythical language would imply that the
theory of meaning of the former would also conflict with Wittgenstein's
theory. The reason a contrast arises is that Wittgenstein's analysis of
convention as arbitrary bedrock would align him with the nominalists
in seeing words as *flatus vocis*. The poet, I have argued, tries and succeeds in making the relation between his physical language and its
meaning nonconventional. The poet fuses the sensuous envelope of
language with the meaning of that language. I shall here state the three
possible relations between Wittgenstein's theory and the theory of
metaphor.

First, if the metaphorical view of language is identical to the mythical view then metaphor will fall under Wittgenstein's criticism of the naming theorists. As noted above, the magical view of language represents the extreme version of confusing a name with its bearer. The magical view does not just confuse the meaning of a name with its bearer, as do the name theorists, but confuses the name itself with its bearer. This relation between metaphor and Wittgenstein is unlikely. A confusion of name and bearer is based on the assumption that a name refers to its bearer or corresponds with its bearer. In the next chapter, in the section "Imagery and Reference", it will be argued that metaphor does not refer to natural objects, in the strict sense of "referring". Metaphor has a conscious distance from the natural world, a distance which is foreign to mythical thought. Further it will be argued that metaphorical language is fused with imagery, not with physical sense impressions, except for auditory impressions. It would be very difficult to argue that metaphor in functioning iconically presents us with its physical bearer as though metaphor somehow caused a thing to pop into one's head or before one's eyes.

The second possible relation between Wittgenstein and metaphor is much more likely. I shall call this second view of metaphor the "weak" view. By "weak" I mean those theorists who would argue that only sound functions iconically in metaphorical language. Such a theory would share the magical view of language only with regard to sound. Sense would be claimed to function as it does in ordinary language. Such theorists would argue that the poem imitates its referent; that is, the poem is like its referent only in an auditory sense just as a photograph is like its referent only in a visual sense. This theory could cite as iconic *only* sound exploitations such as rhyme, alliteration, assonance, agnomination and rhythm.

It is quite significant that none of the theorists presented hold such a view of poetic language. A critic who held such a weak view would have to conduct his literary analysis without ever referring to the metaphorically important element of imagery or seeing as. Wimsatt rejects this view in saying *both* the logical and counterlogical elements in poetry function iconically. He specifically argues that a poem "approximates the intuitive sensuous condition" of painting.[137] He compares the sensuous fullness of the poem to a sculptured object.[138] His whole

---

[137] Wimsatt, *The Verbal Icon*, p. 231.
[138] *Ibid.*, p. 217.

analysis of the poem as an icon leaves no doubt that the poem is iconic
in senses *in addition to* auditory sensations. Valéry's argument that the
poem tends to reproduce itself implies an experience which includes
sensations in addition to auditory sensations. He specifically states that
the mechanism producing this re-created state is the "harmonious exchange between expression and impression".[139] The word "impression"
certainly does not mean just sound. He shows that it is more inclusive
by arguing that poetry in reproducing itself calls up remembered sensations, images and sentiments.[140] Valéry then does not hold the view
that poetry is iconic only in the auditory sense.

However, if there were a literary critic who held this "weak" theory,
then the conflict with Wittgenstein would be either insignificant or
nonexistent. Admittedly Wittgenstein would think the poet had a queer
compulsion to use certain sounds with certain meanings, but there is
no reason in principle why such an understanding of meaning by the
poet could not be assimilated to Wittgenstein's theory of use. In Chapter I I argued (above, p. 52) that the most significant sense of use for
Wittgenstein was the social sense. This sense means that a meaningful
use of language presupposes: (a) public actions, that is, verbal and
nonverbal signs; (b) public objects, that is, a common physical environment; (c) conventional rules, that is, social customs, linguistic and
otherwise. There (above, p. 58) it was also argued that an individual
use had meaning if it could be explained by means of the social sense
of use. The individual use, for example, in saying "abracadabra" while
pointing to the jaw, is given meaning when the explanation "I meant
toothache" tied the private or individual use to a social language. There
is no reason why the poet could not explain his queer compulsion to
use rhyme, meter, etc., in the same way. His use of meter could be explained by the use of a dictionary which gives conventionally agreed
upon accents of words. He could tell us that words in accented positions
were to be emphasized. His use of rhyme could be explained by the quite
physical quality of similar sound. He could tell us that such pairs of
rhyming words were to be related in some especially significant way.
The poet's use would always be queer or odd in the same sense that
"abracadabra" is an odd word for "toothache", but in either case the
individual meanings could be understood. Either case could be explained. Neither explanation would call for a modification of Witt-

---

[139] Valéry, p. 73.
[140] *Ibid.*

genstein's criteria. If the poem were an icon only in that its sound is iconic while its sense is literal, we would never have to refer to any private experiences at all. The critic would never refer to imagery, either his own or that excited in the reader. Of course, I have implied that I doubt if any poet or literary critic would be happy with these strictures.

This clue brings us to the third possible relation between metaphorical meaning and Wittgenstein. I shall call this the "strong" sense of saying that the poem is iconic. By "strong" I mean the view which would argue that metaphor includes *imagery* as well as sense impressions. The weak theorists could claim that only the sensa of sound functioned iconically. Only sound is like its object. The weak theorist can only entertain analogies between poetry and music. The strong theorist can entertain further analogies to the plastic arts. The strong theorist differs from the weak theorist in two very significant ways.

First, the strong theorist argues that the normal function of *meaning* is transformed in the poem to meaning which functions iconically. Not only is the normal function of the sound of literal language transformed in the poem, but also the function of sense. The new function of sense is that it is iconic in exciting imagery. The strong theorist argues with Valéry that the normal pedestrian function of literal meaning is transformed in the dance of poetry and with Wimsatt that *both* the logical and counter logical elements function iconically in the poem. The strong theorist agrees with Langer that in poetry propositions are no longer discursive but presentational. The strong theorist sees an alternative to Brémond's argument that sense must be expurgated from the poem because it is a foreign prose element. Sense is no longer foreign after its poetic transformation into sense functioning iconically. The iconic function of sense can be seen in this example.

> The south-wind strengthens to a gale,
> Across the moon the clouds fly fast,
> The house is smitten as with a flail,
> The chimney shudders to the blast.
>
> (Robert Bridges, "Low Barometer", ll. 1-4)

The sense of the metaphor functions iconically to excite the concrete image of the house being lashed, perhaps by hail. The metaphor excites imagery through the sense of "flail" while the sound of "flail" is iconic in that it resembles its referent. "Flail", in this example, is iconic in a double sense. It excites images of sound as well as being a sound impression which resembles its referent. The strong theorists can recognize that the poem exploits, for example, both an *image* of sound and an auditory *impression* of sound.

Second, the strong theorist differs from the weak theorist because, in speaking of images tentatively defined as *any sense impression remembered,* he ceases to talk merely about language. It is evident that the sound of physical language cannot present, for example, visual sensations, in the same sense that it can present an auditory sensation. As Brooks and Warren note onomatopoetic words can only imitate sounds, not, for example, visual forms. The poem is an iconic *impression* only in an auditory sense.[141] True, written language does have visual characteristics; but very few poets arrange their words in an iconic pattern, that is, a pattern on the page which pictures its object. The shape on the page of print rather divides the poem into lines and stanzas. Thus to contend that the poem imitates its referent in a fully sensuous sense requires the introduction of associative images. The strong critic thus does not talk *just* about the language of the poem, but also includes associative images, accompanying these words, and the experience of seeing as. The strong theorists speak of "the poem" as though it were more than signs on the page or sounds in the air. He speaks of the *poem as it exists while being read or heard.* As Wellek and Warren argue, the poem is not the mere words on the page but is rather "a structure of norms, realized only partially in the actual experience of its many readers".[142] Wellek and Warren's reservation that the poem is only partially realized in a reader's experience is well taken and will be returned to in Chapter III. Richards also defines the poem as a read object. He suggests that Wordsworth's "Westminster Bridge" is neither the mere words on the page nor the experience which prompted Wordsworth to write this poem, "but the class composed of all actual experiences, occasioned by the words, which do not differ within certain limits from that experience".[143] In other words, the poem "Westminster Bridge" is the total experience occasioned by the words of the poem if this experience does not vary excessively from a standard experience.[144]

The question now is how would the strong theorist be affected by

---

[141]   Cleanth Brooks and Robert Penn Warren, *Understanding Poetry,* 3rd ed. (New York, Holt, Rinehart & Winston, Inc., 1961), p. 150.
[142]   René Wellek and Austin Warren, *Theory of Literature* (New York, Harcourt, Brace & Co., 1949), p. 151.
[143]   Richards, *Principles of Literary Criticism,* p. 226.
[144]   *Ibid.,* pp. 226-27.

Wittgenstein's analysis. Wittgenstein clearly recognizes a plurality of language-games. He also clearly recognizes that there can be a game in which the purpose of words is to call up images. In such cases "uttering a word is like striking a note on the keyboard of the imagination".[145] Thus there is no reason why Wittgenstein could not agree with the strong theorist that in reading metaphorical language images *occur* and that it is the *purpose* of such language to arouse such imagery. He could agree that imagery is a type of constant accompaniment of metaphorical language; that imagery is a type of epiphenomena. However, the strong theorist, as will shortly be shown, would never be happy with this epiphenomenal view. The strong theorist often appeals to the experience of imagery and the experience of seeing as in order to *justify* his analysis of the *meaning* of a metaphor. It is in arguing that the experience of imagery and seeing as on the reading of metaphor is essential to metaphorical *meaning* that the significant conflict with Wittgenstein arises. The critic, in appealing to either imagery or seeing as, is appealing to *inner experiences for justification*. The critic will not say that meaning *is* the imagery or the seeing as but will say that both are essential to metaphorical meaning. In short, both *imagery and seeing as play a part in the language-game in which we analyze metaphorical meaning*.

The most important question left open for the next chapter is whether metaphor is iconic in the weak or in the strong sense.

---

[145] *Investigations*, # 6.

III. METAPHOR

The purpose of this chapter is to show that metaphorical language fits the general conclusions of the preceding chapter while still retaining its own distinctive characteristics. The purpose of this chapter is also to see how metaphor settles the outstanding questions of the last chapter. The most urgent of those questions, the one requiring an answer before proceeding to the other two, is whether metaphor is a fusion of sense and sound or a fusion of sense and sensa; whether metaphor supports the weak or strong theory; whether only sound functions iconically in metaphor or whether sense also functions iconically. When this question is answered I can go on to settle the other two questions: What is the referential status of poetic metaphor? How does metaphor achieve both concreteness and universal status?

A. THE WEAK THEORY

It will be recalled that by "weak" I meant those theorists who would claim poetic language is iconic only in an auditory sense. Poetic language uses only auditory exploitation in devices such as rhyme, alliteration, and rhythm. No serious theorists could deny that metaphor is a fusion of sense and sound. Consider this beautiful example.

> And more to lulle him in his slumber soft,
> A trickling streame from high rock tumbling downe,
> And ever-drizling rain upon the loft,
> Mixt with a murmuring winde, much like the sowne
> Of swarming Bees, did cast him in a swowne.
> > (Edmund Spenser, "The Faerie Queene", ll. 136-140)

The metaphor is in lines four and five in the comparison between the "murmuring winde" and "the sowne of swarming Bees". The subject of the comparison is the wind, the "murmuring winde". This one phrase is practically brilliant enough to prove the whole thesis of sense and sound. The sense of the passage is that a wicked monk is lulling a good knight to sleep. The sense of the fourth line is that the wind is one of these devices used by the deceitful monk. Spenser does not just give us the word "winde" in an abstract sense; he is not just asking us to remember the sound of wind; he actually gives us the sound of wind in the word "murmuring". The sonant "m" is a dull sound. The dull monotony of the wind is further captured by the double repetition of the syllable "mur". The word "murmuring" in fact sounds like a murmuring wind. In Cassirer's terms it is a mimetic word. It is examples like this word that the onomatopoetic theory of language cited.

Nor does the exploitation of the auditory resources of language end with the subject of the metaphor. The predicate of the metaphor, "the sowne of swarming Bees", is internally unified by the alliteration between the s and w of "sowne" and "swarming". More important, not only is this predicate tied to "murmuring winde" by the explicit grammatical element "like", but "sowne" is tied to "sowne" by rhyme. Thus the association of the dull sound of swarming bees with the sleepy state of a "swowne" is achieved not only through sense but through the auditory tie between "sowne" and "swowne". We know that the sound of swarming bees is dull and drowsy, fitting the sense of the whole passage and culminating in "swowne", but the similarity is also stressed to our ear. Sense and sound heighten each other in this sound tie, this rhyme.

Poe's "Ulalume – A Ballad" provides us with another example which excellently illustrates the fusion of sense and sound of the weak theory. The author in this poem is taking an imaginary walk with his soul.

> Here once, through an alley Titanic,
> Of cypress, I roamed with my Soul—
> Of cypress, with Psyche, my Soul.
> (Edgar Allen Poe, "Ulalume—A Ballad", ll. 10-12)

This metaphorical walk with his soul is used here to set the stage for the passage to follow. In the following passage Poe gives us a sustained metaphor in which the soul is described as a female angel.

> But Psyche, uplifting her finger,
> Said—"Sadly this star I mistrust—
> Her pallor I strangely mistrust:
> Ah, hasten!—ah, let us not linger!
> Ah, fly!—let us fly!—for we must."
> In terror she spoke, letting sink her

Wings till they trailed in the dust—
In agony sobbed, letting sink her
Plumes till they trailed in the dust—
Till they sorrowfully trailed in the dust.
                    (Edgar Allen Poe, "Ulalume—A Ballad", ll. 49-58)

One immediately notices that this whole stanza is a sustained metaphorical description of the narrator's psyche. The sense of the passage is that the psyche suspects that their following the star is leading to some yet unknown sorrow. The last four lines express in an auditory manner this expected sorrow. Lines seven and nine are extremely smooth. They are smooth because they use the very musical dactylic foot and because they are identical except for the first word in each of the lines. Lines six and eight also have this parallelism and flow easily. The tenth line is exactly identical to the ninth except that "sorrowfully" is used instead of "Plumes" and that it has a different position. The shift in position of "sorrowfully" is quite significant. It changes the last line into one with anapaest feet. Thus, in expecting line ten to continue the free flow of line nine, one is quite surprised that the first syllable of line ten is unaccented. This surprise serves to increase the stress on the accent when it finally does come on the first syllable of "sorrowfully". Thus, "sorrowfully" is in a quite prominent position. "Sorrowfully" is a difficult word, perhaps the hardest to pronounce in the whole stanza. Its difficulty plus its accented position throw it into sharp contrast with the smoothness of lines seven and nine. The very sound of line ten then imitates the expected sorrow of the whole passage. One skips along lines six through nine but has to labor through ten, a labor of sound supporting the sense of the expected sorrow.

These two examples suffice to show that metaphor is a fusion of sense and sound. No longer argument is needed because no serious theorist has wanted to deny that metaphor is a fusion of sense and sound in this weak sense. The weak theorist would argue that the poem is a sensuous object only in an auditory sense. Such a theorist can compare poetry to no other art form but music.

B.   THE STRONG THEORY

The strong theorist argues that both sense and sound function iconically yielding a fusion of sense and sensa. Metaphor involves imagery and seeing as. If the weak theorist will entertain analogies between poetry and music the strong theorists will entertain, *in addition*, analogies to the plastic arts. I have argued that in fact all the theorists examined are strong theorists. Frye emphasizes that the lyric is a fusion of *melos, orsis* and reflection or sense. Wimsatt compared the iconicity of the poem to the sensuous fullness of painting and sculpture. Valéry sees the poem as language which re-creates an experience in its reader. Langer's poem is a presentation of virtual life. All these theorists are theorists in the strong sense. The question now becomes: Does metaphorical language represent a fusion of sense and sensa in the strong sense? Does the sensa of metaphor, its sensuous concreteness, include sensations other than those of sound? My answer is to be yes. In fact, if one wishes to defend, for example, Frye's position that lyric includes *melos* and *orsis*, if one wants to defend a strong theory of the fusion of sense and sensa, one would select metaphor as his stronghold. Of all the devices of poetic language, metaphor most clearly displays this fusion.

However, in trying to substantiate the point that metaphorical language is quite imagistic one is immediately confronted with a methodological problem. In arguing that metaphor is a fusion of sense and sound I could point to sound in a physical way. The meter of a poem is quite as prominent as the beat of a drum. Shifts in meter as enforcement of meaning are quite pronounced. Imitation of sense by sound, rhyme, and alliteration are by no means private. One can point to these elements in the full sense of pointing analyzed by Wittgenstein. This ability to produce physical evidence for his contention is the reason, as noted above, that the weak theorist would not seriously confront Wittgenstein. A weak theory poet would seem odd, like the person who used "abracadabra" for "toothache", but such a poet could give an explanation of his individual use by pointing to the sound exploitations noted in the two above examples. A strong theorist could not point to the experience of imagery or seeing as in the same sense. As noted (above, p. 112) the strong theorist always means more by the phrase "the poem" than the physical words on the page or sounds in the air. The strong theorist understands the poem as a *read object. Reading is the stance appropriate to metaphor.* This apparently innocuous statement will now be given more content in my analysis of reading.

1. Reading

My understanding of reading has some fruitful similarities to Husserl's *epoche.*

a. *Husserl*

Husserl states that by means of the *epoche*:

We put out of action the general thesis which belongs to the essence of the natural standpoint, we place in brackets whatever it includes respecting the nature of Being: *this entire natural world therefore* which is continually "there for us", "present to our hand", and will ever remain there, is a "fact world" of which we continue to be conscious, even though it pleases us to put it in brackets.[1]

The *epoche* does not mean we deny the world like the solipsist, nor that we even doubt it as a sceptic, but rather it *"bars me from using any judgment that concerns spatio-temporal existence (Dasein)".*[2] We set the natural world out of action, disconnect it, place it in brackets. Judgments of perception and judgments of value are suspended.[3]

It is quite important that the *epoche* places in brackets not only the "outside" world of normal perception but also our own selves, " 'I, the man'." [4] "We have 'Suspended' the whole world with all things, living creatures, men, ourselves included." [5] One wonders what would be left after such a radical act. Husserl's answer is clear. The *epoche* leaves consciousness as a residuum. *"Consciousness in itself has a being of its own which in its absolute uniqueness of nature remains un-affected by the phenomenological disconnexion. It therefore remains over as a 'phenomenological residuum'...."* [6] Husserl seems to mean that the *epoche* leaves a stream of experience which is undifferentiated as to whether its contents are perceived or imagined, fact or fancy. As Spie-gelberg puts it, what is left is not a physical self but a "vividly streaming present".[7] Such a streaming present is, as Van Peursen notes, a sus-pension of Descartes' metaphysical soul substance for an anonymous self.[8]

The *epoche* allows us to accept all data on an equal footing, whether that data be contributed by the physical world or by our imagination,

[1] Edmund Husserl, *Ideas: General Introduction to Pure Phenomenology*, trans. W. R. Boyce Gibson (London, George Allen & Unwin Ltd., 1958), p. 110.
[2] *Ibid.*, p. 111.
[3] *Ibid.*, p. 264.
[4] *Ibid.*, p. 233.
[5] *Ibid.*, p. 154.
[6] *Ibid.*, p. 113.
[7] Herbert Spiegelberg, *The Phenomenological Movement* (The Hague, Nijhoff, 1960), I, p. 141.
[8] C. A. van Peursen, "Edmund Husserl and Ludwig Wittgenstein", *Philosophy and Phenomenological Research*, XX (Dec., 1959), p. 191.

whether the data is objective or subjective. The *epoche* allows "*the original right of all data...*".[9]

This phrase that the *epoche* allows "the orginal right of all data" clarifies what I mean by reading in a most significant way. *The reading which is appropriate to metaphor is that reading which allows the "original right of all data" presented by metaphor during the act of reading.* Husserl does not apply these consequences to Locke's analysis of primary and secondary qualities, but I suggest that such an application will clarify what I mean by reading. Primary qualities are those which "are utterly inseparable from the body, in what estate soever it be...".[10] Secondary qualities, on the other hand, "are nothing in the objects themselves, but powers to produce various sensations in us by their primary qualities...".[11] Reading appropriate to poetic metaphor is reading which allows metaphor's primary qualities, the words, and its secondary qualities, the imagery and seeing as, on an equal footing. The *epoche* assures that neither quality will be discriminated against. Neither shall be called more "real" than the other.

Husserl himself recognized a similarity between the neutrality of the *epoche* and the aesthetic stance. In speaking of Dürer's engraving "The Knight, Death, and the Devil" he states:

This *depicting picture-object* stands before us *neither as being nor as non-being*, nor in any *other positional modality*; or rather, we are aware of it as having its being, though only a quasi-being, in the neutrality-modification of Being.

But it is just the same with the *object depicted*, if we take up a *purely aesthetic* attitude, and view the same again as "mere picture", without imparting to it the stamp of Being or non-Being, of possible Being or probable Being, and the like. But, as can clearly be seen, that does not mean any privation, but a modification, that of *neutralization*.[12]

The aesthetic stance is neutral. It lacks positionality or belief content. No belief is held concerning the existence or nonexistence of the objects represented.

My analysis of reading as compared to the *epoche* thus far has this significance. First, the act of reading is neutral. It brackets both the physical world and systems of reality. Second, the act of reading does not have two objects, one the "real" poem and the other the "ideal"

---

9   Husserl, p. 97.
10 John Locke, *An Essay Concerning Human Understanding*, abridged and edited by A. S. Pringle-Pattison (Oxford, The Clarendon Press, 1960), pp. 66-67.
11 *Ibid.*, p. 67.
12 Husserl, pp. 311-12.

poem; one the primary qualities of the poem, the other the secondary qualities. We do not read poetry by having one eye fixed on the page and the other eye watching a movie screen in our heads. In reading, the poem is a unity. We allow all data on an equal footing.

b. *Polemical Dialogue*

This understanding of reading will now be supported and broadened by a polemical dialogue between Croce and Sartre, on the one hand, and Dufrenne, Wittgenstein, Wimsatt and Beardsley, on the other hand. This dialogue will center around the question whether the work of art is an object in or of the imagination or whether it has the status of a perceived object. The relevance of this dialogue to reading is that a methodology of reading which allows that imagery is a part of the poem may be thought to imply that the whole poem is in or of the imagination. The question is: *If* imagery is a part of the poem while reading (I emphasize the "if" because I am at present analyzing the mode, namely reading, which will allow the *possibility* of imagery, but not necessarily the actual occurrence of imagery) then does this make reading more like imagining or more like perceiving? Does the nature of reading suddenly make the poem become an internal object?

The status of the aesthetic object for Croce begins to emerge in his analysis of "expression", the term which gives his theory its name. "Intuitive knowledge is expressive knowledge. ... To intuite is to express; and nothing else (nothing more, but nothing less) than *to express*." [13] It is Croce's doctrine of expression that is of special interest because it states definitely where the poem is. His answer at first seems to mean that the work of art is to be located in the world. "That which does not objectify itself in expression is not intuition or representation, but sensation and mere natural fact." [14] This quote would seem to imply that the aesthetic object is necessarily objectified. Expression seems to be essentially connected with embodiment in a physical medium.

Croce seems to press this interpretation further in his argument that the ordinary inartistic person does not differ from Raphael only in lacking the technical ability to put the Madonna on the canvas. This argument indicating that Raphael had technique lacked by the ordinary person seems to imply that manipulation of material is essential to the

---

[13] Benedetto Croce, *Aesthetic as Science of Expression and General Linguistic*, trans. Douglas Ainslie (New York, Noonday Press, 1962), p. 11.
[14] *Ibid.*, p. 8.

expression of art. However, very close attention to Croce's argument here will show that his point is rather that the average person does not have an *image* of the Madonna in his head. Thus, Croce's point is that Raphael differed from the common man in having such an image.[15] This subtle twist in the argument argues then not for the essential necessity of manipulating material in order to express but for the necessity of having an image in one's head. One then very quickly begins to suspect that the work of art is not to be material. Croce confirms this understanding of "expression".

The aesthetic fact is altogether completed in the expressive elaboration of impressions. When we have achieved the word within us, conceived definitely and vividly a figure or a statue, or found a musical motive, expression is born and is complete; there is no need for anything else.[16]

Externalization of an intuition is purely contingent. Externalization requires will, thus implying the relevance of morality to artistic externalizations.[17] We must "understand the purely external relation between the aesthetic fact or artistic vision and the physical fact or instrument which aids in its reproduction...".[18] Croce leaves no doubt that the work of art is always internal.[19] The physical objects artists produce are mere causes of the reproduction of the image which is the real aesthetic fact.[20] Of the four stages of aesthetic production, the last stage, namely, "translation of the aesthetic fact into physical phenomena..." is quite inessential.[21] The physical object does assist the audience, all other conditions being equal, to reproduce in themselves the aesthetic experience.[22]

That Croce extends this general view of the relation of the physical and the "real" work of art to language in the poem and the "real" poem is clear. "And what else are those combinations of words called poetry, prose, poems, novels, romances, tragedies or comedies, but *physical stimulants of reproduction*...?"[23] Croce then sees the words in the poem, in the metaphor, as physical *stimulants* which assist the reader or hearer in reproducing the "real" poem in himself. The great weak-

---

[15] *Ibid.*, pp. 9-10.
[16] *Ibid.*, p. 50.
[17] *Ibid.*, p. 116.
[18] *Ibid.*, p. 104.
[19] *Ibid.*, pp. 50-51.
[20] *Ibid.*, p. 104.
[21] *Ibid.*, p. 96.
[22] *Ibid.*, p. 97.
[23] *Ibid.*

ness of Croce's theory is that the physical artifact, the body of words in the case of a poem, is merely contingent. As Hospers notes, Croce and Collingwood "tend to view the artist's actual manipulation of a physical medium outside himself as an accident or an afterthought".[24] Hosper's charge is accurate at least with respect to Croce.

Sartre's analysis of the aesthetic object, though more guarded with regard to the contingency of the physical work of art, shares certain fundamental points with Croce. His theory posits two modes of consciousness.

The image and the perception, far from being two elementary psychical factors of similar quality and which simply enter into different combinations, represent the two main irreducible attitudes of consciousness. It follows that they exclude each other.[25]

Images have four characteristics which contrast with perceptions.

First, an image is not an object of consciousness but is a consciousness.[26] The object of perception and imagination may be the same, for example, the chair on which I am sitting. The difference then between imagination and perception is the way the consciousness is related to the chair.[27] Sartre is not exactly clear here but seems to mean that in perception the chair is posited as existing while in imagination it is posited as not existing. It will be seen that in fact this is Sartre's third characterization of the difference between the two acts.

The second characteristic of images, one which will prove to be extremely weak when applied to the aesthetic object, is that images are given immediately. We can learn nothing from turning our image around as we could by walking around an object. We find nothing but what we have put in the image. Objects, on the other hand, are brimming over with qualities. In perception the object overflows consciousness, while in imagination it is never more than consciousness. An image is delivered all in a lump. Our attitude then toward images is not observation but only quasi-observation.[28] Sartre means that images cannot be investigated in the same way that we can investigate an object.

[24]   John Hospers, "The Concept of Artistic Expression", *The Proceedings of the Aristotelian Society, New Series*, LV (June 20, 1955), p. 316.
[25]   Jean-Paul Sartre, *The Psychology of Imagination*, trans. not given (New York, Philosophical Library, 1948), p. 171.
[26]   *Ibid.*, p. 4.
[27]   *Ibid.*, p. 7.
[28]   *Ibid.*, pp. 9-13.

Third, the object of imaginative consciousness is posited as nothingness, while the object of perception is posited as existing. There are four modes in which the object may be posited as nothingness; (a) as non-existent; (b) as absent; (c) as existing elsewhere; and (d) as neutralized and not positing its object as existing.[29] Sartre argues that in these four forms the image "includes an act of belief, or a positional act".[30] Husserl disagrees that (d) is an act of belief. Of the neutrality-modification he states:

We are dealing now with a modification which in a certain sense completely removes and renders powerless every doxic modality to which it is related, but in a totally different way from that of negation, which, in addition, as we saw, shows in the negated a positive effect, a non-being which is itself once more being.[31]

And further: "The neutrality-modification came before us in marked contrast with *real* belief, presumption, and the like...."[32] Husserl would deny that neutralization, Sartre's fourth mode in which the object is posited as nothingness, is a positional act, an act of belief. A neutralized experience, an experience placed under *epoche*, is an immanent experience, an experience whose object exists in itself necessarily. In such an act there is no belief assertion and thus none of the contingency of perception.[33] Further, Husserl specifically notes that the purely aesthetic attitude is such a neutralized experience. In such a stance one sees a picture

as "mere picture", without imparting to it the stamp of Being or non-Being, of possible Being or probable Being, and the like. But, as can clearly be seen, that does not mean any privation, but a modification, that of *neutralization*.[34]

Husserl then concludes that the aesthetic object is taken in the mode of neutralization and that such a stance, contrary to Sartre, is not positional. Sartre then accuses Husserl of being "the victim of the illusion of immanence...".[35] This debate which may seem irrelevant to metaphor-

[29] *Ibid.*, p. 16.
[30] *Ibid.*
[31] Husserl, p. 306.
[32] *Ibid.*, p. 314.
[33] *Ibid.*, pp. 143-45.
[34] *Ibid.*, pp. 311-12.
[35] Sartre, p. 83. It must be noted that this debate between Husserl and Sartre is not primarily a debate over the nature of aesthetic experience. Their argument is much more serious. Husserl seems to think that the *epoche* discovers an immanent consciousness. Precisely here Sartre thinks Husserl failed to take seriously

ical imagery is really quite significant. The question is whether such images are positional, that is, posit their object as nothingness in one of Sartre's four modes or whether such images are non-positional and thus do not posit their object either as existing or not existing as in Husserl's neutralization. I agree with Husserl. The reason I agree with Husserl instead of Sartre is that the stance appropriate to metaphorical meaning involves a step back, so to speak, from literal presuppositions. Metaphorical meaning does not call for a negation of the natural world but a bracketing or holding at a distance of the natural world. Thus metaphor does not posit its object either as existing or not existing. Fuller arguments follow in the sections called "Imagery and Sense Impressions", "Imagery and Reference", and "Imagery and Seeing As".

Finally, images are spontaneous. In perceiving we seem to be passive but in imagining we are active.[36] As Dufrenne notes, here Sartre identifies imagination with freedom as the power to negate and posit, at the same time, the world.[37] Kaelin also notes that images are connected with Sartre's notion of freedom.[38] "For a consciousness to be able to imagine it must be able to escape from the world by its very nature, it must be able by its own efforts to withdraw from the world. In a word it must be free."[39] However, even this transcendence of the world does not mean imagination does not presuppose the world. "Thus, although as a result of producing the unreal, consciousness can appear momentarily delivered from 'being-in-the-world', it is just this 'being-in-the-world' which is the necessary condition for the imagination."[40]

Having sketched Sartre's two modes of consciousness we must now determine which mode is relevant to the work of art, the poem. Sartre answers by saying the work of art "is something unreal (*irréel*)".[41] The beautiful cannot be experienced by perception. In fact concentration on the physical work prevents the appearance of the aesthetic object.

---

the fundamental phenomenological tenet that consciousness is always consciousness *of*. Thus for Sartre a reflective act on consciousness does not discover any residuum of consciousness, but rather discovers that consciousness is nothing but particular consciousnesses. However, a full consideration of this debate is irrelevant here.

[36]   *Ibid.*, pp. 18-19.
[37]   Mikel Dufrenne, *Phénoménologie de l'expérience esthétique* (Paris, Presses Universitaires de France, 1953), I, p. 259.
[38]   Eugene F. Kaelin, *An Existentialist Aesthetic* (Madison, Wisc., The University of Wisconsin Press, 1962), pp. 40-41.
[39]   Sartre, p. 267.
[40]   *Ibid.*, p. 269.
[41]   *Ibid.*, p. 274.

The physical embodiment of the work of art is merely its "material analogue...".[42] The poet uses words as analogues to excite the real aesthetic object. "Esthetic contemplation is an induced dream...."[43] The similarity of Sartre's thought to Croce's here is quite significant, although Sartre would never say that the work of art could occur without the physical analogue. Still for Sartre the status of the work of art is nonactual.

Dufrenne disagrees fundamentally with Sartre's argument that imagination is the mode of consciousness appropriate to the aesthetic object. Of Sartre's analogue he says: "Le chose fabriquée par l'artiste, réalisée parfois avec la collaboration des exécutants, n'est donc qu'un moyen pour l'imaginaire de se manifester, et la perception n'est qu'une occasion d'imaginer."[44] This identical charge could be made against Croce. Dufrenne objects to the reduction of the physical work of art to the status of a stimulus to or occasion of the imagination. "Objet esthétique et œuvre d'art sont distincts en ceci qu'à l'œuvre d'art doit se joindre la perception esthétique pour qu'apparaisse l'objet esthétique; mais cela ne signifie pas que la première soit réelle et le second idéelle, que la première existe comme une chose dans le monde, et la seconde comme une représentation ou une signification dans la conscience."[45] The physical work of art is not just a stimulus to the performance of the "real" work of art which exists in some mental realm, either in Croce's imagination or as an object of the imagination as analyzed by Sartre. They are drawn together because the aesthetic object is *perceived*. "L'objet esthétique est, au contraire, l'objet esthétiquement perçu, c'est-à-dire perçu en tant qu'esthétique."[46] Nor is perceiving aesthetically a queer type of perception. It is to perceive faithfully. "Percevoir esthétiquement, c'est percevoir fidèlement; la perception est un tâche, car il y a des perceptions maladroites qui manquent l'objet esthétique, et seule une perception adéquate réalise sa qualité esthétique."[47] One final passage will clarify further Dufrenne's understanding of perception, the mode appropriate to the work of art.

La perception est perpétuellement le théâtre d'un drame: elle ne cesse de se dépasser vers une autre forme de connaissance qui tente de se délivrer de la

---

[42] *Ibid.*, p. 275.
[43] *Ibid.*, p. 281.
[44] Dufrenne, I, p. 262.
[45] *Ibid.*, I, p. 26.
[46] *Ibid.*, I, p. 9.
[47] *Ibid.*, I, pp. 9-10.

subjectivité et de saisir l'objectivité de l'objet, en sorte que la distinction du
sujet et de l'objet est le résultat et la fin de cet effort, et en même temps
elle ne cesse de revenir à cette expérience et cette assurance initiales où lui
est donnée la présence de l'objet parce qu'objet et sujet ne s'y discernent
encore pas. Et ce drame retentit dans le statut de l'objet perçu: il n'existe
pas seulement en tant que vecu par moi, mais en tant qu'indépendant de moi,
refusant la complicité qui le lie à moi dans la perception et sollicitant une
attitude objectivante qui fasse droit à la vérité de son être objectif.[48]

Dufrenne's fundamental thought is that the aesthetic object is an object
perceived. To perceive faithfully is an accomplishment. Kaelin notes
that Dufrenne is here accepting Merleau-Ponty's description of an object of perception as an "en-soi-pour-nous".[49]

Dufrenne's insistence that perception is the mode appropriate to the
work of art has two very important consequences.

First, if the work of art is perceived it follows that the aesthetic
object is an object belonging to the public world. The aesthetic object
is not private. It accords itself with nature. It acknowledges itself as a
thing among things. It is not ashamed of its inhumanity in its human-
ity.[50] Dufrenne means that the aesthetic work has a certain autonomy as
a thing. It removes itself from us and from objects which we have subordinated to our ends. It communicates the character of *alterité* which our
used objects let us forget. It is a thing in its nakedness.[51]

In saying the work of art is a thing in its independence and fullness
Dufrenne is disagreeing fundamentally with Sartre over the "unreality"
of the work of art, a quality designated by both writers by the term
"irréel". Sartre used this word to indicate that the work of art is an
object of the imagination.[52] One of the consequences of saying that the
work of art is an object of the imagination, as my second characterization of Sartre's understanding of images showed, is that they are given
all in a lump. Dufrenne also wants to use the term "irréel", but he
objects to Sartre's identification of "irréel" with the imagination. Dufrenne uses the term "irréel" to deny that the work of art is given all at
once in a lump. By unreal he means that the work has a certain fullness.
It is never totally grasped because of its richness and our poverty of
sentiment.[53] As Kaelin notes Dufrenne is thus using "irréel" to mean

[48]   *Ibid.*, I, p. 284.
[49]   Kaelin, p. 370.
[50]   Dufrenne, I, p. 127.
[51]   *Ibid.*, I, p. 129.
[52]   Sartre, p. 274.
[53]   Dufrenne, I, p. 264.

"pre-real".[54] The pre-reality of the work of art then does not proceed from a diverted consciousness, from imagination, but from attention to the object while perceiving it. Thus, the pre-reality is internal to the object and is perceived.[55] The pre-reality of the work stems from its perceived fullness, not from its being an image. Sartre has said in his second characterization of images that they are given all at once and are never more than consciousness, while in perception the object overflows consciousness. The object has more qualities than those given. Dufrenne's point is that the aesthetic object has precisely the latter fullness and thus is not given in imagination. "Dire que l'objet est en soi, c'est donc dire qu'il y a de cet objet un être objectif qu'il ne nous est pas donné de saisir absolument parce que toute connaissance commence avec la perception, et que cet ensoi ne peut éviter l'être pour-nous." [56]

Second, Dufrenne's emphasis on perception as the mode appropriate to the work of art, though allowing that work the independence of a thing in the world, does not have to state that in other respects the work is identical to an objective thing. On the contrary, the work of art differs from objective things and from objects subordinated to our usual ends in that only the former reveals its maker. In an artifact the maker is anonymous. The work of art, on the other hand, places us in direct communication with the author.[57] "Le style est donc le lieu ou apparaît l'auteur." [58] Dufrenne's emphasis then on perception, though allowing some differentia between the work of art and other perceived objects such as artifacts and natural objects, must insist that it is *in* the work itself, in style, which is the way the author handled the medium, that the author is revealed. In other words, the perceived object itself tells us its own meaning and standards. Thus we do not interpret the work through biographical details but can only interpret the details through the work. Dufrenne's understanding of perception is beginning to agree with the "new critics" in emphasizing that the work, the poem itself, is definitive of the poet's intention. Like the "new critics" he distinguishes the act of creation from the act of appreciation, the cause of the work from its evaluation. Biographical facts about the creation of a work are no basis for judging that work.[59] The standards of apprecia-

[54] Kaelin, p. 365.
[55] Dufrenne, I, p. 264.
[56] *Ibid.*, I, p. 284.
[57] *Ibid.*, I, p. 141.
[58] *Ibid.*, I, p. 150.
[59] *Ibid.*, I, p. 144.

tion are dictated by the work itself. External norms are not imposed. The work imposes its own norms. Thus if a work is imperfect it is because it fails to realize its own essence. The opposite of beauty is not the ugly, but the abortive.[60]

Wimsatt and Beardsley direct arguments, similar to those of Dufrenne, specifically to Croce in their attack on the "intentional fallacy".[61] The intentional fallacy is based on the assumption that the poet's mind, his inspiration while writing a poem, somehow is specially related to "the poem". Such an emphasis on the quality of the poet's inspiration is an earmark of romanticism, thus leading Wimsatt and Beardsley to refer to Croce's thought as "the culmination and crowning philosophic expression of romanticism".[62] They accurately summarize that for Croce "the intuition or private part of art is *the* aesthetic fact, and the medium or public part is not the subject of aesthetic at all".[63] Croce seems to think "the real poem" is in the poet's imagination. The written poem is somehow less or inferior to the poem in the poet's mind. Wimsatt and Beardsley argue quite to the contrary.

The poem is not the critic's own and not the author's (it is detached from the author at birth and goes about the world beyond his power to intend about it or control it). The poem belongs to the public. It is embodied in the language, the peculiar possession of the public, and it is about the human being, an object of public knowledge.[64]

By emphasizing the special relation of the poet's mind to the "real" poem theorists of Croce's type often want to refer to the quality of such an inner experience, to the quality of the inspiration, as a *standard* by which the poem is judged. Wimsatt and Beardsley disagree. Like Dufrenne, they argue that certainly the poet, as a designing intellect, is the *cause* of the poem, but this is not to grant that his intention or

---

[60]   *Ibid.*, I, p. 21.
[61]   Wimsatt and Beardsley also analyze the "affective fallacy", which is the counterpart to the intentional fallacy. The intentional fallacy confuses the cause of the poem with the poem. The affective fallacy "is a confusion between the poem and its *results*. . .". (Wimsatt, *The Verbal Icon*, p. 21). The affective fallacy puts the poem in the reader's mind. Croce could also be accused of this fallacy because he argues that by means of the physical objects which artists make the audience may re-create the aesthetic object in their imagination (Croce, p. 97). To commit the intentional or affective fallacy is to let the poem vanish respectively either into the poet's mind or the reader's mind.
[62]   Wimsatt, *The Verbal Icon*, p. 6.
[63]   *Ibid.*
[64]   *Ibid.*, p. 5.

design is the *standard* by which the critic judges the work.[65] "Judging a poem is like judging a pudding or a machine. One demands that it work. It is only because an artifact works that we infer the intention of an artificer." [66] The thoughts and attitudes of the poem are imputed to a *dramatic speaker* and to the author only by an act of biographical inference.[67] Lerner makes a similar point by noting that it is not Milton who speaks in "Paradise Lost" but it is "Milton".[68]

The obvious fact is that if intention not shown by the structure of the poem itself is relevant to the poem then it is lost in most cases because the poet is either dead or has forgotten his mental accompaniments to the poem. Even in the case of a living poet who has a good memory, the relevance of his analysis of the poem is questionable. For example, should Eliot be consulted about "The Love Song of J. Alfred Prufrock"? The answer of Wimsatt and Beardsley is clear.

Our point is that such an answer to such an inquiry would have nothing to do with the poem "Prufrock"; it would not be a critical inquiry. Critical inquiries, unlike bets, are not settled in this way. Critical inquiries are not settled by consulting the oracle.[69]

The significant intention of the poet in fact is not private. It is public and "is discovered through the semantics and syntax of a poem, through our habitual knowledge of the language, through grammars, dictionaries, and all the literature which is the source of dictionaries, in general through all that makes a language and culture . . .".[70] Wimsatt and Beardsley note that the poet may have private or semiprivate meanings which he attaches to certain words, and knowledge of these shades over into external facts. These last facts may or may not be relevant to the poem. However, the decision of relevance is based on the first level, "the verbal and hence intellectual composition which is the poem".[71]

Wimsatt and Beardsley's argument that the intention relevant to literary criticism is the intention "discovered through the semantics and syntax . . ." of the poem is quite similar to Wittgenstein's point that intention is not a private accompaniment of language but is shown in

---

[65]   *Ibid.*, p. 4.
[66]   *Ibid.*
[67]   *Ibid.*, p. 5.
[68]   Laurence Lerner, *The Truest Poetry: An Essay on the Question What Is Literature* (London, Hamish Hamilton, 1960), p. 83.
[69]   Wimsatt, *The Verbal Icon*, p. 18.
[70]   *Ibid.*, p. 10.
[71]   *Ibid.*, p. 12.

speaking language. "An intention is embedded in its situation, in human customs and institutions." [72] A person's intention is not the spooky mental surroundings of an utterance. An intention is the way something is said. Wimsatt and Beardsley's emphasis on the poem, on the grammar and syntax as a key to criticism, also connects the relevant poetic intention with the way the poet spoke. Wittgenstein's analysis of intention, extended to poetic language, would emphasize in a similar way a methodological procedure which demands a close attention to the poem, the way the poet spoke. There is nothing private or spooky about intention. Intention is not a mental parallel to the written poem. Nor is the poem some private performance which is parallel to the words of the poem. "The real poem" is in neither the imagination of the poet nor that of the reader. Croce and Sartre both are committed to the erroneous view that "the poem" is something which is parallel to the words of the poem.

c. *Conclusions*

Four consequences for my understanding of reading follow from the polemical dialogue between Sartre, Croce, Dufrenne, Wittgenstein, Wimsatt, and Beardsley. These consequences follow mainly from a comparison of Dufrenne's understanding of perception and my understanding of reading. I say "comparison" because reading is like perceiving in some, but not all senses. Reading and perceiving are alike in that the objects of both acts have sensuous qualities and in that the content of neither act is free or spontaneous. Reading and perceiving are further alike in that neither involves two objects, one the physical cue and the other its mental accompaniment. Reading and perceiving are unlike in that reading involves imagery, while perception does not. If, for example, a supposed case of visual perception is found to involve or include imagery we would with Ryle say that this is a case of "seeing" not seeing. Reading, on the other hand, with regard to metaphor essentially involves imagery. Thus the unique nature of reading is clarified by the following sections entitled "Imagery Occurs", "Imagery and Free Association", "Imagery and Sense Impressions", "Imagery and Reference", and "Imagery and Seeing As". An analysis of metaphorical imagery clarifies the nature of reading equally as much as does this preliminary clarification by the dialogue between Sartre and

[72] *Investigations,* # 337.

Croce, on the one hand, and Dufrenne, Wittgenstein, Wimsatt, and
Beardsley, on the other. The consequences of this dialogue for my
understanding of reading are:

First, the autonomy for the poem which reading as *epoche* implied
in bracketing naturalistic and reality claims is now broadened. Dufrenne, Wittgenstein, Wimsatt, and Beardsley extend this bracketing
to include biographical details, external standards and spooky occurrences either in the mind of the poet or of the reader. Wimsatt and
Beardsley summarize well this broader suspension by saying that the
poem is "detached from the author at birth and goes about the world.
... The poem belongs to the public." [73] Not only is the poem independent of the author's intentions, *if* not embodied in the poem, but also
free from its results on the public. To confuse the poem with its effects
is to commit the affective fallacy. The result of either the intentional
or the affective fallacy "is that the poem itself, as an object of specifically critical judgment, tends to disappear".[74] That Wimsatt and
Beardsley are correct is born out by both Croce and Sartre who do let
the words of the poem become stimuli to the "real" poem which is
either in the author's or public's imagination. My understanding of reading tries to keep the metaphor from vanishing into the thicket of biographical details, external standards or secret events. My understanding
of reading emphasizes, with the type of "new criticism" implied by
Wimsatt and Beardsley, that the poem as we have it is definitive of
intention. *Reading* as I understand it *is a radical openness which seeks
as a methodological ideal to let the poem reveal its intention or meaning. Reading is an active openness to the text.*

Second, *in relating my understanding of reading to Dufrenne's perception instead of Sartre's imagination I provide a mode which is appropriate to and allows the poem to develop a sensuous fullness ap-
proaching that of a perceived object.* The theorists of the preceding
chapter in arguing that the poem is a presentational symbol, a concrete
universal, an icon, a fusion of a sense and sensa, imply that the poem
does have the sensuous fullness of a perceived object. Sartre is quite right
in arguing that objects of perception overflow or are wider than our
consciousness of them. Metaphor as icon, as a fusion of sense and sensa,
has precisely this fullness. In describing objects of perception our descriptions never "get" the thing. My point is that the metaphor as an

[73] Wimsattt, *The Verbal Icon*, p. 5.
[74] *Ibid.*, p. 21.

object of reading has this type of overflow. The metaphor is never "gotten" in *either* a reading *or* a description. Of course, a dream can never be "gotten" in a description either, but it is "gotten" in the act of dreaming. By saying that dream imagery is "gotten" I mean that such imagery has the character of an unrepeatable conscious state. I agree with Sartre that images have this character of being given in a lump. But I argue with Dufrenne that it is precisely this finality and completeness which destroys the analogy between images and works of art. Thus I argue reading is like perceiving not like dreaming.

Since reading is more like perceiving than like dreaming, then metaphorical imagery can be returned to in the sense that the metaphor can be reread while dream imagery, as Sartre correctly notes, is given only once and does not overflow consciousness. Metaphorical imagery is neither given once nor is it limited to consciousness. Metaphorical imagery in concert with other elements of poetry has precisely the fullness noted by Dufrenne, a fullness which, quite unlike imagery of dreams, overflows consciousness as does a perceived object. I deny that metaphorical imagery has Sartre's second characteristic of imagery, namely, being given in a lump not exceeding consciousness.

Third, *in relating my understanding of reading to Dufrenne's perception instead of Sartre's imagination I am implying that the content of such an act is not free or spontaneous.* Here I begin to anticipate my analysis of metaphorical imagery, but this anticipation is tied up with my analysis of reading and thus is appropriate here. Metaphorical imagery is always associated with language, a physical medium; and, as a result, such imagery is never spontaneous like the imagery of dreams. The poem is not an invitation to free association as is sleep. Metaphorical images are always tied to language as a medium. I deny that metaphorical images have Sartre's fourth characterization of imagery, namely spontaneity. The content of the act of reading is not free.

Fourth, Dufrenne, Wittgenstein, Wimsatt and Beardsley also support the consequence that *reading as epoche does not have two objects*, one the "real" poem, the other the physical poem; one the primary quality of the poem, the other the secondary quality of the poem. The *epoche* first had to hold at bay the naturalistic stance which would relegate imagery to the realm of secondary qualities and enshrine the physical words. Now the same *epoche* also holds at bay Croce and Sartre who would enshrine the imagery and relegate words to the realm of secondary qualities. *Reading as epoche*, reading which allows the original right of all data, *refuses to allow the distinction between the actual*

poem and the ideal poem to arise in the first place. Since no initial distinction between subjective and objective is allowed by the *epoche,* then there is no actual and ideal poem or physical and real poem. Reading as *epoche* keeps us from getting a headache from trying to have one eye fixed on the poem on the page and the other eye fixed on a movie screen in our heads. In *reading*, the poem is a unity. Reading a poem, a metaphor, involves two objects no more so than does a painting involve two objects.

I have analyzed reading in order to overcome the methodological problem of how images can be pointed to or cited as evidence by the strong theorist. This problem has not been settled but circumvented in that at least now it is clearer what is meant by saying that the metaphor is a *read* object. Reading permits the original rights of all data although it is not yet known what this data will be. A strong theory has by no means been proved, but a methodology of reading has been established. Of course, I do not claim that my methodology of reading has been formed *in vacuo.* Quite to the contrary, my analysis of reading has been formulated with a view to adequacy to metaphor. Thus my analysis anticipated points about metaphor which I have not, but shall, substantiate. My methodology fits or is appropriate to its content, namely, the metaphor, as a glove fits the hand. Thus the following analysis in clarifying the object of reading, namely, the metaphor understood as seeing as between elements of an imagistic description, clarifies the nature of reading. In other words, the following sections on imagery clarify reading by clarifying the object of reading. In order to cite evidence for the object of reading we must now read metaphors. In reading metaphor in the way analyzed no new and queer way of reading is called for. My analysis of reading makes explicit what we all along implicitly knew of reading poetry. Reading as I have analyzed it is a description, not a prescription.

2. *Imagery occurs*

The first question is: Do images occur on reading metaphor? [75] I argue that metaphor essentially involves imagery while literal writing does not. We are not embarrassed nor do we consider it a lapse of attention if we

---

[75] I emphasize that this section and the following sections on imagery are analyzing only metaphorical imagery. I shall mention other species of imagery only incidentally.

have images while reading metaphors while we consider it both a lapse and are embarrassed if we are reading science. Let us try this experiment. Read this passage from d'Abro's *The Evolution of Scientific Thought from Newton to Einstein.*

So long as we restrict our attention to space and time computations in our frame, we may, as before, appeal to vibrating atoms for the measurement of congruent time-intervals and to rigid rods for the purpose of measuring space. It is when we seek to correlate space and time measurements as between various Galilean frames in relative motion that astonishing consequences follow. We discover that the concepts of spatial and temporal congruence of classical science must be modified to a very marked degree. They lose those attributes of universality with which we were wont to credit them. It is then found that congruence can only be defined in a universal way when we consider the extension of four-dimensional space-time.[76]

Now I ask you: Did you have any images? Most likely you did not. At least it is clear that Wittgenstein would say[77] that if images did occur they are irrelevant to the meaning of the passage. If you did not have images reread the passage and try to have images. Indulge yourself. Now ask yourself: Did the images help my understanding of this explanation or did they not rather detract from its meaning? I rather suspect that in reading such scientific writing we consider our attention lapsed when associative images arise. We call ourselves down. We make a special effort to concentrate. We are ashamed of ourselves

[76] A. d'Abro, *The Evolution of Scientific Thought from Newton to Einstein,* 2nd ed. (New York, Dover Publications, Inc., 1950), p. 82.

[77] I have added the comment that *Wittgenstein* would deny the relevance of such imagery to literal language in order to indicate that I do not necessarily agree with his thought here. I rather suspect that image-laden language does have a function in scientific discourse. Such imagistic words are verbal equivalents of scientific models. Consider this example (an example called to my attention by Professor John J. Compton) from Newton: "Absolute, true, and mathematical time, of itself, and from its own nature, *flows* equably without relation to anything external, and by another name is called duration. . . ." (Italics mine). (*Sir Isaac Newton's Mathematical Principles of Natural Philosophy and his System of the World*, trans. Andrew Matte in 1729, revised by Florian Cajori, Berkeley, University of California Press, 1947, p. 6.) The word "flows" is certainly a metaphorical, image-laden expression. In a very excellent article R. Harre argues that such expressions with a fullness of implicative suggestiveness are not at all foreign to scientific theories. In fact, he suggests that a fruitful scientific theory always has such metaphors or "*picture carrying expressions*" ("Metaphor, Model and Mechanism", *Proceedings of the Aristotelian Society, New Series*, LX, Jan., 1960, p. 112). Such metaphors have accretions of meaning from several contexts; and, as a result, such terms present in a theory "suggest the existence and sketch the character of mechanisms in regions previously inaccessible. . .". (Harre, p. 115). The word "flows" in the above translation from Newton admirably fits Harre's

in a way similar to our self embarrassment when we catch ourselves daydreaming while walking to the bookstore. But now read this metaphor:

> Like waves make towards the pebbled shore,
> So do our minutes hasten to their end;
> Each changing place with that which goes before,
> In sequent toil all forwards do contend.
>> (William Shakespeare, Sonnet LX, ll. 1-4)

And this one:

> The apparition of these faces in the crowd;
> Petals on a wet, black bough.
>> (Ezra Pound, "In a Station of the Metro", entire poem quoted)

Now I ask you: Did you have any images? Did you "see" ocean waves or lake waves? What kind of petals did you "see" on what kind of tree limb? I suspect that your first answer is "yes" and that thus you have an answer to the second and third questions. Now, would you call having these images a lapse of attention? Before answering this question reread the passages like you would read a much-read response in church. Resist the images like you would in reading a scientific description. Which reading involved a lapse? I suspect that you had at least as much difficulty *not* having images on reading these metaphors as you had difficulty in having images on reading the scientific passage. To have images on reading the scientific passage you try to have them; to not have images on reading the metaphors you try not to have them.

---

point. The word "flows" is precisely a "picture carrying expression" which has accretions of meaning from several contexts. Nor is this word from this passage anomalous. Other such words, for example, the use of the term "current" to refer to the flow of electrons in a wire, come readily to mind. Max Black argues similarly that theoretical models in physics are a type of metaphor and further that such models play an essential role in the growth of scientific knowledge (*Models and Metaphors*, pp. 219-43). That in fact such image-laden terms have a role in scientific or literal discourse does not weaken my argument but rather strengthens it. I am arguing, in opposition to Wittgenstein, that imagery is relevant to the meaning of poetic metaphor. If imagery is relevant to models or metaphorical words in literal discourse my argument is strengthened. The argument of this work depends on the point that imagery is relevant to metaphorical meaning, not that it is irrelevant to literal meaning in certain cases. I have accepted Wittgenstein's arguments for the irrelevance of imagery in order to avoid the general semantical considerations which the stronger claims of Harre and Black imply. I am strongly inclined to think that imagery has some relevant relation to meaning in other species of discourse, but I am committed here only to defending this relevance with regard to poetic metaphor.

Conversely, to concentrate on the scientific passage excludes images; to concentrate on the metaphors includes images. A lapse on reading scientific prose is experientially similar to attention to poetic metaphor, and conversely. We do not call ourselves down. We seem to allow images "the original right of all data". I argue that we accept the metaphor's images as having the same right to consideration as does the metaphor's sound. The irrelevance of imagistic embellishments when we are reading scientific prose does not serve to deny their relevance to metaphor, but rather it serves to show that we do not read metaphor like we read science.

The first thought experiment involved comparing a scientific prose passage to two metaphorical descriptions to determine which was more imagistic. A second experiment involves a metaphor as compared to a statement of its content in prose. For example, compare this passage from Eliot

> Here is no water but only rock
> Rock and no water and the sandy road
> The road winding above among the mountains
> Which are mountains of rock without water
> If there were water we could stop and drink
> Amongst the rock one cannot stop or think
> Sweat is dry and feet are in the sand
> If there were only water amongst the rock
> Dead mountain mouth of carious teeth that cannot spit
> Here one can neither stand nor lie nor sit
> There is not even silence in the mountains
> But dry sterile thunder without rain
>   (T. S. Eliot, "The Waste Land", ll. 331-42)

to this translation of the information of the passage.

Some travellers are walking along a mountain road which is dry and dusty. Sharp rocks rise on either side of the road. Thunder sounds overhead but there is no rain.

This translation is quite adequate to the *facts* in Eliot's passage. We could enforce the translation if a hypothetical scientist had travelled Eliot's road and recorded information such as temperature, humidity, and the attitude of the mountains. Even this reinforced version, however, would compete very poorly with the imagery and concreteness in the metaphor in the ninth line quoted above. The implicit metaphor is that mountain rocks encase the road with "carious teeth". That the teeth are the rocks along the road is shown by line three where the road is among the mountains and in line six where we are again "amongst the rock". In this brilliant metaphor Eliot compresses into an image-packed line the dryness and desolation of the preceding lines. The most brilliant exploitation of imagery is that the teeth of the dead mouth cannot spit. The mouth cannot spit because, of course, the mouth of a skeleton, the "dead mouth" with "carious teeth" cannot spit. Not only does the metaphor suggest the dry mouth of a skeleton but the mouth of a man so thirsty that he is unable to spit. I argue that the body of associative imagery which Eliot taps in this metaphor, visual imagery of skulls and kinesthetic-tactile imagery of thirst, will always outstrip the prose restatement as far as imagery goes. Given the tentative definition of imagery in the preceding chapter, namely, that images are sense impressions remembered, then it seems undeniable that these three examples arouse such imagery. Shakespeare's metaphor causes us to "see" waves. Pound's metaphor evokes imagery of petals on a tree limb. Eliot's metaphor evokes visual imagery of skulls and tactile imagery of thirst and desolation. In Langer's terms, to read these metaphors is to have the illusion that one is experiencing life. Wimsatt would argue that in these metaphors sense and sound function iconically. Metaphors which excite imagery with regard to the other senses could easily be cited.

A note on my terminology in the preceding paragraph is significant enough here to deserve treatment in the text. I have said these metaphors "evoke" or "cause" imagery. Such terminology implies that I have slipped into a position like that of Croce and Sartre and am now looking on words as physical analogues of the "real poem". I have used such phrases, and shall continue to use them, because it is grammatically awkward to speak of a relation between words and imagery in any other way. Ideally I should say "words – imagery" implying that the nature of the chain between words and imagery is of no concern to metaphorical meaning so long as the imagery occurs. I have used the quasi-scientific terms "cause" or "evoke" because of grammatical convenience. This convenience should by no means be escalated to ontological status in attempting to decide where the "real poem" is. I then conclude from my examination of these metaphors that they do arouse images while one is reading them. If we read these metaphors with an openness then images do seem given as part of the "original data" of the metaphor.

My generalization from the examples that images occur while reading metaphors is not without theoretical support. Wellek and Warren argue that metaphor is really an analogy or comparison between images which are defined as "the vestigal representatives of sensations...".[78] That their point here is correct and fruitful will be seen below in the section on "Imagery and Seeing As".

The thought of Wellek and Warren is supported by Brooks and Warren. The latter state:

The representation in poetry of any sense experience is called imagery. Imagery does not consist merely of "mental pictures", but may make an appeal to any of the senses. Poetry characteristically appeals continually to the senses; this is another way of saying that poetry is concrete.[79]

Further they explicitly state that metaphor and similes are definitely species of imagistic language, species which compare images.[80] Nor, they state, are images mere stage setting devices or pleasing pictures in themselves, but "are important devices for interpretation".[81] They quite clearly state that "imagery affects meaning...".[82] A strong note of discord with Wittgenstein's theory of meaning is here sounded with the suggestion that images at least are *involved* in the meaning of metaphor. This discord will become heightened as this analysis proceeds because it will be argued that Brooks and Warren are correct on this point.

Stephen Brown makes the same point in a slightly different way. In poetry images are substituted for objects. Brown here perceptively sees that the poet fuses words with imagery. The poet does not see words as fused with their physical bearer as Cassirer noted of the mythical thinker. Metaphor involves a substitution of images for objects with a comparison between the images.[83] A metaphor is a momentary, illuminating identification between the main idea and an imported image, an identification which does not explain itself but rather must be seen by our insight.[84] Brown's emphasis on insight will agree with my emphasis that seeing as between the metaphorical elements is an *irreducible* experience-act.

I thus conclude that an examination of the above examples and the

[78]   Wellek and Warren, p. 191.
[79]   Brooks and Warren, p. 555.
[80]   *Ibid.*
[81]   *Ibid.*, p. 269.
[82]   *Ibid.*
[83]   Stephen J. Brown, S. J., *The World of Imagery* (London, Kegan Paul, Trench, Trubner & Co., Ltd., 1927), p. 2.
[84]   *Ibid.*, pp. 48-54.

testimony of these informed critics justifies the minimal conclusion that images do occur while reading metaphor. The significance of this conclusion is that the question now is not *whether* we accept a strong or weak theory but *which* strong theory we accept. Further the question is can such a theory deal with the basic difficulties raised by Wittgenstein. I shall deal with these problems in the order of their urgency. I shall discuss: imagery and free association, imagery and sense impressions, imagery and reference, and imagery and seeing as.

3. *Imagery and Free Association*

a. *Problem*

The most obvious problem, a problem arising from my analysis of reading, is that imagery seems to open the door to free association. If in reading we allow the original right of all data then it would seem that each of us is launched into his own solipsistic world of free reverie.

Richards formulates the problem in a very clear manner. In saying poetry causes emotion instead of reference Richards intends to include imagery as a part of what is caused by the poem. He recognizes two types of imagery – tied and free. By tied images he means mainly those associated with poetic diction. "The chief of these are the auditory image – the sound of the words in the mind's ear – and the image of articulation – the feel in the lips, mouth, and throat, of what the words would be like to speak." [85] Free imagery means those other sensory images which the poem causes such as visual images. Richards contends that such free images have been too much emphasized because in fact

individuals differ not only in the type of imagery which they employ, but still more in the particular images which they produce. ... Fifty different readers will experience not one common picture but fifty different pictures.[86]

Failure to see the subjectivity of images has led many "an intelligent and sensitive critic" to be merely "praising the picture floating before his mind's eye".[87] Criticism then should concern itself less with the qualities of imagery than with the efficacy of imagery.[88]

Richards, however, does recognize that the qualities of an image and its effects are related.

[85]   Richards, *Principles of Literary Criticism*, pp. 118-19.
[86]   *Ibid.*, p. 122.
[87]   *Ibid.*, p. 123.
[88]   *Ibid.*, pp. 122-23.

In all forms of imagery sensory deficiencies are for many people signs and accompaniments of defective efficacy, and the *habit of reading so as to allow the fullest development to imagery in its sensory aspect* is likely to encourage the full development of this more essential feature, its efficacy, if the freaks and accidents of the sensory side are not taken too seriously.[89] (Italics mine)

Richards' clearheaded warning to the critic to avoid the deep waters of personal association here is well taken. Also his suggestion on how to read a poetic line, the suggestion I have italicized in the above quote, is precisely the type of reading I have suggested in my analysis. Richards is quite legitimately concerned that the experience caused by the poem must not deviate too far "from a standard experience".[90]

Isabel Hungerland agrees with Richards that the poem is not an invitation to free association. However, she notes that connotation within a context is not as free as is the connotation of a single word. The poet by using his context then is able to attenuate certain connotations and heighten others.[91] Virgil Aldrich argues along a similar line that the literary artist, the poet, is a skillful specialist in managing and controlling the images associated with language. The poem has image management not image mongering.[92]

b. *Examples of Metaphor show Image Control*

I intend to heed the caution of the critics who emphazise that imagery varies widely, yet I still contend that the imagery of metaphor is controlled imagery. Certainly the freedom of association varies with regard to different poets and different readers, but is, in fact, never free. Sartre's contention that images are spontaneous or free while we are passive in perception cannot be applied to metaphorical imagery. I fundamentally disagree with Sartre that the analogy between the free imagery of dreams and the imagery of poetry can be defended. Metaphorical imagery is always associated with language and thus is far from being free. Consider this very controlled metaphor by Pope:

[89] *Ibid.*, p. 123.
[90] *Ibid.*, pp. 226-27. For further treatment of the problem of imagery I refer the reader to the following article: Norman Friedman, "Imagery: From Sensation to Symbol", *The Journal of Aesthetics & Art Criticism*, XII (Sept., 1953), pp. 25-37.
[91] Isabel C. Hungerland, *Poetic Discourse* (= *University of California Publications in Philosophy*, Vol. XXXIII) (Berkeley and Los Angeles, University of California Press, 1958), pp. 24-26.
[92] Virgil C. Aldrich, "Image-Mongering and Image-Management", *Philosophy and Phenomenological Research*, XXIII (Sept., 1962), p. 59.

> Who shames a scribbler? break one cobweb thro'
> He spins the slight, self-pleasing thread anew:
> Destroy his fib or sophistry; in vain,
> The creature's at his dirty work again,
> Throned in the center of his thin designs,
> Proud of a vast extent of flimsy lines!
> > (Alexander Pope, "An Epistle to Dr. Arbuthnot", ll. 89-94)

The concrete image of the spider is specified very precisely in its relation to poor writers. Pope clearly stipulates the *relevant* senses in which a poor writer is like a spider. A very precise description here arouses a very "tied" image. Now consider this example by Valéry where the images are not tied but are vague and suggestive. The sun is being addressed:

> Keep off the idolaters, bright watch-dog, while—
> A solitary with the shepherd's smile—
> I pasture long my sheep, my mysteries,
> My snow-white flock of undisturbed graves!
> Drive far away from here the careful doves,
> The vain daydreams, the angels' questioning eyes!
> (Paul Valéry, "Le Cimetière Marin", translated by C. Day Lewis, ll. 61-66)

The poet is shepherd to tombstones, to his mysteries, to thoughts on death and immortality. The imagery excited by the "snow-white flock of undisturbed graves" is so suggestive and rich as to need no comment. The poet here taps a wealth of association in the reader. As Frye notes, poets of the symbolism tradition, including Valéry, Eliot and Rilke, use images which "do not state or point to anything, but by pointing to each other, they suggest or evoke the mood which informs the poem".[93] The whole poem "Le Cimetière Marin", like Eliot's "The Waste Land", is a brilliant display of images, many of which are metaphors, juxtaposed in most significant ways. Valéry's juxtaposed imagery is certainly freer, less precise, than that of Pope, though this is a criticism of neither writer. In fact, Valéry's imagery is vague; it has a vagueness which matches the mysterious vacuousness of death. It is not going too far to suggest that Valéry in his vague imagery is trying to suggest a vague, numinous experience similar to that analyzed by Otto in *The Idea of the Holy*. Valéry successfully communicates a numinous experience in this poem. Wordsworth also communicates this feeling in his "Lines Composed a Few Miles above Tintern Abbey". Wimsatt correctly notes that romantic poetry, such as that of Wordsworth, favor-

[93]   Frye, p. 81.

ing implication rather than overt statement, is closely related to a symbolist poet like Valéry. "As a structure which favors implication rather than overt statement, the romantic is far closer than the metaphysical to symbolist poetry and the varieties of postsymbolist most in vogue today." [94]

But in favoring implication rather than overt statement, the symbolist and romantic are far from favoring free association. Valéry is tapping the wealth of imagery associated with death, not, for example, that associated with life or vitality. The fear of free association is a bogus fear with regard to poetic metaphor. Only an extremely vague or nonsense metaphor will allow free associations. For example, the imagery associated with the metaphor "13 is like $4\frac{1}{2}$" would probably vary considerably because one is quite at odds to notice any *significant* imagery at all. The same could be said for the nonsense metaphor "igglework is like mirgintheaup". That a metaphor whose sense we do not grasp remains a metaphor only by our grammatical convention of "like" or "as" implies that sense is more relevant to poetic metaphor than Brémond stated.

c. *Why Images are not Free*

The reasons why our associations on reading metaphors are not free are not hard to find.

1. *Memory associates language and images of referents*

First, we share a common language; which is to say, we share the common sound and sense of our language and *the nonverbal associations* of that language. Sapir notes that words in all languages develop certain "feeling tones" on their "conceptual kernel". He argues further that these "are naturally of great value to the literary artist".[95] Stevenson also notes that words not only mean but suggest.[96]

However, both Stevenson and Sapir emphasize the tendency of words to accumulate an emotional aura. This particular aura is more important in ethical language than the language of metaphor. Metaphor utilizes *in addit*ion the image evoking power of words. The poet taps the emotive aura of words; but even more important, he exploits *the*

---

[94] Wimsatt, *The Verbal Icon*, p. 116.
[95] Sapir, p. 41.
[96] Charles L. Stevenson, *Ethics and Language* (New Haven, Yale University Press, 1960), p. 69.

aura of imagery which words get by association in our memory of that word with images of its referent. The poet exploits this aura through his choice of concrete words and descriptions.

Schlauch notes the more relevant exploitation by the poet of the image aura of words. Since the poet uses the medium of ordinary language he has special difficulties in exciting imagery. Because of these difficulties the poet often makes up words to retain images or concrete meanings. The poet use etymological rejuvenation.[97] Schlauch's insight here is informative.

The same point has been extremely well put by T. E. Hulme who says that poetic language

is a compromise for a language of intuition which would hand over sensations bodily. It always endeavours to arrest you, and to make you continuously see a physical thing, to prevent you gliding through an abstract process. It chooses fresh epithets and fresh metaphors, not so much because they are new, and we are tired of the old, but because the old cease to convey a physical thing and become abstract counters. A poet says a ship 'coursed the seas' to get a physical image, instead of the counter word 'sailed'. Visual meanings can only be transferred by the new bowl of metaphor; prose is an old pot that lets them leak out.[98]

Association of individual words and images. – The poet's partiality to concrete elements in his poetry, the partiality noted by Schlauch and Hulme, can be seen both with regard to individual words and with regard to complex concrete descriptions. The poet shows a favoritism for concreteness both in the atomic elements of poetry, that is, individual words, and in more complex structures, that is, concrete descriptions. An excellent example illustrating the poet's exploitation of the imagery associated with single words occurs in Hopkins' "The Blessed Virgin Compared to the Air We Breathe". As the title indicates the whole poem is a metaphor which compares Mary's gift in Christ to the life-giving and sustaining qualities of air. There occurs in this line: "Wound with thee, in thee isled...." (Gerard Manley Hopkins, "The Blessed Virgin Compared to the Air We Breathe", l. 125) the verb "isled", a metaphorical substitute for a more prosaic or dead verb. Why did not Hopkins use some word such as "surrounded"? (I am ignoring in my suggested replacement the obvious difference in the number of syllables in "isled" and "surrounded" since this difference does not affect my

[97]   Margaret Schlauch, *The Gift of Tongues* (New York, Modern Age Books, 1942), pp. 229-34.
[98]   T. E. Hulme, *Speculations: Essays on Humanism and the Philosophy of Art*, 2nd ed. (London, Routledge & Kegan Paul Ltd., 1958), pp. 134-35.

point here.) I suggest, with Schlauch, that Hopkins used the fresher word because it is more likely to evoke in the reader images of the nonverbal context to which the word refers. We have forgotten that "surround" comes from the Latin *super*, meaning over, and *undare*, meaning to rise in waves or overflow; but we have not forgotten the association between the verb "isle" and islands. Hopkins uses the relation of which we are still conscious between the word and images of its referent to excite imagery of islands. In short, he uses etymological rejuvenation to make the verb more than a mere sign. Etymological rejuvenation taps the image aura of words which language in conjunction with our memory accumulates, especially around new words. In Hulme's terms Hopkins chose "fresh epithets and fresh metaphors" instead of "abstract counters" in order "to get a physical image". "Visual meanings can only be transferred by the new bowl of metaphor; prose is an old pot that lets them leak out." [99]

Sapir correctly noted that the connotative aura of words was of great significance to the poet. Schlauch and Hulme emphasize that for the poet the most significant aspect of this aura is the image arousing ability of concrete words. I argue that such imagery is not free. Admittedly there is less uniformity with regard to this image aura of words than there is for the denotation of words. No one had succeeded in writing a dictionary of images, a sort of handbook through which the poet can thumb to put together just the right set of imagery. Still Stevenson's argument (that connotations in ethical language, though less precise than denotations, still are not free because such connotations are often involved with descriptive meanings) [100] must be extended to metaphorical language. I argue with Aldrich that a legitimate function of language can be to express or evoke pictures or images. [101] Further there seem to be rules for language functioning in this pictorial way. The poet is an expert in using these rules. [102] Hopkins can reasonably expect that his concrete word, his rejuvenated expression "isled", will excite imagery of islands not turnips. Imagery is not free because we associate words, the atomic elements of poetry, and their context in our memory.

[99]   *Ibid.*, p. 135.
[100]   Stevenson, pp. 69-71.
[101]   Virgil C. Aldrich, "Pictorial Meaning and Picture Thinking", *The Kenyon Review*, V (Summer, 1943), p. 407.
[102]   Virgil C. Aldrich, "Pictorial Meaning, Picture-Thinking, and Wittgenstein's Theory of Aspects", *Mind*, LXVII (Jan., 1958), pp. 75-76.

Association of complex verbal structures and complex images. – Nor is this association merely between words, as atomic entities, and images of their referents. The poet also excites more complex imagery in his concrete descriptions. In such descriptions the poet uses an additional device for image control; namely, the verbal context. Thus, images associated with words in a poetic description are not like images associated with single words in a psychological test. Note the tightly controlled imagistic context of Empson's metaphor

> Twixt devil and deep sea, man hacks his caves;
> Birth, death; one, many; what is true, and seems;
> Earth's vast hot iron, cold space's empty waves:
>
> King spider, walks the velvet roof of streams:
> Must bird and fish, must god and beast avoid:
> Dance, like nine angels, on pin-point extremes.
>
> (William Empson, "Arachne", ll. 1-6)

which compares the tenuous character of human life to the spider's precarious existence as he walks on water. The reported associations which one would get on a psychological test with regard to the words "spider", "beast", or "angel" are not the same as those aroused by this very tight contextual metaphor. The associative imagery of the individual atomic words is much freer than the association of this rigorous context. As Hungerland notes, connotations within a context differ from the connotations of the same words in isolation. The poem presents controlled contextual connotations. Thus, the poet attenuates some connotations while heightening others. The poem is not an invitation to free association.[103]

In summary, the first reason that the images of metaphor are not free is that we share a common language which excites imagery through its sense by fullness of descriptive detail or by etymological rejuvenation of single words. The metaphor controls imagery through its particularity of detail, through its sense, a point neglected by Brémond. Thus, these details are not irrelevant as Ransom's "irrelevant local texture" suggests, but are, as Wimsatt argues, "more than usually relevant".[104] The fullness of detail, the specificity and particularity of sense, might be irrelevant to the usual literal description but is quite essential to control of imagery in metaphorical language. The indefinite imagistic aura of words becomes delineated in the descriptive detail of

---

[103] Hungerland, pp. 24-26.
[104] Wimsatt, *The Verbal Icon*, p. 76.

the metaphorical context. Metaphorical control of imagery utilizes both the association of word and image in an atomic manner in memory, and also the association of complex verbal structures with complex imagistic structure. Language and imagery are fused both with regard to simple elements, such as individual words and images, and with regard to more complex elements, such as a contextual description and complex imagery.

Agreement with the theorists of the preceding chapter is beginning to emerge. To say metaphorical language is a fusion of language and imagery is to imply with Langer that reading such language is an experience, an experience of imagery. Sense as well as sensa can now be iconic, as Wimsatt argued, because metaphorical meaning is fused with metaphorical imagery.

2. *History associates language and selected imagery*

The second reason that the images of metaphor are not free is that we share a common body of historical associations. These, though closely related to a common language, are not identical with language lines. For example, we share many Judaeo-Christian historical symbols although we do not share a language identical with that original culture. The poet then has at his disposal not just the iconic power of a common language, but the iconic associations of wider cultural contexts. The second reason that metaphorical imagery is not free is that historical traditions have established a body of selective imagery around many motifs exploited in metaphor.

Edith Sitwell exploits this type of historical association in her "Still Falls the Rain". The rain may be taken literally for the first few lines, but then we come to:

> Still falls the Rain
> At the feet of the Starved Man hung upon the Cross.
> (Edith Sitwell, "Still Falls the Rain", ll. 12-13)

and:

> See, see where Christ's blood streames in the firmament:
> (Edith Sitwell, "Still Falls the Rain", l. 27)

The literal rain becomes a metaphor for Christ's blood. Sitwell in this metaphor taps the rich body of associative imagery which the Christian tradition has attached to Christ's blood. The species of imagery exploited in this type of metaphor is again far from free. History has selected certain associations and suppressed others with regard to Christ's symbolic blood.

The above two reasons why associations are not free in reading metaphors are reasons deriving from language's association with a common environment, an association which is direct through our memory or indirect through historical and cultural conventions given in our culture. The poet presupposes a language which is not totally removed from its context whether that context is our own experience or the experience of the race embodied in our cultural heritage. Language and its associations, then, are the "stuff" on which the poet works. Language is the poet's medium, having the qualities of sense, sound, and imagery. The *qualities* of the "stuff" given or assumed by the poet are, as the medium theorists argued, *shared by poet and reader*. It is beginning to appear that imagery is one of the qualities of the poet's "stuff". Such imagery is not free, private association but is in some sense shared.

3. *Intention or style controls imagery*

The third reason that associative images are not free goes beyond the iconic possibility of language. The poet does not simply present us with an unformed medium just as the sculptor does not offer an uncut stone. The third reason that images in the metaphor are not free is that they are "stylized" or intended. I can now speak of intention without committing the "intentional fallacy" because I always mean the intention, as my analysis of reading stated, revealed by the structure of the poem itself. I do not argue, nor do Wittgenstein, Wimsatt, and Beardsley, that the poet did not have intentions other than those finally realized in the poem, but I do argue that the *relevant* intention is the intention in the structure of the metaphor. Dufrenne agrees with this emphasis in arguing that style, that factor which for him distinguishes a work of art from a natural object and from a mere artifact, reveals the author. "Le style est donc le lieu ou apparaît l'auteur." [105] Now I shall clarify what is meant by style.

In treating style with regard to painting André Malraux argues that there is no such thing as a neutral style, a style which is completely photographic.[106] The art work always bears the mark of a human will. As Malraux puts it, artists "devalorize reality...".[107] The artist always

[105]   Dufrenne, I, p. 150.
[106]   Weitz, *Problems in Aesthetics*, p. 263.
[107]   *Ibid.*, p. 267.

subdues the physical or objective world in his painting. Applied to poetic metaphor this means that such metaphors never have a neutral style. Metaphorical comparisons are never the neutral, depersonalized comparisons of scientific analogies. Metaphors always bear the poet's mark.

However, Malraux's account is very incomplete. He only notes that style vanishes in stark photographic realism. *Style equally vanishes in complete subjectivism.* In fact, the problem of subjectivism is more pressing here than the problem of realism. The problem here is not whether metaphorical imagery is too photographic or objective but whether such imagery is not pure subjective free association. Pongs deals with this more immediate problem. In his terms the essence of metaphor is to have a tension between "*Gleichnis und Beseelung*", between comparison and animation.[108] Pongs's emphasis on *Beseelung* is especially informative in view of the large number of metaphors which involve personification. In the history of literature both *Gleichnis und Beseelung* have moved between the objective and subjective. *Gleichnis* began to move away from a comparison to the expression of subjectivity, from the objective to "vage sensualistische Assoziationen...".[109] *Beseelung* moved from the pole of perception to pure subjective animation.[110] There is a tension between the associations of the ego and objective nature.

Pongs's analysis has meaning also in view of certain poets in English literature. The metaphysical poets, such as Donne and Marvell, favor the more "realistic" style in their detailed and explicit metaphors which state clearly the relevant sense in which a metaphorical vehicle is like its tenor. The romantic and modern symbolist poets, such as Wordsworth and Valéry, favor, as Wimsatt correctly notes,[111] suggestion and implication rather than overt statement. The metaphysical poet has highly tied imagery while the romantic and symbolist poet has freer implicative association. The point is that imagery in both cases is stylized. The metaphysical poet by no means falls into a neutral or impersonal style because of the rigorous cognitive nature of his comparison. Nor does the romantic or symbolist go off the other

---

[108] Hermann Pongs, *Das Bild in der Dichtung*, Vol. I: *Versuch einer Morphologie der metaphorischen Formen*, 2nd ed. (Marburg, N. G. Elwerte Verlag, 1960), p. 150.
[109] *Ibid.*, pp. 163-74.
[110] *Ibid.*, p. 176.
[111] Wimsatt, *The Verbal Icon*, p. 116.

end into the private association of insanity. Style means that the metaphor always bears marks of the poet's will or intention. It is this mark
of its maker that led Kant to say that an art object involves immediate
recognition that its "shape is attributed to some purpose or other and
to a definite end".[112] *Style, as the imposition of the poet's will on his
medium, rules against the accidental.* Style is where the purpose noted
by Kant, the intention of the poet, appears. Style is, as Dufrenne notes,
the place where the author appears.[113] Purpose in the poem then means
that we must take the totality of its elements *as if* they were intended.

Brooks and Warren apply the intention revealed by style specifically
to imagery. In a good poem one asks

that its imagery shall not be idle and meaningless, dead or inert, or distracting
and self-serving, like some foolish ornament that merely calls attention to
itself. Every bit of image ought to "make sense" and to aid the poem in *its*
making sense. . . .[114]

To regard the imagery one has on reading metaphors as accidental, as
epiphenomenal, would be as gross as to regard the distortion of the
human figure in Cézanne's "Bathers" as accidental. *On reading metaphor one must proceed as if every element given in the act of reading were
intended,* which is to say one must read with openness allowing the
"original right of all data". Every element in the metaphor must be
allowed the possibility of integration with the poem as a whole. Metaphor as stylized rules against the accidental nature of free association.
Metaphorical imagery is controlled because it is part of the intentional
or purposive structure of the poem. To assume that metaphorical imagery is free is to assume that such imagery is a purposeless by-
product which the poet either did not intend or could not control.

Speaking of imagery as intended does not commit the intentional
fallacy analyzed above. Imagery as intended means that *imagery is part
of the intentional structure or style of the metaphor. The metaphor as
a stylized object is definitive of intention.* That the metaphor is definitive of intention is a corollary of my analysis of reading, which
analysis draws from Husserl's *epoche,* Dufrenne's perception and the
type of "new criticism" implied by Wimsatt and Beardsley. Wittgenstein also would agree that intention must be defined by the way the
poet spoke. *The metaphor, in being read, then, presents a stylized or*

---

[112]   Immanuel Kant, *The Critique of Judgment,* trans. James Creed Meredith
(Oxford, The Clarendon Press, 1961), p. 80 n.
[113]   Dufrenne, I, p. 150.
[114]   Brooks and Warren, p. 272.

intentional structure of imagery. This imagery is no more free, no more an epiphenomenon than are the cubic forms in Cézanne's landscapes. The metaphor as a stylized aesthetic form of language counts against an accidental collocation of imagery. Only in poor metaphors in which the poet was unable to impose his will on his matter are the images free.

4. *Seeing as controls imagery*

Fourth, imagery is controlled by the experience-act of seeing as. Seeing as is definitive of imagery. Seeing as selects the *relevant* aspects of metaphorical imagery. This reason why metaphorical imagery is not free is closely related to the third reason because seeing as is part of the intentional structure of the metaphor. However, this reason differs from the third reason because seeing as is, as will shortly be shown, the unique feature of metaphor. The first three means of controlling imagery function in any imagistic, poetic *description.* Seeing as functions only with regard to *metaphor.* Here it suffices to *state* merely that seeing as controls metaphorical imagery. A fuller analysis of the experience-act of seeing as must await a clarification of the problem of images and sense impressions and the problem of images and reference.

I conclude from my examples and four arguments that metaphorical imagery is not free. Metaphorical images thus are not spontaneous like dream images. Metaphorical images are "tied" to language. They are "tied" by our memories, by historical conventions, by the poet's intention as embedded in the metaphor, and by seeing as.

4. *Imagery and Sense Impressions*

Now it is necessary to expand my tentative definition of metaphorical imagery by comparing such imagery to sense impressions. Hume squarely comes to grips with the distinction between sense impressions and ideas of memory or imagination. It is well known that Hume means that ideas are images. In commenting on the *Treatise* I, i, section 1, C. R. Morris states: "Here it is quite clear that Hume is speaking of ideas as mental images. . . ." [115] Thus, Hume's distinction between ideas and impressions is the distinction between images and impressions which is of concern here.

[115] C. R. Morris, *Locke, Berkeley, Hume* (Oxford, Oxford University Press, 1959), p. 119.

An impression in becoming an idea passes through two stages. First, the impression loses some of its vivacity and is intermediate between an impression and an idea. Second, the impression loses even more of its vivacity and becomes a "perfect idea". The ideas in the first stage are ideas of memory; those in the second stage, ideas of imagination. Memory ideas "are much more lively and strong than those of the imagination...".[116]

Hume also notes that ideas of imagination are "not restrain'd to the same order and form with the original impressions; while the memory is in a manner ty'd down in that respect, without any power of variation".[117] Hume is here speaking of a change in order in complex ideas of the imagination. However, this latter difference, a difference in order, is not emphasized. Hume in fact later states that "this difference is not sufficient to distinguish them in their operation...".[118] Most basically, "impressions and ideas differ only in their strength and vivacity".[119] Ideas and impressions further differ in the fact that simple impressions are always prior to simple ideas, except for Hume's famous missing shade of blue. Hume does note that ideas had during sleep, fever, madness, or during "any very violent emotions of soul..." approach very near to the vivacity of impressions.[120] However, he does not seriously consider these cases, a point which considerably weakens his position.

In summary, Hume holds that impressions and images differ only in their degree of vividness and in the order of their occurrence. Applied to metaphor this would mean that images occurring while reading metaphors differ only in being less vivid than sense impressions and in following sense impressions.

Ryle specifically attacks Hume's analysis. Of Hume he states: "His mistake was to suppose that 'seeing' is a species of seeing, or that 'perception' is the name of a genus of which there are two species, namely impressions and ghosts or echoes of impressions."[121] Ryle seems to have in mind two elements in his objection though they are closely related.

First, he accuses Hume of confusing the *act* of seeing with "seeing".

---

[116] David Hume, *A Treatise of Human Nature*, ed. L. A. Selby-Bigge (Oxford, The Clarendon Press, 1958), p. 9.
[117] *Ibid.*
[118] *Ibid.*, p. 85.
[119] *Ibid.*, p. 19.
[120] *Ibid.*, p. 2.
[121] Gilbert Ryle, *The Concept of Mind* (London, Hutchinson & Co., Ltd., 1960), p. 250.

Seeing is a normal perceptual experience; and the term seeing, without quotes, is properly used when something is actually there to be seen. "Seeing" on the other hand, for example, "seeing" snakes while having a delirium tremens, differs in kind from seeing. Ryle argues that in "seeing" one knows he is doing something totally different in kind from cases when he is seeing.[122] Ryle means that concepts of "seeing" usually involve "factual disclaimers".[123] Hume then is guilty of confusing these *acts*.

Second, Hume confused the *content* of the respective acts, thus leading him to suppose that an idea is a weak copy of an impression. To attack this analogy between impressions and ideas Ryle argues that impressions cannot be described as "vivid" while ideas can. Thus, the analogy does not hold. Further, if "vivid" means intense Hume was also wrong. Ryle states, following Wittgenstein, that noises in our fancy are not merely less intense than noises heard. Thus, whatever Hume meant by "vivid" it cannot be predicated of both impressions and ideas, implying that the analogy between ideas and perceptions is weak.[124]

However, Ryle does not totally disagree with Hume. The truth in Hume's account "is that what I see in my mind's eye and what I hear 'in my head' is tied in certain ways to what I have previously seen and heard".[125] However, the relation is not Hume's "para-mechanical" one. Ryle's substitute is that acts involving images, such as make-believe acts, are second order acts which presuppose belief.[126] He states: "Imaging, therefore, is not a function of pure sentience; and a creature which had sensations, but could not learn, could not 'see', or picture, things any more than it could spell." [127] He states that imaging "being one among many ways of utilizing knowledge, requires that the relevant knowledge has been got and not lost".[128] By the above statements Ryle seems to mean that imaginative exercises are more sophisticated than actual exercises and the former presuppose the latter. One learns to imagine one is talking or humming only after one can talk or hum.[129] This is Ryle's more complex and subtle way of saying with Hume that

[122]   *Ibid.*, p. 246.
[123]   *Ibid.*, p. 251.
[124]   *Ibid.*, p. 250.
[125]   *Ibid.*, p. 271.
[126]   *Ibid.*, p. 264.
[127]   *Ibid.*, p. 266.
[128]   *Ibid.*, p. 272.
[129]   *Ibid.*, p. 269.

impressions are prior to ideas. Ryle also agrees with Hume that memory and imagination are related.[130]

Since then imaging is not like seeing, nor are images like percepts, then what is the nature of imaging or images? In commenting on picturing one's nursery Ryle argues:

Roughly, imaging occurs, but images are not seen. . . . True, a person picturing his nursery is, in a certain way, like that person seeing his nursery, but the similarity does not consist in his really looking at a real likeness of his nursery, but in his really seeming to see his nursery itself, when he is not really seeing it. He is not being a spectator of a resemblance of his nursery, but he is resembling a spectator of his nursery.[131]

Ryle also states that "what I imagine is myself seeing, hearing, doing and noticing things . . .".[132] Ryle seems to mean here that in "seeing" in the imagination one is not actually seeing a real likeness of his nursery, but merely seeming to see the nursery when not really seeing it. Emphasis should be placed on the fact that one is not really seeing anything. He seems to mean that one "seeing" his nursery resembles a spectator of his nursery in that he acts as if he were seeing his nursery. Ryle must mean that we speak or act as if we were seeing our nursery.

Ryle's treatment of images is not uncontested. Smythies argues that Ryle is wrong in categorically distinguishing "seeing" of the imagination from actually seeing. He argues that persons under drugs or persons hallucinating do not categorically distinguish the two, but rather confuse them.[133] Ryle does note such extreme cases;[134] but, like Hume, he does not take such exceptional states as serious evidence.

Smythies argues further that we constantly do extend physical object talk successfully to our images, and that further we could have been taught words with relation to images. Ryle could probably agree that we extend talk of public objects by analogy to our images. By saying we resemble a spectator of our nursery he seems to imply that he would permit such an extension. Smythies notes that we do verify images differently from physical objects. We have a second look at our images while we walk around physical objects.[135]

Sartre enters the debate on the side of Ryle in noting that imagina-

[130]   *Ibid.*, p. 273.
[131]   *Ibid.*, pp. 247-48.
[132]   *Ibid.*, p. 273.
[133]   J. R. Smythies, "On Some Properties and Relations of Images", *The Philosophical Review*, LXVII (July, 1958), pp. 389-91.
[134]   Ryle, p. 246.
[135]   Smythies, p. 393.

tion and perception are "the two main irreducible attitudes of consciousness".[136] As the translator of *Being and Nothingness*, Hazel Barnes,
notes: "Sartre rejects the opinion commonly held that imagination is a
vague or faded perception." [137] A restatement of Sartre's distinction,
already analyzed, between images and perception will clarify his position in this debate. For Sartre: (1) images are not objects of consciou-
ness but are a consciousness; (2) images are given immediately while
in perception the object overflows consciousness; (3) the objects of
imaginative consciousness are posited as nothingness while the objects of perception are posited as existing; (4) images are spontaneous
while perceptions affect us.[138] Sartre's second reason leads him to say
that images are not observed but only quasi-observed,[139] a point similar
to Ryle's insistence that images are not seen but "seen". Further Sartre's third characterization of images as posited as nothingness is similar
to Ryle's argument that concepts of "seeing" involve "factual disclaimers".[140] Of course, the means by which Ryle and Sartre reach
these conclusions, and thus the grounds for their conclusions, are quite
different. Ryle is analyzing *concepts* of "seeing". Sartre is doing a
phenomenological analysis of imaginative consciousness. Thus Ryle is
claiming something about language while Sartre is making a claim about
the imaginative consciousness.

The most important questions raised by Hume, Ryle, Smythies and
Sartre are: First, are cases of "seeing", "hearing", etc. (hereafter I shall
use seeing and "seeing" as representative respectively of sense impressions of any sense and imagery of any type), categorically different
from cases of seeing or is there only a difference of quantitative vividness? Involved in this question is the question: On what basis is the
distinction between imagery and percepts made. Second, are there any
characteristics common to images and perceptions? Before I deal with
these questions a warning is appropriate. We need not expect metaphorical imagery to agree with any of the above analyses in detail
because all the analyses are of imagery had while dreaming, having
delusions, etc., while metaphorical imagery is always associated with

---

[136]   Sartre, p. 171.
[137]   Jean-Paul Sartre, *Being and Nothingness: An Essay on Phenomenological Ontology*, trans. Hazel E. Barnes (New York, Philosophical Library, 1956), pp. xii-xiii.
[138]   Sartre, *Psychology of Imagination*, pp. 4-19.
[139]   *Ibid.*, pp. 8-14.
[140]   Ryle, p. 251.

language. At best, there will be some kinship between these different species of imagery.

Following the basic procedural methodology of this book I shall let an example of metaphor help to answer these questions. In this metaphor by Eliot

> At the violet hour, when the eyes and back
> Turn upward from the desk, when the human engine waits
> Like a taxi throbbing waiting
> (T. S. Eliot, "The Waste Land", ll. 215-217)

do we see a taxi or only "see" a taxi? Certainly Sartre and Ryle are correct in that we do not actually perceive a taxi. A taxi does not suddenly pop up on the page before our eyes. Thus, certainly the seeing involved here is categorically different from normal seeing. The "seeing" involved here is certainly deserving of Ryle's quotes. The stickier question is how is this queer type of seeing different from normal seeing. What distinguishes metaphorical imagery from sense impressions? Is such imagery simply less vivid or is there a more qualitative difference here? What is the basis of this distinction?

Ryle's argument that seeing and "seeing" are categorically different hinges on the point that in "seeing" one knows that "what he is doing is something which is totally different in kind from seeing...".[141] Concepts related to "seeing" have "factual disclaimers".[142] Ryle's analysis turns around the obvious point that in imaginative behavior there is no object there to be seen. Investigation of imaginative concepts shows that they are used with regard to cases of "seeing" when there is no object there to be seen. Ryle no doubt would extend his point specifically to metaphorical imagery because he mentions "the novel reader" and "the theatre-goers" as being species of imaginative behavior.[143] However, the obvious fact that one does not really see a taxi in reading Eliot's metaphor is not very helpful in explaining precisely what kind of experience the experience of metaphorical imagery is.

Sartre's phenomenological analysis of this qualitative distinction between images and perceptions promises to be more helpful. However, I seem debarred from using his distinctions because I have argued on the basis of his second, third, and fourth characterizations of imagery that the analogy between images and works of art, images of dreams and

---

[141] *Ibid.*, p. 246.
[142] *Ibid.*, p. 251.
[143] *Ibid.*, p. 256.

images of metaphor, cannot be defended. Metaphorical imagery can be returned to in the sense that the metaphor can be reread while dream imagery, as Sartre correctly notes, is given all in a lump. Second, the object of metaphorical imagery is not given as nothingness but as neutralized. No belief content is either affirmed or denied. Finally, metaphorical imagery is not free while dream associations are apparently free.

However, here it is necessary to reopen my reasons for these objections. Especially urgent is a consideration of my objection to Sartre's third characterization of imagery; namely, that imaginative consciousness posits its object as nothingness ("La conscience imageante pose son objet comme un néant").[144] Now a more detailed consideration of this objection is necessary. In saying that the objects of the imagination are posited as nothingness Sartre means that such objects are posited as nonexistent, or as absent, or as existing elsewhere, or as neutralized.[145] The question now is: Which of these four ways of positing its object as nothingness is appropriate to metaphorical imagery? Sartre does not clearly answer this question. However, this silence does not paralyze my evaluation of his position. The only unobjectionable mode is that the object of metaphorical imagery is absent. If this is Sartre's claim about metaphorical imagery it is identical to Ryle's claim that in cases of "seeing" there is no object there to be seen. However, then Sartre's claim would be no more helpful than Ryle's analysis. The question then becomes: Is one of the other three modes appropriate and helpful? What is objectionable in his analysis?

First, is the object of Eliot's taxi image posited as nonexistent? If Sartre chose this sense of positing its object as nothingness he would be wrong in one sense and misleading in another. He would be wrong in that the object of Eliot's taxi image does exist in one sense. The object of Eliot's image exists in that there does seem to be an *existing similarity* or *relation* between a human heart beat and the throbbing of a taxi engine. Thus to categorically state that the object of metaphorical imagery is nonexistent is at best wrong. However, I have made this point against Sartre in a tongue-in-cheek manner. My real objection is that I doubt the relevance of the terms "existence" and "nonexistence" to metaphorical imagery. The relevance of using such terms with regard to metaphorical imagery is, to say the least, very questionable. "Exist-

[144] Jean-Paul Sartre, *L'imaginaire: Psychologie phénoménologique de l'imagination* (Paris, Librairie Gallimard, 1948), p. 23.
[145] Sartre, *Psychology of Imagination*, p. 16.

ence" and "nonexistence" are terms which function in literal, observational contexts. It is not at all clear what relation the imagery in Eliot's metaphor has to such a literal context. The language-game in which "existence" and "nonexistence" function is quite different from the language-game in which metaphorical imagery functions. My whole analysis of reading implies that such terms are not relevant to metaphorical imagery. To argue that such terms are relevant implies that metaphorical imagery is related, in this case negatively, to some corresponding physical object. To hold such a position makes metaphorical imagery the intervening or corresponding image so effectively attacked by Wittgenstein in the King's College example. The intervening or corresponding image theory cannot be defended. Hume's quasi-scientific truth that simple ideas always have corresponding impressions is relevant to metaphorical meaning only in anomalous cases in which metaphorical imagery either fails to occur or occurs too fully. In the case of failure, if, for example, the reader knew nothing of taxis we might well point out a taxi to him in order to complete the medium which the poet assumes is a "stuff" common to his readers; namely, language and its association with images of impressions. In case the imagery occurs too fully, if, for example, the reader is in a disturbed mental state and acts as if he were actually seeing or hearing Eliot's taxi we would point out that in fact there is no actual corresponding taxi. Only in such anomalous cases is a correspondence between images and impressions relevant to metaphorical meaning. Since such a correspondence is irrelevant it is misleading to speak of the "nonexistence" of the object of such an image. To speak of the "nonexistence" of the object of metaphorical imagery is to misapply a question from one language-game to a foreign language-game. This conclusion will be argued in more detail in the next section on "Imagery and Reference".

An identical argument could be repeated for the next possibility, namely, that the object of metaphorical imagery is posited as existing elsewhere. This possibility obviously refers to physical location and again raises the question of how such physical concepts are related to concepts about metaphorical imagery. To choose this alternative is again to confuse language-games.

Finally, there is the possibility that the object of metaphorical imagery is posited as neutralized. This possibility is not only fruitful but seems to agree with my analysis of reading. However, the difficulty here is that I have argued, with Husserl, that the neutrality of the *epoche* is not a positional or belief act. Thus the neutrality of the aesthetic stance, and thus the neutrality appropriate to metaphorical imagery, does not negate any belief content but rather has no positional or belief content. In short, while agreeing with Sartre that the neutral stance is appropriate to metaphorical imagery, I deny, following Husserl, that such a stance posits its object as nothingness. Sartre's analysis then of the characteristic of imaginative consciousness that it posits its object as nothingness, though making a stronger and more suggestive claim than does Ryle's analysis, still does not provide a means of differentiating metaphorical imagery from perception. An essential difference between metaphorical imagery and sense impressions, namely, that metaphorical imagery is taken neutrally while perception is positional, has emerged in the dialogue with Sartre; but even here Husserl deserves more of the credit.

Sartre's second characterization of imagery, namely, that imagery is quasi-observed, is most fruitful to a clarification of the nature of metaphorical imagery, thus calling for some qualification of my criticism of his thought at this point. Sartre's insight that in perceiving an object is given in profiles because the object has a certain fullness which is not grasped from any one aspect, while images lack this dimensionality, is fruitful. Metaphorical imagery certainly is similar in that it lacks this dimensional fullness. The imagery excited by Eliot's metaphor is certainly not open to discovery and further investigation in the same sense as an actual sense impression of the human heart and a taxi's throbbing engine. Thus in a sense Sartre is correct in that such imagery is given, so to speak, in a lump. It cannot be investigated in the same sense that a physical object can be looked at from an infinite number of different profiles. However, I have argued and shall continue to argue that an emphasis on the unrepeatable character of imagery, that it does not exceed a particular consciousness, while quite adequate to dream imagery, etc., is misleading when applied to metaphorical imagery. The metaphor can always be reread. I can agree with Sartre that in any *one* reading the imagery does not exceed consciousness and thus is given in a lump. Still the fact that the metaphor can be reread places metaphorical imagery in its own unique genus. Nor does rereading simply mean that I can reread the metaphor I have read before and in a significant sense return to the imagery, but that other readers have access to the metaphor's imagery in their reading. If in fact metaphorical imagery had the unrepeatable nature that Sartre's emphasis on being given in a lump implies, then we would expect talk about such imagery to be like *reports* on our dreams. Such reports would be quite incorrigible. I shall argue that this view, namely, that metaphorical imagery is incorrigible, is inadequate to the actual practice of literary critics. Attention to examples of critical discussions of metaphorical *meaning* will show: (1) that the metaphor in the full imagistic sense of the strong theorists is being referred to and (2) that such discussions are precisely *discussions* in a sense in which reports on dreams are not discussions. Critical discussion, the possibility for agreement and disagreement, is based on the assumption that the metaphor is shared in a significant sense. Thus I agree with Sartre that metaphorical imagery does not have the fullness of a perceived object because it does not have the possibility of being investigated from an infinite number of different profiles. Still metaphorical imagery can be "investigated" or lends itself to "discovery" in a weaker sense because metaphors can be reread by the same or different readers. The possibility of returning to the metaphor is part of the reason why I have at several places in this work spoken of "discovering" metaphorical meaning. In view of this partial agreement with Sartre I shall use a term related to his "quasi-observation". I shall say an essential differentia between metaphorical imagery and sense impressions is that the former are "quasi-experienced" while the latter are, of course, experienced in a full sense of the term "experienced". The quasi-experience of metaphorical imagery has the "flatness" of dream imagery in that it cannot be investigated from perspectives while it has the quality of sense impressions in being in some sense sharable. It has this peculiar status because it is imagery associated with poetic language; or, said in another way, imagery excited in the act of reading. However, the full uniqueness of metaphorical imagery has not yet emerged because the imagery of a concrete poetic description is also quasi-experienced. Metaphor will be unique in that it is essentially a seeing as between elements of an imagistic experience. Thus my term "quasi-experience" will finally be clarified only with the analysis of the experience-act of seeing as.

My emphasis on the quasi-experience of imagery can see the partial correctness in Hume's quantitative vividness. The correctness in Hume's analysis is that imagining and perceiving do have some common characteristics. First, as just noted, metaphorical imagery and sense impressions are in some sense sharable. Second, metaphorical imagery and sense impressions both have the characteristic of *qualitative determinacy*. Sartre recognized that images have qualities although these do not exceed consciousness. Thus imagery is quasi-observed. As Smythies noted, we do constantly successfully extend physical object talk to images although we check on images by having a second look instead of walking around them.[146] Images have some qualities common to impressions even though imagining and seeing are qualitatively different. Hume then is correct in saying that images retain some of their perceptual qualities though in a less vivid form. We can perfectly well recognize that we only "see" objects while reading metaphor, while still maintaining that such imagery has qualities which we can discuss. We can recognize with Ryle and Sartre that in reading metaphor we do not see but only "see", yet this in no way denies us the right to talk of the qualities of our images in an analogous way to talking of qualities of perceptions. We can say with Wellek and Warren that images are "the vestigial representatives of sensations..." [147] and with Brooks and Warren that "the representation in poetry of any sense experience is called imagery..." [148] if by these assertions we mean that we can and do extend the qualitative talk of impressions to our imagery.

By metaphorical imagery then I understand those quasi-sensuous experiences, occurring while reading metaphor, experiences which are qualitatively different from impressions because their object is neither posited as existing nor not existing and because such imagery lacks the perspectival fullness of impressions. Further this quasi-sensuous experience is precisely a *quasi-sensuous* experience. We can and do speak of such imagery in qualitative terms.

5. *Imagery and Reference*

Now we must deal with a most significant question: Does metaphorical language refer in a rigorous sense of the word? Are the images which metaphors arouse negatives which are aligned or correspond with natural referents in the physical world? Is Hume's correspondence between simple ideas of the imagination and impressions relevant to metaphorical meaning?

a. *Metaphorical Language and Imagery is Nonreferential*

Ogden and Richards formulate a clear answer to this question. They distinguish the symbolic function of language, a function which causes

---

[146]   Smythies, p. 393.
[147]   Wellek and Warren, p. 191.
[148]   Brooks and Warren, p. 555.

a reference, from the emotive function, a function which causes an emotion.[149] Truth is relevant only to the former. "True reference is reference to a set of referents as they hang together. False reference is reference to them as being in some other arrangement than that in which they actually hang together."[150] In order to emphasize sharply that emotive language, of which poetry is a type, does not refer they argue that such language causes not a reference but an emotion.[151] In such language truth or falsity, the correspondence between a reference and referent, is irrelevant.[152] Ogden and Richards seem to equate "causes emotion" to "functions nonreferentially" because they see only in the black-white terms of the emotive-cognitive dichotomy. I agree with Arnold Isenberg that to say that poetic language functions nonreferentially is not at all to say that such language is thereby emotive.[153] I argue that metaphorical language evokes imagery which is nonreferential, but I deny that metaphor evokes emotion in the strict sense of the term "emotion".

Richards in his *Principles of Literary Criticism,* a work written two years later but still written in the framework of *The Meaning of Meaning,* expands what the poem causes to include imagery.[154] However, these images are always subordinated to their emotional effect.[155] Already in this recognition that images and emotions are not equivalent there is a tension in Richards' thought. He is beginning to suspect with Isenberg that to say a poem causes emotion is not the same thing as to say it causes imagery. I accentuate this tension between imagery and emotion. To say that metaphor evokes imagery is not equivalent to saying it evokes emotion. In fact, the emotion evoked is, as Bouwsma argued, more like Wordsworth's emotion recollected in tranquillity than it is like emotion evoked by bad news. Thus even the emotion evoked is an image of emotion. Emotions evoked by metaphor have Bullough's psychical distance. Bullough argues that in the aesthetic stance the phenomena are put "so to speak, out of gear with our practical, actual self ... by interpreting even our 'subjective' affectations not as modes of *our* being [but] rather as characteristics of the phenom-

---

[149] Ogden and Richards, p. 149.
[150] *Ibid.,* p. 82.
[151] *Ibid.,* p. 149.
[152] *Ibid.,* p. 150.
[153] Arnold Isenberg, "The Esthetic Function of Language", *The Journal of Philosophy,* XLVI (Jan. 6, 1949), p. 20 n.
[154] Richards, *Principles of Literary Criticism,* pp. 117-24.
[155] *Ibid.,* pp. 122-23.

enon".[156] (Bracketed word mine.) The aura exploited by the poet in his metaphor then is not the emotive, action-causing aura of words, which Stevenson noted as significant for ethical language, so much as it is the image aura of words. The question then posed by Richards is do these images refer. Is the image which is excited by an iconic metaphorical description looked through to check its alignment with the natural world or is the image rather looked at?

Sidney Zink argues that poems as poems do not attempt to discover or verify. Thus poetic values can stand quite well without truth.[157] Scientific knowledge involves a comparison between description and described, a point similar to Ogden and Richards' correspondence between reference and referent. Contemplation, the stance appropriate to poetry, is a type of knowledge which has no place for truth. In contemplation "apprehension is fully absorbed in an immediate presentation".[158] The poem is thus an individual object of contemplation, not a proposition claiming truth. Its meanings do not describe and apply but constitute and organize. If one attends to the psychological insights or other scientific truths contained within the poem one shifts away from the poem itself.[159] "The function of the poem is to embody, not to develop or explain." [160] Thus "the poetic desideratum is not 'truth' and 'scope'; it is a qualitative vividness and concentration".[161] Thus for Zink the images excited by metaphor would be contemplated, not compared to the natural world. Their reference would be irrelevant.

Vincent Tomas argues for a similar contemplation in his distinction between aesthetic vision and normal vision. He claims that in aesthetic vision we direct ourselves to the appearance itself without being concerned as to what, if anything, appears. The reality question does not arise in aesthetic vision.[162] Tomas notes that such a stance is like the neutral stance of phenomenology in that the reality question does not arise. For example, on seeing a portrait of a man one neither be-

---

[156]   Weitz, *Problems in Aesthetics*, pp. 647-48. (Originally appeared as Bullough, " 'Psychical Distance' as a Factor in Art and an Aesthetic Principle", *British Journal of Psychology*, V, 1912.)
[157]   Sidney Zink, "Poetry and Truth", *The Philosophical Review*, LIV (March, 1945), pp. 133-35.
[158]   *Ibid.*, p. 135.
[159]   *Ibid.*, pp. 142-43.
[160]   *Ibid.*, p. 145.
[161]   *Ibid.*, p. 148.
[162]   Vincent Tomas, "Aesthetic Vision", *The Philosophical Review*, LXVIII (Jan., 1959), p. 53.

lieves nor disbelieves one is seeing a physical man. One is absorbed simply and solely in the what of the picture.[163]

Tomas' citation of phenomenology is correct in view of Husserl's statement that in perceiving aesthetically one takes the picture "without imparting to it the stamp of Being or non-Being, of possible Being or probable Being, and the like".[164] In being neutral one does not then call the picture an *appearance*. To speak of appearances presupposes a distinction between appearance and reality.

And if I am not aware of what I see as an appearance, I am not obliged to describe it as an appearance when I am asked what I see. The object I aesthetically see when I look at the picture, therefore, is not "the appearance of a man", but "a man".[165]

Tomas then agrees with Husserl, as against Sartre, on the positional status of the *epoche*. Sartre includes neutralization as one of the ways in which the object of imagination is given as nothingness. Tomas' point is that in order to recognize an appearance, to take an object as given as nothingness, one presupposes the distinction between appearance and reality, a distinction which does not exist for aesthetic vision. Tomas would deny Sartre's assertion that the work of art is an unreality. He would argue that metaphorical images are accepted neutrally. They are neither claimed to be appearance nor reality. Isenberg continues this argument by saying "the esthetic attitude is, in fact, indifferent to the distinction between imagination and sensation".[166] The work of art records impressions not convictions.

The arguments here of Tomas and Isenberg that the poet is not held to a correspondence with natural fact are quite significant. They mean that *poetic imagery is not tied to any referent*. The poet is free to introduce persons, places, and events which we know do not exist in the natural world. In a poem we are not bothered by these imaginary events, persons, and places. We do not object to Poe's walk with his psyche in "Ulalume – a Ballad". We are not disturbed by Houseman's trip to the gate of Hell in his "Hell Gate". Our credibility is not strained when we meet the devil in "Paradise Lost". We do not object to the appearance of the ghost of Hamlet's father on the stage. Yet any of the above characters or events would shock us if they appeared in a scientific explanation. If James in his *Psychology* assured us that he

---

163   *Ibid.*, pp. 60-61.
164   Husserl, p. 312.
165   Tomas, p. 62.
166   Isenberg, p. 8.

took a walk with his psyche and noticed that she had wings we would be surprised. If Einstein wrote that space was curved because the devil was bending it we would be appalled.

That we do accept poetic images which have no referents in the natural world reflects on the correctness of my argument that reading as *epoche,* suspending naturalistic judgments, is the way we do read metaphor. My analysis of reading is not so much a prescription as a description. Further, the freedom of imagery from a referent supports the immediate argument of this section that metaphorical imagery does not refer to the natural world or correspond with it. Such images are looked at in their whatness with no concern for correspondence or lack of correspondence with the world.

That metaphorical images are nonreferential ends in themselves is lent and lends support to the theories of poetic language in Chapter II. Langer argued that a poem presents virtual, not a real experience of life.[167] Art forms become an image, an object of sensuous contemplation which is abstracted from the physical and causal order. Thus in poetry discursive language is transformed.[168] Wimsatt argued that the iconicity of the poem, its calling attention to itself by thickening the medium of language, enforces a disparity between itself and reality. The poem is as remote from the natural world as is a sculptured object.[169] The poem becomes a concrete object, not a transparent image. Valéry argued that poetry implies a decision to change the function of language, from the walking of prose to the dance of poetry.[170] Thus these theorists would agree that metaphorical images are not copies of the natural world; they do not refer. These critics would agree that Shakespeare's metaphorical personification here

> Time hath, my lord, a wallet at his back
> Wherein he puts alms for oblivion,
> A great-sized monster of ingratitude.
> Those scraps are good deeds past, which are devoured
> As fast as they are made, forgot as soon
> As done.
> (William Shakespeare, "Troilus and Cressida", III, 3, ll. 145-150)

does not refer to the natural world. The image of time as an ungrateful beggar is not to be held up to physical time. In reading this metaphor

---

[167]   Langer, *Feeling and Form*, p. 212.
[168]   *Ibid.,* p. 227.
[169]   Wimsatt, *The Verbal Icon*, p. 217.
[170]   Valéry, p. 70.

we are no more bothered by the fact that time is not a beggar than we are in seeing "Hamlet" that ghosts do not appear in the physical world. Hume's correspondence between ideas and impressions is irrelevant here.

b. *"Truth" of Metaphor*

However, the denial that metaphorical images "refer" to or picture the world in a strict sense of the word, thus making truth or falsity irrelevant, does not mean that we do not often correctly make statements such as: "Shakespeare expressed a real truth about time here." Or: "This metaphor shows real insight into the nature of time." There are two very good grounds for making such statements.

1. *Verisimilitude as "true"*

First, one may have in mind that truth is verisimilitude. Langer's virtual life represents truth of this type. On reading a poem one has the illusion that he is experiencing life. The most basic factor in verisimilitude is *consistency*. It is this sense of truth which leads Northrop Frye to say: "The poet, like the pure mathematician, depends, not on descriptive truth, but on conformity to his hypothetical postulates." [171] Truth then means consistency, not correspondence.

Peter Carmichael further supports Frye's point. He argues that the artist sets down primitives and derives their conclusion in the work. Thus works of art have analyticity.

Aesthetic knowledge, being *aesthetic*, is wholly internal. If it happens to tally with something found out by natural science or with moral disposition or common sense, that is adventitious, or else we must presume that some confusion between aesthetic and non-aesthetic has occurred.[172]

Existence is no predicate; thus an idea does not entail its existence.[173]

Jarrett has a similar argument but introduces a significant new note. He argues that the realism demanded in poetry is that the poet's assumed premises determine his poem's content. Thus the verification relevant to a poem is an internal or centripetal verification. Strict external verification is not essentially aesthetic.[174] However, Jarrett goes

---

[171] Frye, p. 76.
[172] Peter A. Carmichael, "Aesthetic Knowledge", *The Journal of Philosophy*, LVIII (July 6, 1961), p. 386.
[173] *Ibid.*, p. 387.
[174] James L. Jarrett, "Verification in the Reading of Poetry", *The Journal of Philosophy*, XLVI (July 7, 1949), p. 444.

on to say that truth can be introduced in poetry if it is not extraneous. Poetry means in terms of our experience.[175] Jarrett here, by mentioning the relation of poetry to experience, sounds a note of weakness in the verisimilitude position that the truth of poetry is purely internal. Wimsatt puts his finger squarely on this weakness by noting that if the truth of poetry were internal "then indeed would poetry achieve the status of a pure idealism".[176] Wimsatt notes that poetry also needs truth of a correspondence type. "Poetry is a complex kind of verbal construction in which the dimension of coherence is by various techniques of implication greatly enhanced and thus generates an extra dimension of correspondence to reality, the symbolic or analogical." [177]

2. Correspondence as "true"

We must then move on to the second sense in which we say a poem is "true", namely, in having some type of correspondence to "reality". First, it needs to be noted that one can consistently say that poetic metaphors, metaphorical images, do not refer and yet still say they correspond to "reality". "Refer" is a technical term carrying overtones of strict verification. One can quite easily admit that strict verification is totally irrelevant to poetry while still maintaining that it expresses "reality". Several of the theorists analyzed do precisely this. Wheelwright says that poetic statements assert lightly.[178] Yet he also says: "Poetry has its deepest roots in metaphysics." [179]

Wellek and Warren also attempt the rather delicate task of keeping the poem free from the natural world, free from imitation, while also allowing it some deeper significance. They argue that literary language differs from both ordinary language and scientific language. Signs in science are arbitrary. Also a univocal relation between sign and referent is sought. Literary language, on the other hand, is ambiguous and highly connotative. It not only refers but expresses. Thus literature as art "imposes some kind of framework which takes the statement of the work out of the world of reality".[180] Still the separation must not be too radical. In order to solve this paradox of relatedness yet difference from the world they argue that the referent in literature is in the imagina-

---

[175]   *Ibid.*, pp. 440-43.
[176]   Wimsatt, *The Verbal Icon*, p. 241.
[177]   *Ibid.*
[178]   Wheelwright, *The Burning Fountain*, p. 68.
[179]   *Ibid.*, p. 269.
[180]   Wellek and Warren, p. 14.

tion, not in real space and time. The work thus has fictionality.[181]

John Hospers treats the same problem. He argues that art does not give truth in the same sense as does science. Art does not photograph nature.[182] If the poet were supposed to give such truth he would have to fear the constant invasion of the scientist. Works of literature only incidentally state truth. Hospers would agree with Hungerland that to convert literary insights into science would yield poor literature as well as poor science.[183]

However, Hospers recognizes that literature, of all the arts, is most dependent on life values. Thus literature cannot claim, as can the arts of some visual media, that truth is totally irrelevant.[184] Hospers solves this problem by distinguishing "truth about" from "truth to". Scientific truth is truth about. Truth in literature is always truth to. Some characters show truth to in that in them essential human truths appear. Closely related to characters as true to are actions which are true to life. Finally, a felt quality of experience may be said to be "true to". In these cases "the poet has intuited a viable essence which we too can grasp".[185] "Thus in a way we *can* verify what the artist has presented; we can verify his insights in our own further observations of people and actions." [186] Hospers then would see the truth of Shakespeare's metaphor as truth to, truth to the nature of time as it is related to human accomplishments.

c. *Epoche suspends Naturalistic and "Reality" Judgments*

The above theorists, Jarrett, Wimsatt, Wheelwright, Wellek and Warren, and Hospers, argue then that poetry, and thus metaphorical images, do not refer to the natural world but do refer to reality. To argue that metaphorical images are related to reality would require a treatment of the relation of the poem to reality, a claim which could only be made in the context of a full-blown theory of poetry as well as an epistemology of how reality reveals itself. I leave the problem of whether metaphor reveals reality to the literary critics because such a problem is concerned with the essence of poetry. This book is concerned with metaphorical *meaning*. I have argued that reading as *epoche* is the stance appropriate

---

181   *Ibid.*, p. 16.
182   Hospers, *Meaning and Truth in the Arts*, p. 162.
183   Hungerland, p. 62.
184   Hospers, *Meaning and Truth in the Arts*, p. 213.
185   *Ibid.*, p. 180.
186   *Ibid.*, p. 173.

to discovering such meaning. Tomas argued that in aesthetic vision one suspends naturalistic claims. He explicitly cited such a suspension as the phenomenological method. I argue that Husserl recognized precisely this neutrality of the aesthetic perception, thus justifying Tomas' reference. The other theorists, Ogden and Richards, Zink, Frye, Wimsatt and Langer, although they by no means explicitly recognize the relevance of the *epoche* to the reading of poetry, agree that natural reference is irrelevant to poetic statements. I take their arguments as supporting my contention that we do in fact read poetic metaphor with the openness of the *epoche*, with the suspension of naturalistic judgments. Reference or correspondence is irrelevant to metaphorical meaning because we read with openness. The *epoche* is a stance of contemplation. Thus the images of metaphorical language are looked at, not through. They are not photographic negatives to be lined up with the world.

However, the *epoche* does not just suspend naturalistic assumptions. "The *philosophical epoche*, which we propose to adopt, should consist, when explicitly formulated, in this, that in *respect of the theoretical content of all previous philosophy, we shall abstain from passing any judgment at all, and that our whole discussion shall respect the limits imposed by this abstention.*" [187] Husserl might easily have mentioned all philosophical systems of reality. Thus in reading poetic metaphors we suspend not only the naturalistic stance but reality judgments also. We bracket the "shallow" world of our physical experience and the "deep" world of reality. I am not choosing sides in the debate whether the poem should express reality or be enjoyed in itself, and thus, whether it is criticism or not of a poem if it does not fit such a system. I am arguing that to discover metaphorical meaning, reading, as the first act, suspends both naturalistic and metaphysical categories. The most significant problem with regard to poetic metaphor in this work is what the metaphor means, not is it true. Metaphorical images thus neither refer to the natural world nor do they express reality. In other words, I am arguing that in order to find or discover a metaphor's meaning it is essential, so to speak, to step back from or bracket our naturalistic presuppositions and our reality presuppositions. I am not claiming that once the meaning or relevant sense of a metaphor is found that it is *not* the purpose of poetry to step back into the world or assert about reality. It may be that the essence of poetry is to be myth. Rein-

---

[187]   Husserl, pp. 80-81.

hold Niebuhr correctly argues that myth is poetry believed.[188] Thus to take a metaphor as expressing reality is to take the metaphor mythically. I may read "Lines Composed a Few Miles above Tintern Abbey" as a myth, as an assertion about the cosmos. I may read "Paradise Lost" aesthetically and reject its assertions about the cosmos. At least it is clear that understanding of the *meaning* of either does not require belief in their respective world views; that is, reading them as myths.

Thus far my conclusions are that on reading metaphor: (1) images occur; (2) such images are not free; (3) such images are quasi-sensuous experiences; and (4) such images are contemplated as ends in themselves which do not necessarily correspond with either the physical world or "reality".

I have proposed to show how metaphor fits the general semantical conclusions on poetic language of the former chapter while still having its own peculiarities. The above summary somewhat circumscribes metaphor. Metaphor can now be distinguished from sound exploiting elements in the poem, such as rhyme and rhythm, on the the grounds that the former includes images "seen" or "heard" while the latter exploits impressions actually heard. However, the essential uniqueness of metaphor has not yet been distinguished from *descriptions* in the poem which function iconically. For example, in this stanza of "The Waste Land"

> After the torchlight red on sweaty faces
> After the frosty silence in the gardens
> After the agony in stony places
> The shouting and the crying
> > (T. S. Eliot, "The Waste Land", ll. 322-325)

the first line is highly imagistic yet is not metaphorical. Eliot is highly talented in getting the reader to "see", "hear", "smell", "taste", and "touch" through his descriptions. Metaphor, however, involves an additional essential element.

6. *Imagery and Seeing As*

Metaphor involves not only such iconic descriptions, but *involves the intuitive relation of seeing as between parts of the description. In* Shakespeare's metaphor not only is there an iconic description of time and a beggar but of *time seen as a beggar*. Metaphor involves not only

---

[188] Bewkes *et al.*, pp. 119-20.

a tenor and vehicle, to use Richards' terms, thrown together in a sentence, but the positive relation of seeing as between tenor and vehicle. I shall clarify what I mean by seeing as by analyzing Wittgenstein's understanding of the concept of "seeing as".

a. *Wittgenstein's Analysis of "Seeing As"*

Wittgenstein begins his analysis by noting we use "see" in two senses which have categorically different "objects" of sight. We say "I see this" and also "I see a likeness". Wittgenstein calls the latter seeing "noticing an aspect".[189] To illustrate "noticing an aspect" or "seeing as" Wittgenstein introduces Jastrow's duck-rabbit drawing. (Also he uses other examples.) The question then is: If one viewer sees a duck while another sees a rabbit, or the same person sees both at different times is their or his perception changed or is it the same? Wittgenstein says yes and no. " 'Seeing as . . .' is not part of perception. And for that reason it is like seeing and again not like." [190]

The key to Wittgenstein's thought on how "seeing as" differs from "seeing" turns on the relation of "seeing as" to images or to the imagination.

The concept of an aspect is akin to the concept of an image. In other words: the concept 'I am now seeing it as. . . .' is akin to 'I am now having this image'.

.   .   .   .

Seeing an aspect and imagining are subject to the will. There is such an order as "Imagine *this*", and also: "Now see the figure like *this*"; but not: "Now see this leaf green".[191]

In other words, to see an aspect demands imagination.[192]

Wittgenstein's thought is brilliant here. He means that "seeing" does not require the will but "seeing as" does. Thus the substratum of "seeing as" is "the mastery of a technique".[193] Thus:

It is only if someone *can do,* has learnt, is master of, such-and-such, that it makes sense to say he has had *this* experience. (Seeing as)
And if this sounds crazy, you need to reflect that the *concept* of seeing is modified here.[194] (Parenthetical phrase mine)

---

189   *Investigations*, p. 193.
190   *Ibid.*, p. 197.
191   *Ibid.*, p. 213.
192   *Ibid.*, p. 207.
193   *Ibid.*, p. 208.
194   *Ibid.*, p. 209.

Since "seeing as" is based on ability to execute a technique while "seeing" is not, it is quite conceivable that there are aspect-blind persons who can "see" but cannot "see as". Such a blindness is "*akin* to the lack of a 'musical ear' ".[195]

Further, in answer to the question whether one is seeing something different or merely interpreting what is seen in a different way, Wittgenstein chooses the former alternative. His reason is that when we interpret we form a hypothesis which can be verified while "seeing as" can be verified as little as "I am seeing red". "Seeing as" is not an interpretation.[196]

Wittgenstein concludes from his comparison of "seeing as" to "seeing" and "interpreting" that "the flashing of an aspect on us seems half visual experience, half thought".[197]

It is quite important to note that Wittgenstein denies that he has derived this analysis from introspection. Here again he argues his method is grammatical. He is quite explicit in noting that he is analyzing the *concept* of "seeing as", not the experience of seeing as. This is a conceptual (*begriffliches*) investigation not a causal one.[198] He cautions: "Do not try to analyze your own inner experience." [199] The aspect seen is neither the drawing nor some secret picture which I carry within myself.[200] Careful attention to my psychic state is of no use because it would only discover what is now going on in myself.[201] In order to substantiate this point Wittgenstein argues that if asked what we see while looking at the duck-rabbit we do not say "Now I am seeing it as a picture-rabbit" but simply, "It's a rabbit." [202] Wittgenstein's subtle point here is that the former answer would be a misunderstanding of the question, a misunderstanding eventuating in a statement of what *I* was doing at a certain time instead of a statement of what was seen. Wittgenstein does not deny that the game in which the statement "Now I am seeing this or that" is appropriate can be played. He is not explicit here but seems to mean that when playing this game, a game in which the statement "Now I am seeing..." is appropriate, that the technique of the simpler game, the game in which the statement "It's a rabbit"

[195]   *Ibid.*, p. 214.
[196]   *Ibid.*, p. 212.
[197]   *Ibid.*, p. 197.
[198]   *Ibid.*, p. 203.
[199]   *Ibid.*, p. 204.
[200]   *Ibid.*, p. 196.
[201]   *Ibid.*, p. 219.
[202]   *Ibid.*, pp. 194-95.

is appropriate, is presupposed.[203] Wittgenstein's point here is perhaps similar to his argument that pointing is a complex game. He did not deny there is a game of ostensive defining, but did insist that it assumed a simpler game. A great deal of stage setting in language is presupposed. At any rate, whether this is Wittgenstein's intended meaning or not does not obscure the point that he extends his attack on inner experience to "seeing as". Even in "seeing as" we do not report on our private experiences. Rather the way we are seeing a figure, for example, the duck-rabbit, manifests itself in "fine shades of behaviour".[204]

b. *"Seeing As" and "Recognizing"*

Noel Fleming in an excellent article shows how "seeing as" is related to "recognizing". He argues quite correctly that being able to recognize depends on being able to see as. However, in cases of recognition it is required: (a) that the object in fact be what it is recognized as; and (b) that it was known at the time of recognition that it was that object.[205] On the other hand, "seeing as", for example, in seeing the picture-rabbit, leaves open both the question: (a) whether it is actually a rabbit; and (b) whether the seer thought it was a picture-rabbit or that he recognized a picture-rabbit there.[206] Thus, "recognizing x as y entails but is not entailed by seeing x as y, where seeing x as y and recognizing it as y are no more two different things than Bannister's running the mile in under four minutes is a different thing from his breaking the world record".[207] Stated slightly differently, "to recognize x as y is to see x as y, knowing or believing correctly that x is y".[208]

It is quite important to emphasize that the relation between metaphorical tenor and vehicle is one of "seeing as" not one of "recognition". We do not on reading Shakespeare's metaphor recognize that time is a greedy beggar; we only see time as a greedy beggar. Only with regard to dead metaphors is it correct to say we "recognize" the object named. For example, if I am leading a hike and see a broken bottle and say: "Watch out, there is a sharp bottleneck", I would correctly be

---

[203]   *Ibid.*, pp. 208-09.
[204]   *Ibid.*, p. 203.
[205]   Noel Fleming, "Recognizing and Seeing As", *The Philosophical Review*, LXVI (April, 1957), p. 161.
[206]   *Ibid.*, pp. 173-74.
[207]   *Ibid.*, p. 174.
[208]   *Ibid.*

said to have recognized a bottleneck. I would satisfy Fleming's conditions in that: (a) it actually is a bottleneck; and (b) it was known at the time to be a bottleneck. Shakespeare's metaphor does not fill the first condition. The fact is that time is not a beggar, while the bottleneck now is taken to mean quite literally the narrow top of the bottle.[209] It is conceivable that time as a beggar could become, through an idiomatic quirk, a literal phrase. Perhaps instead of "time causes us to forget past deeds" this hypothetical language might say "time begs", meaning by this last hypothetical idiom no more and no less than the former phrase, just as "neck of a bottle" means no more and no less than the top, narrowed portion of a bottle. Then we could recognize cases in which "time has begged" just as we recognize cases in which a "bottleneck" is seen.

Fleming correctly argues that seeing as leaves open the possibility, with relation to the duck-rabbit, as to whether it is actually a duck or a rabbit. Aldrich argues that seeing as does not just leave open the possibility that x is not y. Rather to see x as y means that x is not y.[210] "Seeing as" applied to poetic metaphor requires Aldrich's stronger statement. Not only in Shakespeare's metaphor is the possibility left open that time is not a beggar, but this possibility is actualized. Time not only might not be a beggar; it is not a beggar. The tension theories of metaphor see this point quite clearly. Berggren quite correctly notes that metaphors involve at least dual references which are separated by recognized type boundaries. In metaphor such boundaries are transgressed but not obliterated.[211] I have argued in the Introduction that this tension between the metaphorical parts, between tenor and vehicle, is lost either in literal dead metaphors or in mythical metaphors. As Barfield argued, poetic metaphors presuppose a body of prose knowledge because such metaphors represent a *deliberate* yoking of unlikes by an individual artificer.[212] In being a deliberate yoking of unlikes metaphor differs from three similar cases. First, it is not the unconscious identification of the metaphorical subject and predicate of the mythical thinker noted by Barfield. Second, it is not the dead literal metaphor in which the relation between subject and predicate is no

---

[209] There is not necessarily a category mistake *in* a metaphor since a metaphor may compare members of the same logical type. The category mistake would be to take the metaphor as a literal statement.
[210] Aldrich, *Philosophy and Phenomenological Research*, XXIII, p. 57.
[211] Berggren, "An Analysis of Metaphorical Meaning and Truth", p. 383.
[212] Barfield, p. 81.

longer fruitful, in which, for example, the neck of a bottle no longer suggests anything about the top of a bottle. Third, it is not a false case of recognition, though this is perhaps the nearest relative of the three to poetic metaphor. In a case of recognition which fails, when our distant friend Jack turns out not to be Jack at all, we are likely to explain our mistake by saying: "So-and-so had on a suit like Jack's." In metaphor we also are interested in the *relevant* relation between x and y, between Jack's appearance and that of the person thought to be Jack; but metaphor differs in that we are not looking for a reason to explain our mistake since we have not strictly committed a mistake. We never did think time was a beggar. Thus Fleming's argument that seeing as leaves open the possibility that, for example, x is not y is not strong enough for poetic metaphor. In poetic metaphor this possibility is actualized; time is not a beggar. Explicit metaphors have grammatical red flags to disclaim a literal interpretation. Implicit metaphors are recognized by their tension with scientific knowledge.[213] We recognize Hopkins' implicit metaphor

> Oh the mind, mind has mountains; cliffs of fall
> Frightful, sheer, no-man-fathomed. Hold them cheap
> May who ne'er hung there.
> (Gerard Manley Hopkins, "Carrion Comfort", ll. 23-25)

because of its tension with our body of knowledge. In neither implicit nor explicit metaphor is the metaphorical vehicle "recognized' as the tenor, but always "seen as" the tenor.

Recognition is appropriate to the naturalistic stance, as Fleming's first condition emphasizes in saying that x must not only be seen as y but *actually* be y. Metaphor, in always keeping a tension between x and y because x is not y, forces the reader out of the natural, literal stance, thus supporting my contention that reading as *epoche,* which establishes precisely the same type of distance, is appropriate to metaphor. The metaphor itself helps to establish the distance necessary to the first step in discovering metaphorical meaning; namely, the step of reading. The metaphor calls for a relevant relation between x and y, between time and beggars, minds and mountains, but not for a relation of recognition. A relevant relation is one in which x is like y in *some* senses but not *all* senses.

---

[213] This remark is not inconsistent with my claim that reading is an *epoche* because I have not identified, though I have related, reading, recognition and analysis of the metaphor.

c. *Extension of Wittgenstein's Analysis of "Seeing As" to Poetic Metaphor*

Virgil Aldrich perceptively sees that Wittgenstein's analysis of "seeing as" is a propitious place to extend Wittgenstein's analysis to poetry. He notes, following Wittgenstein, that the aspects of the duck-rabbit example are not strictly perceived. Thus reporting on the aspects seen is similar to reporting on images.[214] Aldrich is, of course, closely following Wittgenstein where he argued that reporting an aspect is akin to reporting on images and that seeing an aspect requires imagination.

Aldrich goes beyond Wittgenstein in arguing that the image exhibiting function of language is fused with literal language and that both are initially present in plain talk. There seem to be rules for this image exhibiting function of language, this "picture thinking", which is related to seeing an aspect; and the poet is precisely an expert in these rules.[215] Aldrich is correct in noting that the pictorial, the iconic, the image exciting power of language, is latent in ordinary language. The poet is not a magician whose images in his metaphorical expression appear *ex nihilo*. The power to function iconically is in the language, in the medium of the poet in as real a sense as ability to be formed in certain ways is in the medium of the sculptor, in the marble. The poet transforms the function of language, but it is still language which is transformed.

Aldrich further notes that the thrill of revelation, and I might add the thrill of reading Shakespeare's metaphor and seeing time as a beggar, is the same type of thrill one has on seeing an aspect in the duck-rabbit.[216] Speaking of the thrill of seeing an aspect of the duck-rabbit may seem to be a trivial point which borders on psychologism. I shall not debate this point. However, this thrill is significant in poetic metaphor. Without the thrill, the freshness of the seeing as, a metaphor is a trite metaphor. Triteness is a valid ground for literary criticism of a poetic metaphor. No poet now could dare use the metaphor: "My love is like a red, red rose...."

Aldrich's clue that Wittgenstein's "seeing as" is relevant to poetic language is left as a clue. This work further develops Wittgenstein's thought in the following ways. Metaphor involves seeing as in a quite significant way. In fact, *seeing as is the fundamental distinguishing*

[214] Aldrich, *Mind*, LXVII, p. 73.
[215] *Ibid.*, pp. 75-76.
[216] *Ibid.*, p. 78.

characteristic of metaphor in poetry. Wittgenstein's understanding, however, needs modification.

1. *Differences with Wittgenstein*

First, "seeing as" with regard to the duck-rabbit is "seeing as" connected with a physically existing *Gestalt* on the page. The seeing as with
regard to Shakespeare's brilliant metaphor in which time is seen as a
beggar is not related to a physical *Gestalt* on the page. The visual similarity between the words in the metaphorical tenor and the metaphorical
vehicle is trivial to say the least. *Metaphorical seeing as is a seeing as
between elements of an imagistic description.* I have used the phrase
"imagistic description" instead of "images" because the seeing as is not
necessarily between two imagistic elements. Either the tenor or the
vehicle in a metaphor may be "image poor". In fact, the tenor in
Shakespeare's metaphor, the tenor "time", is quite abstract. The iconic
language in this metaphor, the imagistic fullness of this description, is
all in the vehicle, the "beggar". Quite often the reason for using metaphor instead of an iconic description is that only through the metaphor
or perhaps most economically through the metaphor can the abstract
tenor be iconicized. Shakespeare would have had quite a difficult task
in trying to get a description of time to reach the iconicity which his
metaphor so economically achieved. Further, there are cases, though
rare, in which the vehicle is abstract or at least less iconic than the tenor.
For example, in Eliot's metaphor

> Streets that follow like a tedious argument
> Of insidious intent,
> To lead you to an overwhelming question. . . .
>   (T. S. Eliot, "Love Song of J. Alfred Prufrock", ll. 8-10)

the vehicle, the tedious argument, is less iconic than the street. In
summary, the first difference between my analysis of seeing as and
Wittgenstein's analysis is that my analysis is about a seeing as between
elements of an imagistic description.

Second, Wittgenstein quite clearly states that he is analyzing the
concept of "seeing as".[217] He argued that his analysis of "seeing as" is
not an analysis of an internal state on which he introspects. His investigation here as always is claimed to be grammatical. Thus, in using the
words "seeing as" we are not interested in internal and private experi-

---

[217] *Investigations*, p. 203.

ences but in fine shades of behavior. Such subtle ways of behavior tell us whether the person is seeing the duck-rabbit as a duck or as a rabbit. Thus there are "tokens" (*Anzeichen*) which indicate "seeing as"; there are fine shades of behavior.[218]

Wittgenstein's use of the word "token" is very interesting here. "Token" implies that even though fine shades of behavior reveal that we are seeing something a certain way, such fine shades of behavior are not equivalent to or definitive of "seeing as". If Wittgenstein is taken seriously here he implies that the experience of which these fine shades of behavior are a *token of* is at least relevant to the language-game in which "seeing as" functions. Words which are tokens imply the relevance of that which they are tokens of. This is a very queer way for Wittgenstein to be talking. In his analysis of "pain" he went to all extremes to deny that pain words and pain behavior were "tokens" for some internal sensation. I argued that his refusal to admit the relevance of the sensation of pain to the language-game in which pain words are used led him to make the meaning of "pain" equivalent to certain behavior. I argued that such an equivalence leaves his analysis of "pain" in grave difficulties. "Token" then could mean that Wittgenstein recognized that "seeing as" is some type of intellectual act which one's language and behavior indicate. If this is the case Wittgenstein would seem to admit for "seeing as" what he would not admit for "pain", namely, that the words are indications or tokens of an experience. Whether or not Wittgenstein meant for his word "token" to be taken this seriously is pure conjecture. I rather doubt that he did. The only way that the act of seeing as could be distinguished in some minimal way from verbal and subtle behavioral manifestations is if some internal experience of seeing as were recognized as relevant to the game in which "seeing as" is used. Thus Wittgenstein would have to appeal to some type of self-examination or introspection, an appeal which he definitely intended to avoid.

However, even if Wittgenstein does not distinguish the act of seeing as from the tokens of seeing as, I argue that such a distinction must be made. I quite agree with Wittgenstein that unless seeing as manifests itself in the public game of analyzing poetic metaphors, unless there are fine shades of behavior, then seeing as is irrelevant to metaphorical meaning. Production of an analysis is a necessary condition of knowing a metaphor's meaning. I here agree with Wittgenstein that the verb

---

[218] *Ibid.*, pp. 206-07.

"know" is closely related to the verb "can" or "is able". However, I also emphasize that reading is a necessary condition for grasping metaphorical meaning. Thus one's analysis of Shakespeare's metaphor, one's analysis of the relevant senses in which time is a beggar, is a token or clue indicating that one has sensitively read the metaphor. The evidence of seeing as is not equivalent to the act of seeing as. Thus I am analyzing not just the concept of "seeing as" but the act of seeing as. I intentionally remove the quotes from seeing as.

By *insisting on the distinction between the act and its result,* the seeing as and the analysis it produces, *I provide a logical means by which such an analysis is denied equivalence with seeing as,* a means which Wittgenstein failed to provide with regard to pain statements and pain behavior. Thus the statement of the relevant aspects of a metaphor is never equivalent to the experience-act of seeing as with regard to that metaphor. The essential reason no equivalence relation is possible is that in seeing as thought and sensation are fused. Because of the element of sensation language about the metaphor is never equivalent to the experience of reading that metaphor. Wittgenstein recognized this fusion of thought and experience in arguing that seeing as with regard to the duck-rabbit is a queer type of perception in which the seer is both active and passive. "Seeing as" is a technique; it requires imagination. One can see the duck-rabbit figure and still be aspect-blind and be unable to see either a duck or a rabbit. Wittgenstein recognized that "seeing as" has the queer status of being "half visual experience, half thought".[219] Wittgenstein would agree with Kant that in this type of perception the self is active. Here concepts and percepts touch. Since in seeing as thought and sensation are fused, statements about the experience-act of seeing as can no more get the totality of an experience-act of seeing as than can statements about red get the sensation of red. Both types of statements have, in Wittgenstein's terminology, ostensive meaning. The purpose of language in both cases is to indicate or point to a context, not to be a verbal equivalent of that context. The explicitly formulated analysis of a metaphor is open to reinterpretation in view of the experience-act of seeing as. There is never a closed case in which we have got the meaning of a metaphor. An analysis of a metaphor's meaning is always openended.

In summary, my analysis of seeing as differs from Wittgenstein's in that metaphorical seeing as: (1) is between elements of an imagistic de-

[219]   *Ibid.*, p. 197.

scription; and (2) requires a distinction between the experience-act of seeing as and tokens or manifestations of this act. I am not just analyzing the concept of "seeing as" but also the act of seeing as. The nature of seeing as, being an experience-act, requires the distinction between itself and verbal analyses of its content.

2. *Positive analysis*

I shall now more positively analyze the act of seeing as. The duck-rabbit figure which can be seen in two ways is an ambiguous figure. The duck-rabbit *Gestalt* then is a figure common to both ducks and rabbits. I argue that the relation between the duck, the duck-rabbit and the rabbit is a transitive relationship. I shall symbolize the three by A, B and C respectively. If A is like B, the duck like the duck-rabbit, and B is like C, the duck-rabbit like the rabbit, then A is like C, the duck like the rabbit. In Wittgenstein's example we are given B and the problem is to see A and C. In metaphor the problem is different though the act of seeing as is similar. *In metaphor we are given A and C and the problem is to see B*. B in the duck-rabbit is the common *Gestalt* form between ducks and rabbits. In the metaphor B is the relevant senses in which A is like C. In Shakespeare's metaphor we are given A and C, time and a beggar; and the purpose of seeing as is to discover B, the senses in which time is like a beggar, the common *Gestalt,* figuratively speaking, between time and beggars.

In reading metaphor with openness we let the image auras of A and C play against each other in order to discover B. As Richards would put it, we must develop "the habit of reading so as to allow the fullest development to imagery in its sensory aspect . . .".[220] As Empson argues poetic language carries with it a wealth of ambiguous implication. The form of ambiguity forces the reader to open his mind to possible associations.[221] Implicative fullness is the distinguishing mark of poetic language.[222] As Kaplan and Kris argue poetic language does not simply tolerate ambiguity but demands it.[223] As Berggren notes, one of the basic tendencies of metaphor is to be "centrifugal"; that is, it implicates wider contexts.[224] These theorists agree that *the ambiguous image aura of language is essential to metaphorical seeing as.*

[220]   Richards, *Principles of Literary Criticism*, p. 123.
[221]   William Empson, *Seven Types of Ambiguity* (London, Chatto & Windus, 1956), p. 91.
[222]   *Ibid.*, pp. 29-30.
[223]   Kaplan and Kris, p. 422.
[224]   Berggren, "An Analysis of Metaphorical Meaning and Truth", pp. 399-401.

However, *seeing as*, in being the means by which relevant aspects of the imagery are selected, is *definitive of imagery*. In performing the experience-act of seeing as we decide which of the body of imagery aroused[225] by the metaphor is essential to the metaphor, and thus which aspects of the imagery are part of the intentional structure of the metaphor. *Seeing as is an intuitive experience-act by which one selects from the quasi-sensory mass of imagery one has on reading metaphor the relevant aspects of such imagery.* I shall explain my generalization more fully.

First, in saying that seeing as is an "experience-act" which is definitive of imagery or selects the relevant aspects of the imagery excited by a metaphor, I mean to emphasize that seeing as has the inherent duality of having both active and passive stages which merge into each other. As my reading as *epoche* emphasized, we must read the metaphor so as to allow the original right of all data. Such a reading is an active passivity which allows, in Richards' words, "the fullest development to imagery in its sensory aspect...".[226] Quite often the relevant way in which the metaphorical vehicle is like the tenor seems to dawn on us as an insight. For example, in reading Shakespeare's metaphor the sense in which time is like a beggar seems to dawn on or come to us. We feel as if something has been shown us. The word "experience" in my phrase "experience-act" emphasizes the necessity of experiencing in a full sense the auditory qualities of the metaphor and the necessity of quasi-experiencing the imagery involved. The word "experience" emphasizes an open receptivity to the metaphor. On the other hand, the relevant aspects of metaphorical imagery may be seen only after our active interrogation of the metaphor in an inner dialogue or actual verbal dialogue with oneself or others. The poet may require considerable effort on our part to see the vehicle as the tenor. The word "act" in my phrase emphasizes the necessity of an act of formulating the relevant sense of the metaphor. This emphasis on the active nature of seeing as agrees with Wittgenstein's statement that: "The grammar of the word 'knows' is evidentally closely related to that of 'can', 'is able to'."[227] I argue similarly that a necessary condition of being said to "know" or "understand" a metaphor's meaning is doing something; namely, analyzing the sense of the metaphor. In summary, we try to let the meta-

---

[225] The phrase "imagery aroused" should not be taken as separating the metaphor from its imagery. See above, p. 137.
[226] Richards, *Principles of Literary Criticism*, p. 123.
[227] *Investigations*, # 150.

phor reveal itself and at the same time we interrogate it. This duality of activity and passivity merge into each other and both function in every act of reading a metaphor. Thus in clarifying this dual tendency of seeing as I clarify further the nature of reading, for seeing as is a specialized form of reading.

Seeing as is the experience-act where the second and third necessary conditions for understanding a metaphor's meaning, namely, the conditions of reading and analyzing the metaphor, come to focus. This activity and passivity are the metaphorical counterparts of the "half visual experience, half thought" which Wittgenstein correctly asserted of seeing an aspect with regard to the duck-rabbit.[228] If we are successful in seeing the metaphorical vehicle as the tenor then we see the relevant aspects of the metaphorical imagery. Seeing as is then another and very basic reason why metaphorical imagery is not free. Only relevant imagery functions in the experience-act of seeing as. As Kahn argues, the critic is one gifted in selecting relevant aspects of the experience which is the work. [229]

The second clarification of my generalization above is latent in my allusion in the prior paragraph to a "successful" case of seeing as and latent in my calling seeing as an *"intuitive* experience-act". I mean that seeing as is an irreducible, primitive accomplishment which either occurs or does not occur. This irreducible nature of seeing as is related to the point already argued that the experience-act of seeing as must be distinguished from language about that experience-act. Seeing as is not reducible to a specific analysis. Nor is seeing as reducible to a specific set of procedural rules. There is no set of rules which will inevitably overcome aspect-blindness. Literary analysis is an art, and like all arts it is a step beyond its rules. Still the critic is able to communicate with other readers of the metaphor. In analyzing Shakespeare's metaphor appeal to conventions or physical objects might help. If someone did not understand the word "wallet" in Shakespeare's metaphor we might refer him to a dictionary or we might show him a wallet. Criteria can help fill in gaps in our background and thus help to understand the metaphor. In fact, knowledge of the criteria of the words in Shakespeare's metaphor is a necessary condition for understanding the metaphor's meaning. However, knowledge of criteria is not a sufficient

[228]   *Ibid.,* p. 197.
[229]   Sholom J. Kahn, "What Does a Critic Analyze? (On a Phenomenological Approach to Literature)", *Philosophy and Phenomenological Research*, XIII (Dec., 1952), p. 242.

condition for understanding the metaphor. One might well know the criteria for "time" and the criteria for a "beggar" and still not be able to see time as a beggar. An understanding of the metaphor, a grasp of the relevant senses in which time is like a beggar, requires an openness to the text, a sensitivity to the imagery involved. Shakespeare in this particular text does not leave much room for intuition because he lists some of the relevant senses in which time is a beggar. In a metaphor such as this one by Dickinson

> After great pain a formal feeling comes—
> The nerves sit ceremonious like tombs;
> (Emily Dickinson, "After Great Pain a Formal Feeling Comes", ll. 1-2)

intuition is much more important. Here, since the poet does not fully develop the relevant senses in which nerves sit like tombs, one is more dependent on the intuitive talent of seeing as.

If the reader is unable to see in what sense nerves sit like tombs, one would proceed to help that person see nerves sitting as tombs in a way similar to that one would use to help one see the duck-rabbit as a duck or a rabbit. In this latter case of aspect-blindness we might say: "Don't you see that these narrow pointed peninsulas are the rabbit's ears and this round curve is his nose. The rabbit's eye is here", and so on. We identify parts of the common *Gestalt* with the rabbit or duck. If we are successful the person is apt to say: "Oh, yes. Now I see", meaning that he sees the duck or the rabbit. One would proceed in a similar way in getting an aspect-blind person to see how nerves sit like tombs. The hypothetical conversation might run: "Don't you see that a great pain, a great tragedy, stuns one into a stupor. One goes about one's daily tasks in a formal, unfeeling way. The nerves sit like tombs. Instead of the warmth of life which they formally felt, now all is precise, numb, ceremonious and cold like stones in a cemetery." We try to help someone see as with regard to metaphor by citing relevant senses in which the vehicle is seen as the tenor. Metaphorical seeing as differs from seeing as with respect to the duck-rabbit in that in the latter case one is given the common *Gestalt* and the problem is to see the duck or rabbit. In the metaphor nerves and tombs are given and the problem is to see their common form. If we are successful the subject will say: "Oh, yes. Now I see", meaning that he sees the common qualities. If we are not successful all we can do is try some more loose and informal reasoning, more metaphors and analogies. As Bouwsma would argue, the meaning is in the language. It cannot be gotten out strictly in translations or restatements. We can only suggest that the metaphor be reread.[230] As Wimsatt perceptively argues: "Criticism of poetry is like 1.414 ... or 3.1416 ..., not all it would be, yet all that can be had and very useful."[231] Wimsatt means that the critic in explaining, in trying to get one to see as, cannot hand over a meaning in a clean, neat package. The critic points to the poem and calls on analogies in much the same way that one does in trying to get someone to see the duck-rabbit as a rabbit. *In either case seeing as is an irreducible intuitive experience-act. It is categorically impossible to reduce seeing as to a set of rules or criteria.* There are no magic three or magic seven number of rules which will guarantee that everyone will now be able to analyze metaphors, now see nerves sit as tombs.

Now I move on to the third clarification of my understanding of the experience-act of seeing as. The word "intuition" as understood here not only emphasizes that seeing as is irreducible but also that seeing as has "grounds". "Intuition" usually implies, and certainly does here, some type of insight. In arguing that seeing as is irreducible to rules or specific analyses I am not saying that seeing as will occur with regard to metaphorical elements juxtaposed on the basis of fiat. Shakespeare and Dickinson were active in creating their metaphors in that time had not been compared to a beggar nor nerves sitting to tombs; but in neither case did the poet achieve a metaphor by the sheer force of his or her creative will, by sheer fiat. *The metaphor establishes a relation but also reveals a relation.* Saying that metaphor reveals a relation seems to deny my methodology which brackets the natural world and reality because a relation revealed implies that *in fact* the metaphorical parts were similar to begin with. Thus we seem back in a correspondence view between metaphorical imagery and the world or reality. My answer is that what we call "similar" is defined ex post facto by the act of seeing as. Our smaller minds can apply the word "similar" after a greater mind has led us to the experience-act of seeing as. Seeing as defines similarity, not vice versa. Only a trite metaphor yokes a tenor and vehicle which we all know to be similar. A great poet always surprises us. We are surprised to see time as a beggar or nerves sit like tombs. As Murray puts it, the revelation of metaphor is concerned with uncharted areas.[232]

---

[230]   Elton, p. 95.
[231]   Wimsatt, *The Verbal Icon*, p. 83.
[232]   Irving J. Lee (ed.), *The Language of Wisdom and Folly: Background Reading in Semantics* (New York, Harper and Brothers, 1949), p. 84. (Originally appeared in Gilbert Murray, *Tradition and Progress*, Boston, Houghton Miffin Co., 1922.)

This is another way of saying that metaphor in any creative field, whether literature or physics or philosophy, is always on the cutting edge. The statement of the relevant sense of a metaphor, the similarity between tenor and vehicle, is based on our experience-act of seeing as which occurs while reading metaphor, not vice versa. Metaphor *reveals* a similarity.

If metaphor not only establishes but reveals a relation then one would expect grounds for cases of seeing as which fail. There are grounds for such failures. Of course, the successful cases of seeing as have the qualities lacked by these negative cases.

First, it is quite a valid ground for criticism if the imagery which the poet tries to yoke in his comparison is inconsistent and thus has no validity beyond a forced togetherness. For example, in Joyce Kilmer's metaphor in which a tree is compared to a human person we find these two ajoining couplets.

> A tree whose hungry mouth is pressed
> Against the earth's sweet flowing breast;
> A tree that looks to God all day,
> And lifts her leafy arms to pray;
>
> (Joyce Kilmer, "Trees", ll. 3-6)

Brooks and Warren accurately note the inconsistency of metaphorical imagery here. In the first couplet the roots of the tree are its mouth while in the second its branches are arms. Such a contorted position in which the roots are a mouth and the branches are arms would represent "a strangely deformed human being".[233] The imagery does not yield itself to a consistent seeing as. The imagery which methodologically our reading must assume as purposive does not here bear out this assumption. The imagery here displays the inconsistent or accidental. To use Berggren's term, the imagery here is not "centripetal".[234] It lacks integration.

The second reason the act of seeing as fails is when the imagery is not inconsistent, but undeveloped. A likely candidate for this charge is Hart Crane in his very difficult metaphor in "At Melville's Tomb".

> And wrecks passed without sound of bells,
> The calyx of death's bounty giving back
> A scattered chapter, livid hieroglyph,
> The portent wound in corridors of shells.
>
> (Hart Crane, "At Melville's Tomb", ll. 5-8)

---

[233] Brooks and Warren, p. 288.
[234] Berggren, "An Analysis of Metaphorical Meaning and Truth", pp. 399-402.

The difficulty of this metaphor in the second and third lines (plus other difficulties) provoked the editor who first published this poem, Harriet Monroe, to write Crane for his explanation. Crane replied:

This calyx refers in a double ironic sense both to a cornucopia and the vortex made by a sinking vessel. As soon as the water has closed over a ship this whirlpool sends up broken spars, wreckage, etc., which can be alluded to as *livid hieroglyphs*, making a *scattered chapter* so far as any complete record of the recent ship and her crew is concerned.[235]

Max Eastman quite justifiably reacts to Crane's analysis thus:

No one will deny that these lines with their exegesis reveal in the author a genuine and rare poetic mind and feeling. It is equally certain that without exegesis they reveal little or nothing at all. But this fact does not disturb Hart Crane in the least. *It does not even occur to his mind.* He is not defending his skill in communicating experience. He is defending his integrity in the art of talking to himself in public.[236]

Eastman accuses, sometimes justifiably, certain modern poets, Crane explicitly, of "talking to themselves in public" and practicing the "cult of unintelligibility".[237] The point is that the relation of seeing as between the debris of a wrecked ship and the "livid hieroglyph" is not clear. The intentional structure in the poem seems insufficient for a qualified reader to see the ship's wreckage as a "livid hieroglyph" from the metaphor alone. Since the metaphor's intention is not clear one has to consult the poet's intention, thus becoming susceptible to the "intentional fallacy".

A third reason seeing as may fail is when the imagery is trite or overworked. In Sidney Lanier's "My Springs" a metaphor comparing lover's eyes to springs occurs.

> In the heart of the Hills of Life, I know
> Two springs that with unbroken flow
> Forever pour their lucent streams
> Into my soul's far Lake of Dreams.
>
> (Sidney Lanier, "My Springs", ll. 1-4)

As Brooks and Warren note, such a comparison is by no means new.

The comparison of eyes to pools or springs ... is another cliche, equally dull. These two worn-out images could be given new strength only if the relationship established between them were really expressive and imaginatively justifiable.[238]

---

[235] Quoted in Brooks and Warren, p. 322.
[236] Max Eastman, *The Literary Mind: Its Place in an Age of Science* (New York, Charles Scribner's Sons, 1935), p. 96.
[237] *Ibid.*, pp. 57-122.
[238] Brooks and Warren, p. 302.

Such extremely conventional metaphors border on becoming literal terms. To call eyes springs is not very far from becoming like calling the top of a bottle its neck. In Lanier's metaphor there is a danger that seeing as will be changed to recognition, the tension being lost between tenor and vehicle. A trite metaphor is no longer suggestive. The ambiguous image aura essential to metaphorical seeing as vanishes. In Berggren's terms, trite metaphors no longer are "centrifugal".[239]

The fourth case in which seeing as fails is not due to the poem but the reader. The reader may be inattentive or uninformed in some way which hinders his seeing as. Cases in which one reads a metaphor and finds it unintelligible but then changes his verdict on reading a critical analysis of the metaphor are too numerous to mention specifically. In such cases the reader decides that in fact imagery in a significant relationship of seeing as was embodied in the metaphor but was missed on his first reading.

I have analyzed above four reasons or grounds why seeing as with regard to metaphor fails. In negating these cases we get the reasons metaphorical seeing as occurs. The metaphor is read with an attentive openness; metaphorical imagery yields itself to a consistent seeing as; metaphorical imagery in a relation of seeing as is embodied in the intentional structure of the metaphor; and metaphorical imagery in a relation of seeing as is suggestive and fresh, not degenerating into a case of recognition. Now I shall relate metaphorical seeing as to the two preceding chapters.

C. METAPHOR AND THEORISTS OF POETIC LANGUAGE

Seeing as embodied in the metaphor is the fundamental way in which metaphor fits the generalization on poetic language of the previous chapter. That generalization is that poetic language is that language in which both sense and sound function iconically, thus yielding a fusion of sense and sensa. The poem is a particular thing, a sensuous object, an experience which also means. The poem is particular and universal. Langer argued for the sensuous particularity of the poem which as a presentational symbol is abstracted from the physical and causal order, becoming an image of sensuous contemplation.[240] According to her the poem achieves particularity by being an experience of virtual

---

[239]   Berggren, "An Analysis of Metaphorical Meaning and Truth", p. 399.
[240]   Langer, *Feeling and Form*, p. 47.

life. The poem also is universal in that it is constructed by symbolic transformation, which is Langer's equivalent to Kant's understanding in accordance with the categories. Thus the presentational form of the poem is based in human rationality just as basically as are discursive forms.[241] For Wimsatt the poem is particular through its fullness of descriptive detail which, contrary to Ransom, is not irrelevant but more than usually relevant to the poem.[242] The poem as an icon approaches the sensuous fullness of painting or music.[243] The language of the poem is thick or opaque. The poem is universal because it is of the nature of language to be universal and poetry is an art form of language. Since the logical and counterlogical function iconically the poem has fullness and particularity and, at the same time, more universal meanings. Thus there can be some incomplete mediation between the poem and a critical analysis of it in general terms.[244] The medium theorists recognized that the qualities of the poet's medium are sound and sense. Poetic meaning is fused with its sensuous vehicle. Thus it is untranslatable. To forget either quality of the medium leads to a perversion. The poem is not Brémond's pure sensuous sound nor Herschberger's literal truth vehicle. Further, following Frye a point implicit in Valéry's thought was made explicit; namely, that the poem has sensuous qualities in addition to auditory stimulations. In view of the quasi-sensuous nature of imagery the more comprehensive phrase "fusion of sense and sensa" was chosen over "fusion of sense and sound". The poem fuses sense, sound and imagery.

My analysis of metaphor shows that it, as a specialized part of poetic language, fits the conclusions of these theorists. The minimal or weak conclusion that metaphor is a fusion of sense and sound was established at the beginning of this chapter. The stronger conclusion that metaphor involves imagery related by the experience-act of seeing as has now been established. *Metaphor is a fusion of sense and sensa because the seeing as in the metaphorical structure is half thought, half experience.* On the reading of metaphor one experiences imagery and sound, that is, sensa. This imagery between the tenor and vehicle is related by the experience-act of seeing as thus yielding the relevant senses in which the metaphorical tenor is seen as the vehicle, that is, sense. Thus *in reading metaphor one experiences imagery and sound − sensa −*

[241]   Langer, *Philosophy in a New Key*, pp. 88-91.
[242]   Wimsatt, *The Verbal Icon*, p. 231.
[243]   *Ibid.*
[244]   *Ibid.*, p. 83.

related in a relevant way – sense. In reading, the metaphor presents us with an organized or cognitively significant structure of sound and imagery. The meaning of the metaphor, as is the meaning of other art forms, is in the sensuous structure itself. Here the gap established by Wittgenstein between meaning and its bearer, the bearer with regard to metaphor being imagery and sound, does not exist. The poet is here more akin to the word magician than to Wittgenstein's understanding of meaning.

I emphasize that metaphor is a *fusion* of sense and sensa. One would have more difficulty dividing sense from sensa in a metaphor than in any other poetic element. Metaphorical seeing as between elements of an imagistic description is a quasi-experience. Yet it is also an experience-act eventuating in the meaning or relevant sense of a metaphor. Thus metaphorical imagery related by seeing as is not an interesting sensuous flourish, an embellishment tacked on to metaphorical meaning. As Brooks and Warren argue, poetic imagery must "not be idle and meaningless, dead or inert, or distracting and self-serving, like some foolish ornament that merely calls attention to itself".[245] With Coleridge we must see that image and sense are fused and thus that: "Images are not pillars supporting vacancy, but caryatids sustaining weight; they are not empty casks, but barrels containing meaning." [246] I argue that here thought and sensation are inseparable because the object of reading is a *sensuous object interpreted.* Seeing as is half thought, half experience. The form-content dichotomy does not exist here. Meaning and the quasi-experience of imagery are here fused. The metaphorical imagery which is *quasi-experienced* also *means* in that this fullness of imagery eventuates in relevant common qualities in the experience-act of seeing as. The same imagery which *occurs* also *means.* Metaphor most significantly achieves the poetic ideal that sense and sound shall function iconically, achieving a fusion of sense and sensa in poetic language.

D. WITTGENSTEIN AND METAPHOR

I now argue that this analysis of metaphor, showing that it includes imagery and seeing as, is not susceptible to Wittgenstein's criticism of the inner meaning or inner experience theory. One cannot defend the

---

[245]   Brooks and Warren, p. 272.
[246]   James Volant Baker, *The Sacred River: Coleridge's Theory of the Imagination* (Louisiana State University Press, 1957), pp. 195-96.

analogy between images had while fetching a red flower or continuing a series and images had while reading metaphor.

First, showing one understands the order "fetch me a red flower" and the order "continue the series" can be done in several ways. There are *alternate* ways which will demonstrate understanding. In showing one knows how to continue a series, Wittgenstein notes that several things may happen. The subject may cite the formula and apply it; or he may feel the relief of mental tension and then continue the series; or he may say: "Yes, I know that series", and then continue it; or he may say nothing but simply continue the series.[247] Similarly, when ordered to fetch a red flower the person ordered may carry a color chart, may conjure up a mental image of red and compare it to the flower, or may simply pick a red flower. There is no one process here.[248]

If we construe the poet's order as one directing us to read the poem we can readily see how it differs from the above two orders. The poet is not saying go from the first word in the poem to the last in any of several ways. He is not saying have whatever mental events you wish so long as you get from the first word to the last. The poem with its devices to control imagery, with its seeing as, eliminates alternate routes in an important sense. The poet's order is very confining. He is saying read these lines and have these experiences while reading these lines. I argue that there are no grounds for saying the imagery of poetry is like the imagery one has while fetching the red flower or continuing the series. In the former case the imagery is controlled; in the latter, it is free. In the latter case imagery is irrelevant to the success of the act. In the former case imagery is quite necessary to a successful seeing as. The poet's order specifies by means of the intentional structure of the metaphor the imagery to be experienced while reading. A part of the poet's order is to have these images related by seeing as. The imagery which is inessential to showing one understands the order "fetch me a red flower" or "continue the series" is essential to the poet's order. Thus one cannot defend the analogy between images had while fetching a red flower or continuing a series and images had while reading metaphor.

Second, Wittgenstein is able to convincingly argue for the irrelevance of inner processes to the justification of one's understanding of meaning because there are definite achievement *criteria* for showing, for

---

[247] *Investigations*, # 151.
[248] *Blue Book*, pp. 3-4.

example, that one knows how to "continue a series" or how to "fetch a red flower". In the former case the act must be performed in accordance with a body of conventions. In the latter case the act must produce a flower commonly called "red". Appeal to criteria, as Wittgenstein defines them, is not a sufficient condition for showing that one understands the meaning of a metaphor, although knowledge of criteria may be a necessary condition for understanding a metaphor's meaning. If appeal to criteria is not a sufficient condition for showing one's understanding of a metaphor's meaning, then the argument against imagery is considerably weakened. The success of Wittgenstein's argument is based on the ability to cite criteria for all types of uses. As my analysis has shown, criteria for Wittgenstein are *observable* features selected by convention. Appeal to the poem as read in order to justify one's understanding of the metaphor is not an appeal, strictly speaking, to observable features selected by convention. Only the weak theory would say the poem as read consists of observable features. The strong theory demanded by metaphor recognizes imagery as a part of "the poem". I shall argue in the next chapter that literary discussion makes precisely an appeal to the poem understood in the strong sense, and thus that the game of literary discussion implies some criticism of Wittgenstein's conception of criteria. A discussion of metaphorical *meaning* presupposes not only Wittgenstein's: (1) common actions; (2) common physical environment; (3) common body of accepted conventions; but also (4) the experience-act of seeing as on reading the metaphor. A different sense of justification of the correctness of one's understanding of meaning is called for here.

Third, images with regard to literal language are at best intervening images. In the King's College example such an inner image is really a shadow of the objective application, an inner picture which represents by means of its similarity to its outward referent. Such an intervening shadow becomes useless if the spoken sentence can serve as the shadow, a shadow which does not picture by similarity. In this particular example explanations using ostensive definitions make the shadowy image totally useless.[249] I argued above that metaphorical imagery is nonreferential; thus such imagery is in no sense a shadowy picture, a negative transparency which is aligned with the natural world. Since naturalistic and reality claims are suspended while reading metaphors such images

---

[249]   *Ibid.*, p. 37.

become objects of contemplation. They become thick like Wimsatt's icon. They are looked at not through.

The question now, in view of the breakdown of the analogy between images had while fetching a red flower or continuing the series and images had while reading metaphor, is: Does metaphorical seeing as, involving imagery, now avoid Wittgenstein's criticisms by passing them, as it were, on a different plane or is there still a significant clash? In favor of the first suggestion is Wittgenstein's clear recognition of a plurality of language-games, and further that there is a game in which the purpose of words is to excite imagery.[250] However, even in view of these liberal types of remarks one must take care not to soften Wittgenstein's clear contention that meaning *is* not an inner experience nor does meaning *involve* inner experience. Wittgenstein would have to say that images and the experience-act of seeing as were *epiphenomena* as far as the public language game of using words is concerned. Wittgenstein could not recognize that imagery and seeing as between elements of an imagistic description function *essentially* in the language-game in which metaphorical meaning functions.

It is now evident that the relegation of metaphorical imagery involved in the experience-act of seeing as to the realm of the epiphenomenal will not do. Cassirer's remark that the magical view of language and, by extension, the poet's view of language never see such language as the nominalists' *flatus vocis* touches the essential point of conflict. The poet rejects the nominalists' *flatus vocis* because he tries to achieve a verbal form in which sense, sound and imagery are fused. The poet does not see word and bearer as fused, as does the magical actor, but word, sound and imagery. As Hulme correctly argues, poetic language, since it cannot bodily hand over sensations, at least does second best in handing over images.[251] The poet uses Schlauch's etymological rejuvenation and Wimsatt's iconic exploitation in order to make it difficult to read poetry without images. The poet rejects the nominalists' *flatus vocis* because it is these particular words in this configuration that achieve a marriage between sense, sound and imagery. The poet reveres words because he tries to make them more than meanings. He tries to imprison sound and imagery in these words. One would then expect the poet to act, as does the primitive magician, to words as though they actually had some precious content in the very words. The

---

[250]   *Investigations,* # 6.
[251]   Hulme, pp. 134-35.

poet tries to fuse images and meaning, thus making images involved with meaning.

Metaphor achieves this fusion in a very significant way. On reading metaphor one experiences imagery and sound, that is, sensa, related in a relevant way by the experience-act of seeing as, that is, sense. Of all the poetic elements one would have most difficulty in dividing metaphorical sense from sensa. The same metaphorical imagery *quasi-experienced* also *means* in that it is formed, controlled, or relevant imagery. A fundamental contrast here with Wittgenstein's analysis is implied. The whole point of Wittgenstein's attack on the inner meaning theorists and the name theorists is that meaning is not predicated respectively either of an inner experience or a physical bearer. This analysis of metaphor does not agree with the inner meaning theorists in saying that meaning *is* an inner image or is predicated of an inner image. However, it is essential to metaphor that imagery is *involved* in metaphorical meaning through the experience-act of seeing as. In justifying his analysis of a metaphor the critic points to the metaphor as read. In this type of pointing the critic is in somewhat the same predicament as one who claims to justify his pain statements by reference to some internal criteria. Both the critic and the person referring to internal criteria for his pain statements would be citing grounds which would not be criteria in Wittgenstein's full sense of the word. I shall argue that in fact the literary critic does appeal to something other than criteria in appealing to the metaphor as read. A discussion of the meaning of a metaphor then presupposes not only Wittgenstein's: (1) common actions; (2) common physical environment; (3) common body of accepted conventions; but also (4) a common intersubjective experience-act of seeing as. Inclusion of the fourth prerequisite for critical discussion is another way of emphasizing that seeing as is not reducible to criteria. In fact, the existence of a language-game in which metaphorical seeing as functions, the game of critical analysis, implies that Wittgenstein's conception of criteria is inadequate with regard to this game. I argue that the critic does in fact successfully point to the metaphor to justify his analysis, thus using a type of pointing which Wittgenstein denied in the case of pain. The strong theory critic who has been defended here points to the metaphor as read. Such a theorist can be expected to justify his analysis of metaphorical meaning on the basis of the experience-act of seeing as, an act requiring imagery.

IV. LANGUAGE OF LITERARY DISCUSSION

The purpose of this chapter is to analyze in what sense the critic justi-fies his analysis of a particular metaphor. The sense or meaning of a metaphor is the relevant way the metaphorical vehicle is seen as the tenor. The question is how does the critic substantiate his statement of the relevant sense of a metaphor. Is there any basis for choosing one critical analysis over another? There are three possible senses or ways of justification relevant to critical analysis. First, a critic might claim he derived his analysis from the metaphor in an analytical manner. Second, the critic might justify his analysis by pointing or referring to the meta-phor in one of two ways. First, he might point to the metaphor in the full sense of pointing analyzed by Wittgenstein; that is, he might point to the words in a physical sense as print on the page or sound in the air. Second, he might point to the metaphor as read. I have implied that this type of pointing would not be allowed by Wittgenstein because it would *involve* reference to experiences which are not strictly physical; namely, imagery involved in seeing as. Very shortly it will be argued that in fact critical explanations of metaphorical meaning are justified in this way. However, I shall show first why the former alternative senses of justification are inadequate. I shall show this inadequacy mainly by referring back to conclusions arrived at in Chapters II and III.

A. ANALYTICAL OR VERBAL JUSTIFICATION

No one has ever claimed to justify his analysis of poetry in the strictly logical way used by symbolic logicians. One would have great difficulty in finding logical symbols in the writings of literary critics. The more plausible and relevant type of analytical justification is a looser, common sense type of analysis. However, even in this loose sense this type of justification is impossible to defend and thus will be dismissed rather summarily here. This type of justification would be based on two assumptions which are clearly wrong.

First, this type of justification would assume that poetic meaning in the metaphor is replaceable by an equivalent in the sense that the phrase "a man who has not married" is an equivalent replacement, according to *Webster's New Collegiate Dictionary*, of the word "bachelor". Applied to poetry this would mean that a critical explication of metaphorical meaning is a near equivalent to the meaning in the metaphor. This assumption would fundamentally oppose all the theorists analyzed in Chapter II. An important point of the theories, that the poem is a presentational symbol, a concrete universal, an icon, a fusion of sense and sensa, is that *poetic meaning is fused with its sensuous vehicle*. Thus the precise shade of poetic meaning is expressible in this and no other way. A change of words, a change which affects sound and imagery, affects a change in meaning. Certainly ordinary language has few, if any, exact synonymous replacements. The word "bachelor" may differ in subtle ways from *Webster's* synonymous replacement, and certainly the particular context in which the word occurs lends it fine shades of meaning which *Webster's* definition does not have. However, poetic meaning's lack of synonymous replacements is qualitatively more radical because the sound of the words and the imagery excited by the words are significant in the meaning of the words.

The medium theorists, noting the untranslatability of poetry most explicitly, emphasized the involvement of poetic meaning with its sensuous vehicle. Bouwsma notes that meaning is in the language in the poem in a way in which ordinary meaning is not in its vehicle. Since the meaning is in the poem it cannot be gotten out in a translation. "The meaning of sentences is translatable, but the 'meaning' of poems, of music, is not." [1] If you do not grasp the meaning all you can do is reread the poem.[2] Hospers argues that not only is a poem untranslatable but unrestatable. Such a prose restatement is nothing but an empty shell. To assume that a poem is translatable or restatable is to assume that the poem is a sugar-coated message, a sugar-coated pill. Translatability assumes the poem expresses in pretty words what could be expressed with less beauty in prose.[3] Wimsatt perceptively sees that: "Criticism

---

[1]   Elton, p. 95.
[2]   *Ibid.*
[3]   Hospers, *Meaning and Truth in the Arts*, pp. 132-33.

of poetry is like 1.414 ... or 3.1416..., not all it would be, yet all that can be had and very useful." [4] Wimsatt's point is that the critic does not get out all that is in the poem. The critical restatement only approximates poetic meaning.

I have shown that metaphor fits these conclusions most significantly. Of all the elements of poetry one would have most difficulty in drawing a sharp line between metaphorical sense and sensa. Sense and sensa are fused in the experience-act of seeing as. The same sound and imagery which is experienced also means. Because metaphor achieves this fusion it is neither possible nor desirable that critical language about the metaphor is to replace or be an equivalent of the metaphor's meaning. Arnold Isenberg perceptively sees that it is not the function of critical language in the arts to "*afford* the experience which it purports to describe...".[5] Rather "it is a function of criticism to bring about communication at the level of the senses; that is, to induce sameness of vision, of experienced content".[6] Isenberg's last phrase, that criticism tries to "induce sameness of vision, of experienced content" is significantly reminiscent of my hypothetical example in Chapter III. That example showed how one would proceed to help an aspect-blind person see the metaphorical vehicle as its tenor. In that example one cited relevant ways in which nerves sit like tombs *in order to get the reader to see nerves sitting as tombs*. Since seeing as is an irreducible experience-act, talk about the metaphor, analysis of its relevant senses, cannot guarantee that the aspect-blind person will be able to see the vehicle as the tenor, but it is the purpose of such talk to "induce sameness of vision, of experienced content".

Frank Sibley advances an argument significantly similar to those above. He correctly notes that it is reasonable that we can cite nonaesthetic features in support of our application of aesthetic terms. For example, in support of our contention that a particular painting lacks "balance", an aesthetic quality, we point out the nonaesthetic fact that certain figures in the painting are too far to the left of center.[7] However, such nonaesthetic characteristics count only for or against the application of an aesthetic term. The aesthetic and nonaesthetic are not logically related. Such aesthetic terms are characteristically, not conditionally,

---

[4] Wimsatt, *The Verbal Icon*, p. 83.
[5] Elton, p. 142.
[6] *Ibid.*, pp. 137-38.
[7] Frank Sibley, "Aesthetic Concepts", *The Philosophical Review*, LXVIII (Oct., 1959), pp. 423-24.

associated with nonaesthetic features.[8] In saying that aesthetic and non-aesthetic terms are "characteristically" related Sibley means they are related in some weak inductive sense. There is no number of nonaesthetic conditions which logically imply or require the application of an aesthetic concept. Only a weaker, characteristic relation is possible. Thus having taste, being able to apply aesthetic terms correctly, does not depend on analytic acumen in relating the nonaesthetic to aesthetic terms but on having "ability to *notice* or *discern* things . . .".[9] Applied to metaphor this means that *language about the metaphor*, the critic's analysis, is characteristically related to *language in the metaphor*. There is no logically conditional or analytical relation here.

Second, an analytical justification of a critical analysis presupposes that there is a body of conventions, such as a dictionary, to which one could appeal in cases of dispute. Unfortunately, often to the critic's chagrin, there seems to be no such source of appeal. Even in cases in which metaphors have been much analyzed, for example, those of Shakespeare, there is no final, definitive and closed meaning. Thus one cannot justify his understanding of a Shakespearean metaphor in the same sense in which one justifies his understanding of how to "continue a series". There are conventional criteria for the tenor "time" and the vehicle "beggar" but no conventional criteria telling in what sense time is seen as a beggar. One cannot produce other signs, namely, language about the metaphor, in accordance with a rule because there is no definitive source of such rules. There is no conventionally accepted standard or criteria which can be the basis of a verbal justification of one's understanding of a metaphor. Wittgenstein's body of social conventions cannot here provide sufficient conditions for showing the correctness of one's understanding of a metaphor in the same sense that such conventions provide a sufficient condition for showing one's understanding of how to "continue a series". The lack of a definitive source of *convention* is the first clue that criteria, as understood by Wittgenstein, cannot be a sufficient condition for justifying the correctness of one's understanding of metaphor's meaning.

Further, it follows from the arguments against an analytical justification of critical analyses that there is no dictionary of metaphor not because no one has bothered to compile such a work, but because the nature of poetic meaning, and metaphorical meaning in particular,

---

[8]   *Ibid.*, p. 429.
[9]   *Ibid.*, p. 423.

makes such a compilation impossible. Metaphorical meaning is always open because of the experience-act of seeing as. No dictionary is possible because it is not possible to give in words the equivalent of the experience of reading the metaphor.

I conclude for these reasons that the critic cannot claim analytically to derive his analysis of a metaphor even in a loose, logical way. Some other sense of justification must be sought.

B. JUSTIFICATION BY REFERENCE OR OSTENSIVE JUSTIFICATION

That the critic justifies his analysis of the metaphor by referring to it is a more defensible position. In fact, it is not only defensible but correct when "reference" is properly understood. The following critics argue that the purpose of critical language about the poem is to refer to the poem or clarify its meaning, not give an equivalent meaning in different words. A function of critical language is *explanation* of the meaning of the work. An explanation is not an equivalent to the original but a clarification of that original.

1. *Purpose of Critical Language is Referential Explanation*

Richard Blackmur argues that the critic's job is to clarify the work by referring to it. He explicitly rejects the view just analyzed because it fails to realize that there is "as much difference between words used about a poem and the poem as there is between words used about a painting and the painting. The gap is absolute." [10] The critic's analysis of a metaphor is not an equivalent substitution for the metaphor. The critic's language by referring to the metaphor clarifies it. But: "The object remains, and should remain, itself, only made more available and seen in a clearer light." [11]

Stevenson also recognizes that one facet of attention in art is dissective. Like Blackmur he notes that the purpose of dissective attention is not accounting for an experience but getting it.[12] When such analysis becomes persuasive then it is literary criticism.[13]

---

[10] Weitz, *Problems in Aesthetics*, pp. 667-68. (Originally appeared in Blackmur, *Language as Gesture*, London, George Allen & Unwin Ltd., 1935.)

[11] *Ibid.*, p. 665.

[12] Charles L. Stevenson, "On the 'Analysis' of a Work of Art", *The Philosophical Review*, LXVII (Jan., 1958), p. 40.

[13] Charles L. Stevenson, "On 'What Is a Poem?' ", *The Philosophical Review*, LXVI (July, 1957), p. 353.

I. A. Richards, in treating the language of criticism, contends that it has two parts: "the part which describes the value of the experience we shall call the *critical* part. That which describes the object we shall call the *technical* part." [14] Richards hopes that psychology, by leading to a further understanding of values, will be of great assistance to the first part of criticism.[15] The purpose then of critical language in referring to the poem is to clarify its technical fineries and evaluate them. Richards thus agrees with Stevenson that the purpose of literary criticism is dissective and evaluative.

Wimsatt objects to Richards' implication that evaluation and analysis are two acts. Wimsatt also has in mind Eliot whom he quotes as saying: "The critic must not coerce, and he must not make judgments of worse or better. He must simply elucidate: the reader will form the correct judgment for himself." [16] Wimsatt rejects the implication of both Richards and Eliot that explication and criticism are two distinct acts. "The extreme theory of explicative criticism cuts apart understanding and value...." [17] More correctly the critic's main problem "is always how to push both understanding and value as far as possible in union, or how to make our understanding evaluative".[18] I do not intend to settle the issue between Wimsatt and Richards or Eliot as to whether criticism does or should sharply distinguish the evaluative from the descriptive function of criticism. I leave this question to the literary critics. However, even in view of this open question Blackmur, Stevenson, Wimsatt, Richards, and Eliot would certainly agree that explication is *a* function of the literary critic even though they cannot agree that it is *the* function of literary criticism. They could agree with Lalo that the critic's explanation of his judgment is at least as important as the judgment itself.[19] Since this work is about metaphorical meaning it is precisely this function of explanation that is of interest.

I shall now clarify what I meant by saying in this section heading that the purpose of critical language is to be a "referential explanation".[20]

---

[14]   Richards, *Principles of Literary Criticsm*, p. 23.
[15]   *Ibid.*
[16]   Wimsatt, *The Verbal Icon*, p. 246.
[17]   *Ibid.*, p. 251.
[18]   *Ibid.*
[19]   Lalo, p. 283.
[20]   It must be noted that critical language in referring to the metaphor, in having as its purpose the clarification of the meaning of the metaphor, is a quite different kind of language from the language in the poem. I have argued that metaphorical language and imagery are nonreferential. I argued that metaphorical

First, I shall clarify why I use the word "explanation". Then in the sections following on justification by reference in the strong or weak sense I shall clarify the term "referential". I choose the term "explanation" in order to emphasize that a synonymous relation does not exist between meaning in the metaphor and a critical analysis of that meaning. Implicit in the agreement of the above critics that a function of criticism is explanation is the recognition that such explanatory analyses are precisely *explanations*, not deductions. Sibley's argument that aesthetic and nonaesthetic terms are related characteristically, not by logical conditions,[21] must be extended to the relation between critical explanations and the poem. An explanation of the meaning of a metaphor, since it is a type of explanation, has some limited similarities to scientific explanation. In both cases the explanation only *approximates* its object. Wimsatt and Blackmur clearly note that literary explanations only approximate the meaning in the literary work of art. In Blackmur's terms there is a gap between the explanation and the poem. The poem remains and should remain. Explanations only make the object accessible in a clearer light. They do not replace the object.[22] Wimsatt recognizes that explanations of poetry only approximate poetic meaning in his statement that: "Criticism of poetry is like 1.414 ... or 3.1416..., not all it would be, yet all that can be had and very useful." [23] In both cases the explanations are, as it were, parasitical on the explained. Scientific explanations and explanations of metaphorical meaning mean in terms of their respective objects. Scientific explanations and explanations of metaphorical meaning are ostensive types of language.

However, here the similarity abruptly ends. Great differences between critical, literary explanation and scientific explanation arise from basic differences in their respective *objects*. One of the qualities of the metaphor is that it has meaning, while raw scientific data strictly speaking has no meaning. Thus critical explanation clarifies or elucidates meaning the metaphor already has, while scientific explanation gives the data meaning. The literary critic is analyzing an art ob-

---

imagery is not a negative photograph to be aligned with the world. Critical language, on the other hand, according to Blackmur, Stevenson, Richards, Eliot and Wimsatt, is precisely referential. Its role is to refer to the poem. Thus the semantical generalizations about poetic language and metaphor specifically do not apply to explanations of metaphorical meaning.

[21]   Sibley, p. 429.
[22]   Weitz, *Problems in Aesthetics*, p. 665.
[23]   Wimsatt, *The Verbal Icon*, p. 83.

ject while the scientist is analyzing a natural object. A second important difference in the objects is that the metaphor includes imagery while scientific data does not. An explanation of a metaphor is not a scientific explanation or hypothesis because the metaphor has meaning and imagery.

Further, a difference in the respective objects of scientific and critical explanation leads to different types of *justification*. It is important to emphasize that the type of justification being sought here is not a scientific type of justification. An analysis of a metaphor is an explanation of the *meaning* of that metaphor. To confuse a question of meaning with a question of fact is to confuse, in Wittgenstein's terminology, criteria with symptoms.[24] I am not here asking if the critic justifies his analysis by reference to symptoms, but if he justifies his analysis by reference to criteria as Wittgenstein understands them. Of course, I have argued and shall continue to argue that in the metaphor sense and sensa are fused; and this contention may be taken as denying in some sense the radical distinction between criteria and symptoms. My reply is that this fusion still does not turn a question of meaning into an empirical question. Even though meaning in the arts is embodied in a sensuous vehicle, there is still a fundamental difference between a question of fact about such an object and a question of interpretation or analysis of the meaning of that object. To take a question of meaning as a request for symptoms or empirical generalizations is to take the poem as a natural object. Of course, I am not denying that the poem can be investigated as a natural object, thus leading to empirical generalizations about it. However, I am saying that a question about the meaning of the metaphor is not a request for such a generalization. A question of meaning is a question about style, the distinctively human mark on the object, and thus is a question emphasizing the nonnatural aspects of the art object. To ask for the meaning of an unstylized or unformed material is to ask a meaningless question. Only stylized objects have meaning. As Dufrenne argues, style removes the art object from the realm of natural objects and from the realm of objects subordinated to our ends.[25] The question then being asked here is not does the critic appeal to symptoms but does the critic appeal to criteria, as Wittgenstein understands them, in justifying his analysis of a metaphor's mean-

---

[24] *Blue Book*, pp. 24-25. The question of symptom has been raised because a statement about the poem, since the poem is a type of concrete object, might be confused with an ordinary hypothesis about an object of experience.
[25] Dufrenne, I, p. 147.

ing. Does the critic "refer" to the poem in a full sense of "referral" or does the critic "refer" to the poem in some weaker sense?

2. *Justification by Reference in the Strict Sense*

Wittgenstein does not use the term "reference". However, he uses a near equivalent in his analysis of words with "ostensive definitions". Wittgenstein recognized ostensive defining or pointing only in an overt, physical sense, as his analysis of pain statements most clearly shows. He refused to recognize that the meaning of pain words could have any relation to an internal act of pointing. In other words, pointing is an overt act justifiable by appealing to an independent source. An independent source is one publicly accessible in the full sense emphasized in my analysis of the social senses of "use". The independent source for Wittgenstein is criteria. Criteria are *observable* features selected by convention. Thus both in his understanding of criteria and in his understanding of pointing or ostensive meaning Wittgenstein is oriented to physical observation. The question of criteria and the question of pointing or reference are tied up with each other. In order to cite criteria as observable features one presupposes that reference or pointing in the full sense is possible. Thus the only type of justification by pointing which Wittgenstein can recognize is a reference or pointing in the full physical sense.

My objection to this type of justification is already clear from chapter III. This type of critic would have to be a weak theory critic. A critic who is required in justifying his analysis to point to the poem in a rigorous sense of the word "point" could only indicate auditory exploitations such as rhyme, rhythm and alliteration. These are quite physically experienced and can be pointed to in the full sense analyzed by Wittgenstein. This type of critic could justify his understanding of the metaphor in a way quite similar to the way one justifies his understanding of "red". In both cases a fully public context could be indicated. In both cases one could appeal to criteria or observable features selected by convention. I have argued at length that this weak theory is inadequate to poetic metaphor. Metaphor essentially involves imagery related by seeing as. An adequate analysis of any particular metaphor must refer to these essential elements. Imagery cannot be included in or be a part of criteria because criteria are quite clearly understood by Wittgenstein as *observable* features selected by convention. In the criticism of an analytical justification of one's understanding of a metaphor the conventional nature of criteria was challenged by the lack of a body of definitive conventions of metaphorical meaning. Here the other aspect of criteria, namely, the observable features, is being challenged. My first and most basic objection to the view that an explanation of metaphorical meaning can be justified by appealing to criteria in the full sense of the word "criteria" is that such a view implies that metaphor is only a fusion of sense and sound. Demand for this type of justification immediately excludes imagery. Thus I conclude that the critic does not refer to the metaphor in the full sense of "referral" because the metaphor includes imagery.

3. *Justification by Reference in the Weak Sense*

The critic must refer to the metaphor in a weaker sense of "referral". Many theorists recognize that though the language of critical discussion does not involve reference or pointing in the strict sense, still some mode of justification is appropriate to such language. Arnold Isenberg asks:

What is the semantical relationship between the language of criticism and the qualities of the critic's or the reader's experience? I have argued that this relationship is not designation (though I do not deny that there *is* a relationship of designation between the critic's language and *some* qualities of a work of art). But neither is it denotation: the critic does not *point* to the qualities he has in mind.[26]

Critical terms such as "splendor", "eloquence", or "wit" would have no meaning if strict ostensive verification were demanded. The correctness of an application of such terms is found by a second or third reading. No stricter justification is required.[27] Such normative terms are *based* on inductive generalizations, though they *are not* inductive generalizations.[28] The immediate which such terms are applied to cannot then be identified with the sensuous.[29]

  Isenberg's argument that the correctness of an application of critical

---

[26]   Elton, p. 143.
[27]   Isenberg, p. 9.
[28]   Elton, pp. 132-33.
[29]   Arnold Isenberg, "Perception, Meaning and the Subject-Matter of Art", *The Journal of Philosophy*, XLI (Oct. 12, 1944), p. 575.

terms is checked by a second or third reading is very perceptive. I
am arguing that a critical explication of a metaphor's meaning is justified in terms of its adequacy to the metaphor as read. Further, his
argument that the immediate is not identical to the sensuous is similar
to my argument that the original given data of metaphor includes
imagery as well as sound.

Margaret Macdonald makes a similar point.

Criticism, is therefore, I suggest, an indefinite set of devices for 'presenting'
not 'proving' the merits of works of art. It has none of the stability of logical
truth, scientific method, legal and moral law. It varies with time, place and
audience, while not being completely subject to these limitations.[30]

Critical analyses are not thus true or false but better and worse.[31] Critical
analysis is more like the verdict of a judge and jury than a scientific or
logical conclusion. "It affirms a decision reached by a definite procedure
but unlike that of relating evidence to conclusion in deductive and inductive inference." [32] Critical justification then differs from the justification of the scientist or logician. Critical explanations cannot appeal to
"criteria" in the strict sense of the word because works of art "are not
simple objects of sense perception".[33] Both Isenberg and Macdonald
would argue that some mode of justification is appropriate to critical
analysis though such discussions cannot be justified by appeal to criteria
in the strict sense.

A difference between the arguments of Isenberg and Macdonald
and my argument may seem to vitiate my acceptance of their conclusions as valid for the relation between explanations of a metaphor and
the metaphor. They are both analyzing critical judgment which includes *both* critical explanation *and* critical evaluation. This work is
concerned with justification of a critical explanation, not with the wider
problem of also justifying an evaluation. I argue that their conclusions
with regard to the larger problem hold for the smaller problem of how
an explication of a metaphor is justified. The conclusions hold because:
First, negatively I have shown in the first part of this chapter that an
analytical justification of an explanation will not do. Isenberg and Macdonald also rule out logical justification of an explanation. Second, negatively I have shown that the metaphor is not strictly words on a page

---

[30]   Elton, p. 129.
[31]   *Ibid.*, pp. 121-30.
[32]   *Ibid.*, p. 121.
[33]   *Ibid.*, p. 114.

or sounds in the air. Isenberg states that contemplation of works of art cannot be identified with the contemplation of sensuous form alone.[34] Macdonald also argues that works of art "are not simple objects of sense perception".[35] On these grounds both would agree that a strict justification in terms of observable features of the object is impossible. Third, and more positively, there is some mode relevant to the substantiation of an explanation. Isenberg states that the correctness of an application of such explanatory terms can be checked by a second or third reading.[36] Macdonald argues that though such explanations are not justifiable in logical or inductive ways, and thus are not strictly right or wrong, still such explanations can be said to be "better" or "worse" than others.[37] On these grounds I argue that the conclusions of the larger problem apply *mutatis mutandis* to the lesser problem of justification of an explanation.

The weaker sense of justification appropriate to explanations of metaphorical meaning has been significantly anticipated by Isenberg in his argument that critical terms are checked by a second or third reading. If the metaphor is a read object, if adequacy to metaphor demands the fullness of the strong theory as I argued in Chapter III, then it follows that *critical explanations must be justified by referring to the metaphor as a read object.* One would expect *examples* of critical explanation to show that in fact critical discussion does refer to the metaphor as it is realized in its fullness while being read. Such examples can be cited almost ad infinitum. For example, of Eliot's well-known metaphor

> Let us go then, you and I,
> When the evening is spread out against the sky
> Like a patient etherized upon a table;
> (T. S. Eliot, "The Love Song of J. Alfred Prufrock", ll. 1-3)

Brooks and Warren state:

Twilight is the atmosphere of the poem. It is an evening "Like a patient etherized upon a table", and with this image the twilight world becomes also the world of twilight in another way, the realm between life and death. Here, too, enters the notion of a sick world, the atmosphere of the operating room: the quiet is not that of natural sleep—it is an ominous hush.[38]

---

[34]   Isenberg, *The Journal of Philosophy*, XLI, p. 575.
[35]   Elton, p. 114.
[36]   Isenberg, *The Journal of Philosophy*, XLVI, p. 9.
[37]   Elton, p. 130.
[38]   Brooks and Warren, p. 391.

In this explanation which states the relevant senses in which the metaphorical tenor is seen as the vehicle, the evening against the sky as the
patient upon the table, Brooks and Warren are clearly not just referring
to the physical metaphor. They are referring to the ambiguous, implicative, suggestive fullness of imagery realized while reading. Brooks
and Warren here show Richards' suggested "habit of reading so as to
allow the fullest development to imagery in its sensory aspect...".[39]
With Husserl they have read so as to allow *the original right of all
data...*".[40]

It is also worth repeating that though the metaphor referred to is not
strictly the physical metaphor the conclusion of Croce that it is in the
imagination or of Sartre that it is of the imagination is unwarranted. I
have argued at length in Chapter III Macdonald's conclusion: "But if
a work of art is not a physical object, it does not follow that it is a
mental state or ghost." [41] The imagistic fullness and the experience-act of
seeing as referred to by Brooks and Warren are *associated with language*. This association with language destroys the analogy between
metaphorical imagery and the imagery of dreams or of the imagination. I argue with Dufrenne that reading is more like perceiving than
like dreaming. Thus metaphorical imagery and the experience-act of
seeing as are not private and incorrigible as are reports on dreams or
imaginative experiences. Brooks and Warren are not giving a report
on some private movie screen in their imagination. They are explicating
the relevant imagery defined by the experience-act of seeing as. Such
imagery is part of the intentional structure of the metaphor. Brooks and
Warren are not talking of two different metaphors, one scanned or
heard by the physical eye or ear and the other "seen" or "heard" by a
mental eye or ear. In reading, the metaphor is a unity.

Reference to the metaphor in the full strong sense displayed by this
example from Brooks and Warren is by no means anomalous. For
example, of Wordsworth's metaphor in the first line quoted here

> The talking boat that moves with pensive sound,
> Or drops his anchor down with plunge profound;
> (William Wordsworth, "An Evening Walk", 1793 ed., ll. 297-298)

F. W. Bateson remarks: "The 'talking boat' is particularly brilliant – the
perfect epithet for the chatter of the little lake waves against the boat's

---

[39]   Richards, *Principles of Literary Criticism*, p. 123.
[40]   Husserl, p. 97.
[41]   Elton, p. 123.

side." [42] An equally characteristic example is Florence Marsh's comments on a metaphor in Wordsworth's "There Was a Boy".

> Then sometimes, in that silence, while he hung
> Listening, a gentle shock of mild surprise
> Has carried far into his heart the voice
> Of mountain-torrents; or the visible scene
> Would enter unawares into his mind
> With all its solemn imagery, its rocks,
> Its woods, and that uncertain heaven received
> Into the bosom of the steady lake.
> (William Wordsworth, "There Was a Boy", ll. 18-25)

Marsh states:

The figures here—the boy *hung listening, far into* his heart, the *voice* of mountain torrents—are certainly not decorative; they are, as Wordsworth would put it, "a constituent part and power or function in the thought". The thought deals with the way feelings—here of surprise—impress images upon the mind. The boy's mind is viewed spatially and the images of sound and sight are endowed with activity in order to convey the thought.[43]

She further suggests that this metaphorical imagery has "the latent suggestion that the visible scene enters unaware into the boy's mind very much as the uncertain heaven is received into the bosom of the lake".[44] Bateson and Marsh are both evidently referring in their analyses to the metaphor understood in the strong sense of Chapter III. The same remarks made about the explication of Eliot's metaphor by Brooks and Warren could be repeated here. In all three cases the metaphor is being referred to as it is realized in the act of reading. These examples show that not only does *critical theory* argue that metaphor demands a strong theory, but *critical practice* shows reference to the metaphor as read. Critical theory and critical practice agree. Examples such as these could be endlessly cited, but such a multiplication of evidence is unnecessary here.

I conclude from these examples and from my analysis in Chapter III which showed that adequacy to metaphor demands a strong theory that critical explanations of metaphorical meaning are justified by pointing to or referring to the metaphor as a read object. As a read object the

---

[42] F. W. Bateson, *Wordsworth: A Re-Interpretation*, 2nd ed. (London, Longmans, Green and Co., 1956), p. 75.

[43] Florence Marsh, *Wordsworth's Imagery: A Study in Poetic Vision* (New Haven, Yale University Press, 1952), p. 21.

[44] *Ibid.*, p. 26.

metaphor has the peculiar status of being somewhat shared but not fully public. Thus a critical explication is not true or false, as Macdonald argued, either in the logical or inductive sense, but better or worse.[45] As Isenberg argues, the correctness of an application of critical terms is found by a second or third reading. No stricter justification is required.[46] In view of the status of the metaphor as a read object which is shared but not physically experienced in the full sense I argue that the metaphor must be intersubjective but not public. Critical explication presupposes a continuity between the critic as an excellent, experienced reader and the average reader. There is a quantitative difference between the critic and the normal reader, not a qualitative one. The critic does not talk in a vacuum. We expect him to be talking of the metaphor as we read it. Thus critical explication, analysis of the meaning of poetic metaphors, presupposes not only Wittgenstein's (1) public actions; (2) common physical environment; (3) common body of accepted conventions; but also (4) the intersubjective experience-act of seeing as with regard to metaphorical imagery. The game in which poetic metaphors are analyzed presupposes this wider context of shared experience. The only way to avoid these conclusions is to say: (1) that critical literary explanation of metaphors is not a legitimate language-game at all; (2) that critical explanations are all on an equal footing – none are better or worse than others (critical explanations are incorrigible, like statements about our dreams, because they refer to a subjective experience. This view of critical explanation in effect also denies that literary analysis is a legitimate game); (3) that critical analyses are justifiable, but justifiable by reference to analytical criteria; (4) that critical analyses are justifiable, but justifiable by reference to observable features selected by convention. All of these alternative answers are unacceptable.

C. WITTGENSTEIN AND CRITICAL EXPLANATION

I have stated explicitly that the need with regard to metaphorical meaning to expand Wittgenstein's three presuppositions to include also the intersubjective experience-act of seeing as with regard to metaphorical imagery implies some inadequacy in Wittgenstein's criteria at least with regard to this particular language-game. Criteria, as observable features

---

[45] Elton, pp. 121-30.
[46] Isenberg, *The Journal of Philosophy*, XLVI, p. 9.

selected by convention, are inadequate to poetic metaphor for two reasons.

First, as the rejection of an analytical justification of critical explanation of metaphorical meaning showed, it is in principle impossible for there to be a definitive *conventional* source which can be appealed to to settle questions about metaphorical meaning. Poetic metaphors are, as are metaphors in other fields, always on the cutting edge. Because of the irreducible nature of the experience-act of seeing as, this act defines similarity, not vice versa. We apply words such as "similar" after the act of seeing as. There are no criteria which can be appealed to to show the metaphor's meaning although, of course, there are criteria for both the tenor and vehicle of a metaphor alone. With regard to Shakespeare's metaphor there are criteria for "time" and criteria for "beggars" but no criteria for time seen as a beggar. Criteria are then inadequate to this game because the game is played without any definitive conventional source of appeal.

Second, criteria are inadequate because of emphasizing *observable* features selected by convention. Metaphorical meaning introduces imagery. Wittgenstein in his attacks on the inner meaning theory and the naming theory quite correctly argued that meaning *is* not respectively either an inner experience or a physical bearer. If Wittgenstein's objections were left at this point no siginificant conflict would occur with the poet and literary critic. Neither claims that the meaning in poetry *is* the imagery. However, I have shown that Wittgenstein intends to make a stronger claim. He intends to deny not only that meaning *is* an internal experience but also that meaning *involves* internal experience. Wittgenstein clearly reveals his stronger claim in his treatment of pain statements. In his classical beetle in the box example he denies the relevance of the beetle to the language-game. "The thing in the box has no place in the language-game at all; not even as a *something:* for the box might even be empty." [47] Nor does a more adequate understanding of sensations show them to be relevant to the game. The critic and the poet would be quite upset if the irrelevance of the beetle were extended to metaphorical imagery. Such an extension would imply that in the game of metaphorical meaning the kind of imagery, or even if one has imagery at all, is totally immaterial to the game. Such an extension would imply that in reading metaphor one can have whatever images one wishes or have no imagery at all. These conclusions are unacceptable

---

[47] *Investigations,* # 293.

both to the general theories of poetic language analyzed in Chapter II and to metaphor in particular as analyzed in Chapter III.

The conclusion of Chapter II was that in poetic language sound and sense function iconically yielding a fusion of sense and sensa. Poetic language is a fusion of sense, sound and imagery. If imagery is *fused* with meaning it is not, in the words of Brooks and Warren "idle and meaningless, dead or inert, or distracting and selfserving, like some foolish ornament that merely calls attention to itself. Every bit of image ought to 'make sense' and to aid the poem in *its* making sense...." [48]

Metaphor supports the arguments of the general theorists in that its imagery is not epiphenomenal to its sense; the imagery is not an ornament irrelevant to meaning. The same imagery quasi-experienced means in that it leads to the relevant sense of the metaphor through the experience-act of seeing as. Metaphorical imagery is involved with metaphorical meaning. Thus it is reasonable to expect what my examples of critical analyses have shown; namely, that discussions of metaphorical meaning refer to or point to the metaphor as read. There is every reason to think that Wittgenstein would have said imagery is as irrelevant to the language-game in which statements of metaphorical meaning function as is the sensation of pain to the language-game in which pain statements function, or as irrelevant as the imagery in the game in which the statement "fetch me a red flower" or "continue the series" functions. There is good reason for thinking that he would deny that the metaphor as a read object can be pointed to or indicated as a justification of one's understanding of that metaphor on grounds similar to his denial that pain can be pointed to or indicated in any relevant sense. Both would be cases of internal pointing. Neither pain sensations nor the quasi-sensory experience of imagery are accessible as are physical objects or public actions. Certainly Wittgenstein has liberal remarks in which he recognizes a plurality of language-games, even recognizing a game in which the purpose of words might be to arouse images. [49] However, these liberal remarks must not be allowed to soften his clear contention that the meaning is not an inner experience nor does meaning involve inner experience. In order to be consistent with regard to the game recognized whose purpose is to arouse imagery Wittgenstein would have to say that the relation between meaning and images in this particular game is one-way. His metaphor for this particular game is that: "Uttering a word is like striking a note on the keyboard of the imagination." [50] This metaphor is particularly appropriate because the relation between piano keys and the notes sounded is one-way. The key affects the note but not vice versa. Wittgenstein could not recognize the two-way influence between meaning and imagery demanded by metaphor.

The basic shortcoming with regard to Wittgenstein's criteria is that their physicalism does not allow extension to the intersubjective but not physical assumption on which discussions of metaphorical meaning are based. Reference to the poem as read in order to justify the correctness of a critical explication cannot be made solely in terms of Wittgenstein's criteria. Numerous critics analyzed in Chapter I noted the inadequacy of this conception of criteria especially with regard to pain statements. It is needless to repeat all of their criticisms here, but the specific criticism of Wellman is especially lucid and incisive and thus is worth reiterating. Wellman argues that Wittgenstein failed to see that there can be public language with private criteria. Such a recognition enables us to see that our justification of pain statements by other minds is indirect; that is, on the basis of our own experience. "My reason for saying 'He is in pain' is that he has hit his finger with a hammer, but this is a reason only because hitting and hurting have been associated in my own experience." [51] "To insist that one have direct justification for every statement is to make indirect justification under any circumstances either impossible or unnecessary." [52] In short, Wellman implies that the language-game in which pain statements operate presupposes more than Wittgenstein's criteria. It presupposes the intersubjective but not public sensation of pain. My argument is precisely parallel to Wellman's in that I have argued that discussions of metaphorical meaning presuppose not only Wittgenstein's criteria but the intersubjective experience-act of seeing as. A discussion of metaphorical meaning presupposes the metaphor as read.

Moreland Perkins extends an argument similar to that of Wellman and of this book to statements in Gestalt psychology. He notes that in defining observation physically in terms of physiology and behavior that a large class of apparently valid findings in Gestalt psychology is excluded. He notes that reports in this type of psychology seem to be

---

[50] *Ibid.*
[51] Wellman, *The Journal of Philosophy*, LVIII, p. 290.
[52] *Ibid.*, p. 293.

intersubjective though not physicalistic.[53] In view of this apparent validity Perkins suggests that the notion of publicity must "be reworked and developed in such a manner as to include the actual processes of confirming these statements within the class of intersubjective confirmations in general".[54] Perkins' argument is particularly interesting in view of Wittgenstein's duck-rabbit example which is precisely the sort of example used in Gestalt psychology. Further, Wittgenstein explicitly notes that an aspect is not strictly seen,[55] thus agreeing with Perkins that physical observation cannot account for such seeing. Of course, Wittgenstein does not follow Perkins' suggested route of solution. Rather, he retreats again into his grammatical investigation. This book could not beat a similar retreat because adequacy to the fullness of metaphor demanded treatment of the mode appropriate to the realization of this fullness, namely, reading, of which seeing as is a part. Thus I have in fact followed a route similar to that suggested by Perkins. My analysis of the act of reading, of which the experience-act of seeing as is a specialized part, is an attempt to analyze the publicity relevant to metaphor. In clarifying the publicity relevant to metaphor I have clarified the way in which a critical explanation of a metaphor's meaning is justified. A critical analysis is adequate or inadequate in the degree that it is adequate or inadequate to the metaphor as read. Discussions of metaphorical meaning presuppose not only Wittgenstein's (1) public actions; (2) common physical environment; (3) common body of conventions; but also, (4) an intersubjective experience-act of seeing as; a shared metaphor as read. The existence of a game in which these presuppositions operate with some degree of success, namely, the game of literary analysis, implies the criticisms stated of Wittgenstein's conception of criteria.

---

[53]   Moreland Perkins, "Intersubjectivity and Gestalt Psychology", *Philosophy and Phenomenological Research*, XIII (June, 1953), pp. 449-50.
[54]   *Ibid.*, p. 449.
[55]   *Investigations*, p. 197.

CONCLUSION

A conclusion looks back on particular arguments in a work and forward to the wider significance of these arguments. I have analyzed Wittgenstein's attack on the inner meaning theory, an attack which led him to conclude that meaning is not nor does meaning involve inner experience. Instead meaning is use. Use relates words to their context or gives words their meaning. Central to Wittgenstein's understanding of meaning as use is his conception of criteria as observable features selected by convention. Linguistic correctness, the correctness of one's understanding of a word's meaning, is settled by reference to criteria. To decide if a word is correctly used or is correctly understood one appeals to criteria.

Poetic language taken generically begins to diverge from Wittgenstein's understanding of literal language. Poetic language tries and succeeds in achieving a fusion of sense and sensa. "Sensa" includes sound and imagery, and both become the context of poetic meaning, replacing in this particular game the literal context of public actions and public objects. If you will, the poem's referent is its own sound and imagery. The poem in becoming, in Cassirer's words, "a self-contained cosmos with its own center of gravity . . ." [1] places a distance between itself and normal language usage or function. Thus, the theory of meaning as use which was quite subtle and agile with regard to literal language becomes quite clumsy and inept here because the use of poetry is not at all evident. The only use we seem to make of poems is that we talk about them. They are very poor guides to building houses or putting men on the moon. The use of the poem is that it fuses sense, sound and imagery while being read. This use is tantamount to having no use in Wittgenstein's sense since a part of this use involves imagery, a non-public context. By definition for Wittgenstein use can involve no private aspects. Even more divergent from Wittgenstein's understand-

---

[1]   Cassirer, I, p. 26.

ing of literal language is the suggestion that meaning and imagery are fused in poetic language, implying that imagery in this game is involved in meaning. If imagery in this game is involved in meaning then appeal to criteria as *observable* features selected by convention will not settle disputes over the correctness of one's understanding of a metaphor's meaning.

Metaphor supports the general conclusion that poetic language achieves a fusion of sense and sensa. In fact, metaphor of all the elements of poetic language provides a very well entrenched position from which to defend the thesis of the fusion of sense and sensa. The same metaphorical imagery *quasi-experienced means* through the experience-act of seeing as. Here the ultimate point of divergence with Wittgenstein is reached. Here meaning does involve imagery, leading one to expect that discussions of metaphorical meaning involve reference to this imagery.

Examples of literary discussions of metaphorical meaning confirm this expectation. Critical explanations refer to the metaphor as read. Having lost Wittgenstein's independent source of appeal for settling disputes concerning meaning, namely, the independent source of criteria, in that *conventions* cannot give definitive definitions of metaphor and in that reference to the metaphor is not reference to *observable* features, the critic refers to the independent source of the metaphor as read. Knowledge of criteria is a necessary, but not a sufficient, condition for understanding a metaphor's meaning. Critical discussions of metaphorical meaning presuppose that the metaphor is shared in some sense though it is not fully public. In view of this prerequisite I have suggested that the metaphor as read is *intersubjective but not publicly observable.* This wider base of sharability is necessary to supplement Wittgenstein's social senses of use.

The wider significance of this dialogue between Wittgenstein and poetic language has been hinted in several places in my allusions to the role of metaphor in other fields. For example, above (footnote 77, pp. 134-135) I suggested that image-laden metaphors function even in modes of discourse as abstract as theoretical physics. Newton states: "Absolute, true, and mathematical time of itself, and from its own nature, *flows. . . .*" [2] (Italicizing mine.) Harre correctly argues that such "*picture carrying expressions . . .*" [3] do have a function in literal, scientific language and theories. Their function is in making theories fruitful in

---

[2]   Newton, p. 6.
[3]   Harre, p. 112.

that they "suggest the existence and sketch the character of mechanisms in regions previously inaccessible . . .".[4] An example equally as picture-laden as Newton's expression is the term "current", a metaphorical extension of that word from its normal reference to the flow of a liquid to the flow of electrons in a wire.

Max Black explicitly notes similarly that the "use of theoretical models resembles the use of metaphors in requiring analogical trans-fer of vocabulary".[5] Such models are further similar to metaphors in that they need not necessarily be an actually constructed model, but can simply be a suggestive description.[6] Newton's word "flows" and the word "current" are examples of what Black means by a description which is not an actually constructed model. Black notes that the purpose of a good model is to provide "implications rich enough to suggest novel hypotheses and speculations in the primary field of investigation".[7] This implicative fullness which Black attributes to a good model, of course, is quite parallel to my argument that metaphor is an image-laden, ambiguous, implicatively full form of language.

Nor is science the only area in which cousins of poetic metaphor function. Stephen Pepper argues that the essence of metaphysics is to expand the implications of its chosen root metaphor. He thinks all metaphysical systems are based on one or several of four possible root metaphors. The root metaphors are formalism, mechanism, contextu-alism and organicism.[8] Pepper not only admits but proclaims that any of these root metaphors can consistently explain all the facts.[9] This quality, namely, that such world hypotheses are remote from data, of course, makes them quite different from scientific hypotheses.[10] In view of this explicit statement, a statement which is tantamount to saying that no evidence counts for or against any of the root metaphors, one begins to suspect that the old charge that such root concepts are thus meaningless has some force. Pepper's only reply is that the refined data of science always has a certain "thinness", and we are thus driven to form world hypotheses of unlimited scope.[11]

---

[4] *Ibid.*, p. 115.
[5] Black, *Models and Metaphors*, p. 238.
[6] *Ibid.*, p. 229.
[7] *Ibid.*, p. 233.
[8] Stephen C. Pepper, *World Hypotheses: A Study in Evidence* (Berkeley and Los Angeles, University of California Press, 1948), pp. 98-99.
[9] *Ibid.*
[10] *Ibid.*, pp. 82-83.
[11] *Ibid.*, pp. 63-78.

Further, as early as the Introduction (above, p. 28), I noted that metaphorical transference is a process which operates in ordinary language growth and a change in language is a change in the way the world is conceived. Almost any word will show a metaphorical origin if its etymology is studied. The word then loses its image aura through custom or habitual use, thus becoming a "dead" metaphor such as the "neck of a bottle" or the "arm of a chair". No serious linguist denies that metaphorical transference is *a* principle of language growth, though equally no serious linguist would say such transference is *the* only principle of such growth. That in fact metaphorical transference is a force operating in, for example, contemporary English can easily be seen from some of our newly invented space terminology. We have extended the word "satelite" from its usual denotation of natural bodies in orbit around other natural bodies to include man-made space vehicles in orbit around natural bodies. We give our satelites names such as "Liberty Bell", implying a physical similarity between the shape of the space vehicle and the shape of an actual bell and, of course, implying political and social similarities between our satelite and the Liberty Bell. In inventing new names and terminology we usually cast about for words which emphasize some similarity between the new context and an old one, which is to say we make up a metaphor. We deliberately choose words which are suggestive, a suggestiveness quite similar to the implicative fullness of poetic metaphor. Of course, I am embarrassed by our naming our space plane the "X-15" since, to say the least, this name has very little metaphorical significance! However, I am not really embarrassed by this example because I am not by any means denying that quite often we purposely create an abstract, non-suggestive word or symbol. I am only saying that metaphorical transference is *a* principle operating in normal language growth.

The first circle of significance, if I may be permitted to use a metaphor, of this analysis of the meaning of poetic metaphor is that it suggests the above fruitful similarities to relatives of poetic metaphor in other fields. This wider family of metaphor suggests that metaphorical meaning is by no means a freak which is confined to one artistic form of language, namely, poetry. Metaphorical meaning seems to be a resource of language which is much more common and useful than its scant treatment in many theories of meaning would imply. The specific challenge which this widespread image-laden form of language presents to a general theory of meaning is that such metaphorical language suggests new reasons for its *flexibility* yet *stability* of meaning. Poetic metaphor, as a species of image-laden language, introduces, through its imagery and experience-act of seeing as, a flexibility and stability different in kind from the flexibility and stability of Wittgenstein's open class concepts. Open class concepts are those whose criteria of meaning are "a complicated network of similarities overlapping and criss-crossing: Sometimes overall similarities, sometimes similarities of detail." [12] Open class concepts are flexible because convention has chosen no one set of defining observable characteristics. Open class concepts are stable because convention is an accepted body of social custom. The new flexibility and stability of meaning which metaphor introduces is suggested in my referral throughout this book to the "discovery" of metaphorical meaning. "Discovery" as used here means flexibility of meaning and yet stability or accessibility to meaning. In short, "discovery" is a fitting word to be applied to the act of reading. Reading is a discovery.

The *flexibility* of metaphorical meaning is different in kind from the flexibility of open class concepts because there are no definitive criteria, as Wittgenstein understands them, for metaphorical meaning. There is no definitive source of appeal which can tell in what relevant sense time is like a beggar or nerves sit like tombs. The experience-act of seeing as is irreducible to any specific analysis or any specific set of procedural rules. Since metaphorical meaning is, so to speak, on the cutting edge where convention has been left a step behind, the flexibility of such meaning is not simply due to the fact that convention has arrived at no precisely delimited meaning. The suggestiveness of metaphorical imagery is always a step beyond criteria. Metaphorical meaning has the flexibility implied by the word "discovery" because in reading a two-way influence is allowed, or rather demanded, between language and its image aura. The flexibility of metaphorical meaning is not due to the fact that convention has chosen no one set of observational features, but to the mutual involvement of meaning and imagery. Metaphorical meaning is always open-ended. The lack of a definitive source of convention for metaphorical meaning does not mean one has to forsake such meaning as hopelessly vague, but rather means that the main source of appeal to justify one's understanding of the metaphor is that metaphor as read.

The *stability* of metaphorical meaning is due to the accessibility to the metaphor as read. The word "discovery" is appropriate to reading

---

[12]   *Investigations,* # 66.

because the metaphor can be returned to and reread by the same and different readers. The stability of metaphorical meaning is dependent on the experience-act of seeing as during reading, not on criteria as observable features selected by convention. Seeing as is a cognitively significant act and thus is not confined to a single reader. Seeing as has grounds. Further, a theory flexible enough to account for such a form of image-laden language as poetic metaphor need not suddenly become the ghost in the machine theory simply because criteria, in a rigorous sense of that word, are not sufficient to settle disputes about such meaning. The metaphor as read is not inaccessible, though, of course, it is not public in a physical sense either. Wittgenstein readers who criticize his treatment of statements about other minds, for example, Wellman and Hardin, imply that his naive acceptance of the conditions of physical observation seriously weakens his treatment of statements about other minds. While this book does not rest on the validity of their criticism, I have argued that the basic physicalism of criteria for Wittgenstein makes them incapable of accounting for metaphorical meaning. The only alternative to such a physicalism is not a ghostly or spooky theory of meaning. I rather tried to redefine the publicity relevant to metaphorical meaning in my analysis of the metaphor as read. We must not be led by the presuppositions of physical observation to cry "ghost" too soon. The stability of metaphorical meaning is not due to accessibility to an accepted body of social conventions but due to accessibility to the metaphor as read. The metaphor as read serves metaphorical meaning in the same way that criteria, as understood by Wittgenstein, serve literal meaning. In summary, the *flexibility* introduced by metaphorical meaning stems from the two-way influence between language and imagery in the metaphor. The *stability* of metaphorical meaning stems from accessibility to the metaphor as read.

The widest circle of significance of this book, a circle which is like the outermost concentric circle of a pebble's splash in being most remote from the initial point of impact and in being the circle which most disturbs the water, is the suggestion raised by metaphor that the form-content dichotomy must be revised at least with regard to this particular game. Metaphor demands this revision in view of its fusion of sense, sound and imagery. This particular revision raises the question of revision in other areas. Of course, the most basic case of this dichotomy, in fact the dichotomy itself, is the analytic-synthetic distinction. Wittgenstein's whole methodology as a grammatical analysis is based on the validity of this dichotomy because it is fundamental to his thought that his methodology has no factual content. If the whole analytic-synthetic dichotomy needs overhauling as Quine suggests,[13] then a grammatical or analytical or philosophical inquiry would have content at least in a limited sense. As Morton White puts it: "Analytic philosophy will no longer be sharply separated from science, and an unbridgeable chasm will no longer divide those who see meaning or essences and those who collect facts." [14] Quine and White suggest that concepts and percepts overlap at least in some areas. It is implied that concepts and percepts should not be so radically distinguished. Some theory of meaning is needed which takes seriously the Kantian maxim that: "Thoughts without content are empty, intuitions without concepts are blind." [15] Of course, while saying this Kant explicitly recognized the analytic-synthetic dichotomy.[16] However, it must be added that for Kant analytic statements are philosophically trivial and do not include mathematical and geometrical meanings. Thus Kant, Quine and White would say that at least *some philosophical analysis* is of areas where concepts and percepts touch. At least some philosophical concepts or categories are not empty of synthetic implication or significance. It is not incidental that the Neo-Kantianism of Cassirer and Langer lends valuable support to my analysis of poetic metaphor. Cassirer extends Kant's categories of the understanding to include the conceptual, constitutive mode of language. Poetry, as an art form of language, supports this extension in that it is a type of language where conceptual and sensory elements are fused. Seeing as, the essential element in metaphor, is an experience-act in which thought and sensation touch. In metaphor concepts and percepts overlap in the fusion of sense, sound and imagery. Of course, I in no way intend to claim that I have established the strong conclusion of Quine and White, a conclusion which has very significant implications for the question of what is the philosophical method or what is philosophical analysis. I have argued the particular conclusion that metaphorical meaning fuses sense, sound and imagery, and thus is a type of meaning where concepts and percepts touch. If my analysis has been fruitful then it is implied that other species of meaning can be analyzed in a similar way. If my general procedure is extended

---

[13]   W. V. Quine, "Two Dogmas of Empiricism", *The Philosophical Review*, LX (Jan., 1951), pp. 20-34.
[14]   Leonard Linsky, *Semantics and the Philosophy of Language* (Urbana, Ill., The University of Illinois Press, 1952), p. 286.
[15]   Smith, p. 93.
[16]   *Ibid.*, p. 48.

to philosophical meaning or analysis then it is suggested that such analysis is not as "clean" or "pure" of content as Wittgenstein's grammatical method leads us to expect, though I agree with Wittgenstein that the content of philosophical analysis is certainly not empirical. Perhaps the content of such analysis is phenomenological or conceptual.

BIBLIOGRAPHY

BOOKS

Baker, James Volant, *The Sacred River: Coleridge's Theory of the Imagination* (Louisiana, Louisiana State University Press, 1957).

Barfield, Owen, *Poetic Diction: A Study in Meaning* (London, Faber & Faber, 1952).

Bateson, F. W., *Wordsworth: A Re-Interpretation*, 2nd ed. (London, Longmans, Green and Co., 1956).

Berry, Francis, *Poetry and the Physical Voice* (London, Routledge & Kegan Paul, 1962).

Bewkes, Eugene Garett, *et al.*, *The Nature of Religious Experience: Essays in Honor of Douglas Clyde Macintosh* (New York, Harper & Brothers, 1937).

Black, Max, *Models and Metaphors: Studies in Language and Philosophy* (Ithaca, N.Y., Cornell University Press, 1962).

Bloomfield, Leonard, *Language* (New York, H. Holt & Co., 1933).

Bosanquet, Bernard, *Three Lectures on Aesthetics* (London, Macmillan and Co., Ltd., 1923).

Brémond, Henri, *La poésie pure: avec un débat sur la poésie par Robert de Souza* (Paris, Bernard Grasset, 1926).

Brooks, Cleanth, and Warren, Robert Penn, *Understanding Poetry*, 3rd ed. (New York, Holt, Rinehart & Winston, Inc., 1961).

Brown, Stephen J., S. J., *The World of Imagery* (London, Kegan Paul, Trench, Trubner & Co., Ltd., 1927).

Cassirer, Ernst, *The Philosophy of Symbolic Forms*. Vol. I: *Language*. Vol. II: *Mythical Thought*. Vol. III: *The Phenomenology of Knowledge*. Translated by Ralph Manheim (New Haven, Yale University Press, 1957-1961).

Croce, Benedetto, *Aesthetic as Science of Expression and General Linguistic*. Translated by Douglas Ainslie (New York, Noonday Press, 1962).

D'Abro, A., *The Evolution of Scientific Thought from Newton to Einstein*, 2nd ed. (New York, Dover Publications, Inc., 1950).

Decker, Henry W., *Pure Poetry, 1920-1930: Theory and Debate in France* (Berkeley and Los Angeles, University of California Press, 1962).

Dufrenne, Mikel, *Phénoménologie de l'expérience esthétique* (Paris, Presses Universitaires de France, 1953).

Eastman, Max, *The Literary Mind: Its Place in an Age of Science* (New York, Charles Scribner's Sons, 1935).

Elton, William (ed.), *Aesthetics and Language* (Oxford, Basil Blackwell, 1959).

Empson, William, *Seven Types of Ambiguity* (London, Chatto & Windus, 1956).

Foss, Martin, *Symbol and Metaphor in Human Experience* (Princeton, Princeton University Press, 1949).

Frye, Northrop, *Anatomy of Criticism: Four Essays* (Princeton, Princeton University Press, 1957).

Hamburg, Carl H., *Symbol and Reality: Studies in the Philosophy of Ernst Cassirer* (The Hague, Martinus Nijhoff, 1956).

Hospers, John, *Meaning and Truth in the Arts* (Chapel Hill, N.C., The University of North Carolina Press, 1948).

Hulme, T. E., *Speculations: Essays on Humanism and the Philosophy of Art*, 2nd ed. (London, Routledge & Kegan Paul Ltd., 1958).

Hume, David, *A Treatise of Human Nature*. Edited by L. A. Selby-Bigge (Oxford, The Clarendon Press, 1958).

Hungerland, Isabel C., *Poetic Discourse* (= *University of California Publications in Philosophy*, Vol. XXXIII) (Berkeley and Los Angeles, University of California Press, 1958).

Husserl, Edmund, *Ideas: General Introduction to Pure Phenomenology*. Translated by W. R. Boyce Gibson (London, George Allen & Unwin Ltd., 1958).

Kaelin, Eugene F., *An Existentialist Aesthetic* (Madison, Wisc., The University of Wisconsin Press, 1962).

Kant, Immanuel, *The Critique of Judgment*. Translated by James Creed Meredith (Oxford, The Clarendon Press, 1961).

Langer, Susanne K., *Feeling and Form: A Theory of Art* (New York, Charles Scribner's Sons, 1953).

Langer, Susanne K., *Philosophy in a New Key: A Study in the Symbolism of Reason, Rite, and Art* (New York, A Mentor Book, 1959).

Lee, Irving J. (ed.), *The Language of Wisdom and Folly: Background Reading in Semantics* (New York, Harper & Brothers, 1949).

Lerner, Laurence, *The Truest Poetry: An Essay on the Question What Is Literature* (London, Hamish Hamilton, 1960).

Lewis, C. Day, *The Poetic Image* (London, Jonathan Cape, 1947).

Linsky, Leonard, *Semantics and the Philosophy of Language* (Urbana, Ill., The University of Illinois Press, 1952).

Locke, John, *An Essay concerning Human Understanding*. Abridged and edited by A. S. Pringle-Pattison (Oxford, The Clarendon Press, 1960).

Marsh, Florence, *Wordsworth's Imagery: A Study in Poetic Vision* (New Haven, Yale University Press, 1952).

Morris, Charles, *Sign, Language and Behavior* (New York, Prentice-Hall, Inc., 1946).

Morris, C. R., *Locke, Berkeley, Hume* (Oxford, Oxford University Press, 1959).

Newton, Sir Isaac, *Sir Isaac Newton's Mathematical Principles of Natural Philosophy and his System of the World*. Translated by Andrew Matte in 1729, revised by Florian Cajori (Berkeley, University of California Press, 1947).

Ogden, C. K., and Richards, I. A., *The Meaning of Meaning*, 10th ed. (London, Routledge & Kegan Paul Ltd., 1960).

Pepper, Stephen C., *World Hypotheses: A Study in Evidence* (Berkeley and Los Angeles, University of California Press, 1948).

Pole, David, *The Later Philosophy of Wittgenstein* (London, The Athlon Press, 1958).

Pongs, Hermann, *Das Bild in der Dichtung*. Vol. I: *Versuch einer Morphologie der metaphorischen Formen*, 2nd ed. (Marburg, N. G. Elwert Verlag, 1960).

Ransom, John Crowe, *The New Criticism* (Norfolk, Conn., New Directions, 1941).

Richards, I. A., *The Philosophy of Rhetoric* (New York, Oxford University Press, 1936).

Richards, I. A., *Principles of Literary Criticism* (New York, A Harvest Book, First published in 1925).

Ross, W. D. (ed.), *The Works of Aristotle*, 12 vols. (Oxford, The Clarendon Press, 1959).

Ryle, Gilbert, *The Concept of Mind* (London, Hutchinson & Co., Ltd., 1960).

Sapir, Edward, *Language: An Introduction to the Study of Speech* (New York, A Harvest Book, 1949).

Sartre, Jean-Paul, *Being and Nothingness: An Essay on Phenomenological Ontology*. Translated by Hazel E. Barnes (New York, Philosophical Library, 1956).

Sartre, Jean-Paul, *L'imaginaire: Psychologie phénoménologique de l'imagination* (Paris, Librairie Gallimard, 1948).

Sartre, Jean-Paul, *The Psychology of Imagination*. Translator not given (New York, Philosophical Library, 1948).

Schlauch, Margaret, *The Gift of Tongues* (New York, Modern Age Books, 1942).

Smith, Norman Kemp (trans.), *Kant's Critique of Pure Reason* (London, Macmillan & Co., Ltd., 1958).

Spiegelberg, Herbert, *The Phenomenological Movement*, 2 vols. (The Hague, Nijhoff, 1960).

Stevenson, Charles L., *Ethics and Language* (New Haven, Yale University Press, 1960).

Valéry, Paul, *The Art of Poetry*. Translated by Denise Folliot (New York, Vintage Books, 1961).

Webster's New Collegiate Dictionary (Springfield, Mass., G. & C. Merriam Co., 1956).

Weitz, Morris (ed.), *Problems in Aesthetics: An Introductory Book of Readings* (New York, The Macmillan Co., 1959).

Wellek, René, and Warren, Austin, *Theory of Literature* (New York, Harcourt, Brace & Co., 1949).

Wheelwright, Philip, *The Burning Fountain: A Study in the Language of Symbolism* (Bloomington, Ind., Indiana University Press, 1959).

Wheelwright, Philip, *Metaphor and Reality* (Bloomington, Ind., Indiana University Press, 1962).

Wimsatt, W. K., Jr., *The Verbal Icon: Studies in the Meaning of Poetry* (New York, The Noonday Press, 1958).

Wittgenstein, Ludwig, *Notebooks: 1914-1916*. Edited by G. H. von Wright and G. E. M. Anscombe. Translated by G. E. M. Anscombe (Oxford, Basil Blackwell, 1961).

Wittgenstein, Ludwig, *Philosophical Investigations*. Translated by G. E. M. Anscombe (New York, The Macmillan Co., 1960).

Wittgenstein, Ludwig, *Preliminary Studies for the "Philosophical Investigations"*, generally known as: *The Blue and Brown Books* (Oxford, Basil Blackwell, 1960).

Wittgenstein, Ludwig, *Tractatus Logico-Philosophicus*. Translated by D. F. Pears and B. F. McGuinness (London, Routledge & Kegan Paul, 1961).

ARTICLES AND PERIODICALS

Albritton, Roger, "On Wittgenstein's Use of the Term 'Criterion' ", *The Journal of Philosophy*, LVI (October 22, 1959), pp. 845-57.

Aldrich, Virgil C., "Image-Mongering and Image-Management", *Philosophy and Phenomenological Research*, XXIII (September, 1962), pp. 51-61.

Aldrich, Virgil C., "Pictorial Meaning and Picture Thinking", *The Kenyon Review*, V (Summer, 1943), pp. 403-12.

Aldrich, Virgil C., "Pictorial Meaning, Picture-Thinking, and Wittgenstein's Theory of Aspects", *Mind*, LXVII (January, 1958), pp. 70-79.

Berggren, Douglas, "The Use and Abuse of Metaphor, I", *The Review of Metaphysics*, XVI (December, 1962), pp. 237-258.

Black, Max, "Some Questions about Emotive Meaning", *The Philosophical Review*, LVII (March, 1948), pp. 111-26.

Carmichael, Peter A., "Aesthetic Knowledge", *The Journal of Philosophy*, LVIII (July 6, 1961), pp. 378-87.

Cavell, Stanley, "The Availability of Wittgenstein's Later Philosophy", *The Philosophical Review*, LXXI (January, 1962), pp. 67-93.

Daitz, Edna, "The Picture Theory of Meaning", *Mind*, LXII (April, 1953), pp. 184-201.

Feyerabend, Paul, "Wittgenstein's *Philosophical Investigations*", *The Philosophical Review*, LXIV (July, 1955), pp. 449-83.

Fleming, Noel, "Recognizing and Seeing As", *The Philosophical Review*, LXVI (April, 1957), pp. 161-79.

Friedman, Norman, "Imagery: From Sensation to Symbol", *The Journal of Aesthetics & Art Criticism*, XII (September, 1953), pp. 25-37.

Hardin, Clyde Laurence, "Wittgenstein on Private Languages", *The Journal of Philosophy*, LVI (June 4, 1959), pp. 517-28.

Harre, R., "Metaphor, Model and Mechanism", *Proceedings of the Aristotelian Society. New Series*, LX (January, 1960), pp. 101-22.

Herschberger, Ruth, "The Structure of Metaphor", *The Kenyon Review*, V (Summer, 1943), pp. 433-43.

Hervey, Helen, "The Private Language Problem", *The Philosophical Quarterly*, VII (January, 1957), pp. 63-79.

Hospers, John, "The Concept of Artistic Expression", *The Proceedings of the Aristotelian Society. New Series*, LV (June 20, 1955), pp. 313-44.

Hudson, H., "Why We Cannot Witness or Observe what Goes on 'In Our Heads'", *Mind*, LXV (April, 1956), pp. 218-30.

Isenberg, Arnold, "The Esthetic Function of Language", *The Journal of Philosophy*, XLVI (January 6, 1949), pp. 5-20.

Isenberg, Arnold, "Perception, Meaning and the Subject-Matter of Art", *The Journal of Philosophy*, XLI (October 12, 1944), pp. 561-75.

Jarrett, James L., "Verification in the Reading of Poetry", *The Journal of Philosophy*, XLVI (July 7, 1949), pp. 435-44.

Kahn, Sholom J., "What Does a Critic Analyze? (On a Phenomenological Approach to Literature)", *Philosophy and Phenomenological Research*, XIII (December, 1952), pp. 237-45.

Kaplan, Abraham, "Referential Meaning in the Arts", *The Journal of Aesthetics & Art Criticism*, XII (June, 1954), pp. 457-74.

Kaplan, Abraham, and Kris, Ernst, "Esthetic Ambiguity", *Philosophy and Phenomenological Research*, VIII (March, 1948), pp. 415-35.

Lalo, Charles, "The Aesthetic Analysis of a Work of Art: An Essay on the Structure and Superstructure of Poetry", *The Journal of Aesthetics & Art Criticism*, VII (June, 1949), pp. 275-93.

Linsky, Leonard, "Wittgenstein on Language and Some Problems of Philosophy", *The Journal of Philosophy*, LIV (May 9, 1957), pp. 285-93.

Malcolm, Norman, "Wittgenstein's *Philosophical Investigations*", *The Philosophical Review*, LXIII (October, 1954), pp. 530-69.

Mellor, W. W., "Three Problems about Other Minds", *Mind*, LXV (April, 1956), pp. 200-17.

Moore, G. E., "Wittgenstein's Lectures in 1930-33", *Mind*, Part I, LXIII (January, 1954), pp. 1-15. Part II, LXIII (July, 1954), pp. 289-316. Part III, LXIV (January, 1955), pp. 1-27.

Perkins, Moreland, "Intersubjectivity and Gestalt Psychology", *Philosophy and Phenomenological Research*, XIII (June, 1953), pp. 437-50.

Quine, W. V., "Two Dogmas of Empiricism", *The Philosophical Review*, LX (January, 1951), pp. 20-43.

Ransom, John Crowe, "Positive and Near Positive Aesthetics", *The Kenyon Review*, V (Summer, 1943), pp. 443-47.

Rhees, R., "Wittgenstein's Builders", *Proceedings of the Aristotelian Society. New Series*, LX (March 14, 1960), pp. 171-86.

Sibley, Frank, "Aesthetic Concepts", *The Philosophical Review*, LXVIII (October, 1959), pp. 421-50.

Smythies, J. R., "On Some Properties and Relations of Images", *The Philosophical Review*, LXVII (July, 1958), pp. 389-94.

Stevenson, Charles L., "On the 'Analysis' of a Work of Art", *The Philosophical Review*, LXVII (January, 1958), pp. 33-51.

Stevenson, Charles L., "On 'What Is a Poem?' ", *The Philosophical Review*, LXVI (July, 1957), pp. 329-62.

Strawson, P. F., "*Philosophical Investigations*", *Mind*, LXIII (January, 1954), pp. 70-99.

Tomas, Vincent, "Aesthetic Vision", *The Philosophical Review*, LXVIII (January, 1959), pp. 52-67.

Van Peursen, C. A., "Edmund Husserl and Ludwig Wittgenstein", *Philosophy and Phenomenological Research*, XX (December, 1959), pp. 181-97.

Walsh, Dorothy, "The Poetic Use of Language", *The Journal of Philosophy*, XXXV (February 3, 1938), pp. 73-81.

Warren, Robert Penn, "Pure and Impure Poetry", *The Kenyon Review*, V (Spring, 1943), pp. 228-54.

Weitz, Morris, "The Role of Theory in Aesthetics", *The Journal of Aesthetics & Art Criticism*, XV (September, 1956), pp. 27-35.

Wellman, Carl, "Our Criteria for Third Person Psychological Sentences", *The Journal of Philosophy*, LVIII (May 25, 1961), pp. 281-93.

Wellman, Carl, "Wittgenstein and the Egocentric Predicament", *Mind*, LXVIII (April, 1959), pp. 223-33.

Wellman, Carl, "Wittgenstein's Conception of a Criterion", *The Philosophical Review*, LXXI (October, 1962), pp. 433-47.

Wimsatt, W. K., Jr., "Poetic Tension: A Summary", *The New Scholasticism*, XXXII (January, 1958), pp. 73-88.

Zink, Sidney, "Poetry and Truth", *The Philosophical Review*, LIV (March, 1945), pp. 132-44.

UNPUBLISHED MATERIAL

Berggren, Douglas Charles, "An Analysis of Metaphorical Meaning and Truth". Unpublished Doctor of Philosophy dissertation, Department of Philosophy, Yale University (1959).

INDEX OF NAMES

INDEX OF SUBJECTS